NATIONAL GEOGRAPHIC

TRAVELER
Shanghai

NATIONAL GEOGRAPHIC

TRAVELER
Shanghai

Andrew Forbes
Photography by David Butow

National Geographic
Washington, D.C.

Contents

How to use this guide 6–7 About the authors & photographer 8
The regions 61–228 Travelwise 229–266
Index 267–270 Credits 270–271

Page 1: Gongqing Forest Park amusement ride
Pages 2–3: Skyline of Pudong
Left: Nanjing pagoda

How to use this guide

See back flap for keys to text and map symbols

The *National Geographic Traveler* brings you the best of Shanghai in text, pictures, and maps. Divided into three main sections, the guide begins with an overview of history and culture. Following are eight regional chapters with featured sites selected by the author for their particular interest and treated in depth. Each chapter opens with its own table of contents for easy reference.

A map introduces each area of the city, highlighting the featured sites. Walks, plotted on their own maps, suggest routes for discovering an area. Features and sidebars offer detail on history, culture, or contemporary life. A More Places to Visit page generally rounds off the regional chapters.

The final section, Travelwise, lists essential information for the traveler—pre-trip planning, getting around, communications, money matters, and emergencies—plus a selection of hotels, restaurants, shops, and entertainment.

To the best of our knowledge, site information is accurate as of the press date. However, it's always advisable to call ahead.

Color coding

116

Each region is color coded for easy reference. Find the region you want on the map on the front flap, and look for the color flash at the top of the pages of the relevant chapter. Information in **Travelwise** is also color coded to each region.

Shanghai Museum

(Shanghai Bowuguan)

🅰 Map p. 62 2B

www.shanghaimuseum.net/en/

✉ 201 Renmin Dadao

☎ 6372 3500

🕐 Mon.–Fri. 9 a.m.–5 p.m.

💲 $

Visitor information

for major sites is listed in the side columns (see key to symbols on back flap). The map reference gives the page where the site is mapped. Other details are the address, telephone number, days closed, and entrance fee ranging from $ (under $5) to $$$$$ (over $25). Visitor information for smaller sites is provided within the text. Admission fees are based on the prices foreigners pay.

Hotel and restaurant prices

An explanation of the price bands used in entries is given in the Hotels & restaurants section beginning on p. 239.

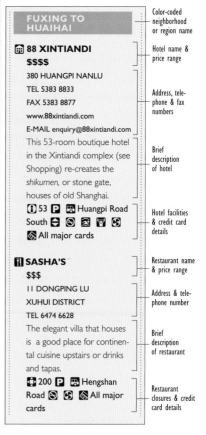

TRAVELWISE

FUXING TO HUAIHAI — Color-coded neighborhood or region name

🏨 **88 XINTIANDI**
$$$$ — Hotel name & price range

380 HUANGPI NANLU
TEL 5383 8833
FAX 5383 8877
www.88xintiandi.com
E-MAIL enquiry@88xintiandi.com — Address, telephone & fax numbers

This 53-room boutique hotel in the Xintiandi complex (see Shopping) re-creates the *shikumen*, or stone gate, houses of old Shanghai. — Brief description of hotel

🛏 53 🅿 🚇 Huangpi Road South 🔄 🔲 📠 📺 🖥 🞧 All major cards — Hotel facilities & credit card details

🍴 **SASHA'S**
$$$ — Restaurant name & price range

11 DONGPING LU
XUHUI DISTRICT
TEL 6474 6628 — Address & telephone number

The elegant villa that houses is a good place for continental cuisine upstairs or drinks and tapas. — Brief description of restaurant

🍽 200 🅿 🚇 Hengshan Road 🔲 🞧 🞧 All major cards — Restaurant closures & credit card details

AREA MAPS

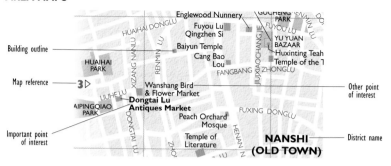

Building outline

Map reference

Important point of interest

Other point of interest

District name

- A locator map accompanies each area map and shows the location of that area in the city.

WALKING MAPS

Point of interest not on walk route

Direction of route

Featured site (in bold) on walk route

Red numbered bullets link sites on map to descriptions in the text

Walk route

- An information box gives the starting and finishing points, time and length of walk, and places not to miss along the route.

Navigating Shanghai: *Lu* means road, *jie* street, and *xiang* lane. North is *bei*, East *dong*, south *nan*, west *xi*, and center, *zhong*. Frequently these are combined as in *donglu*. Odd or even numbers can be on either side of the street.

EXCURSION MAPS

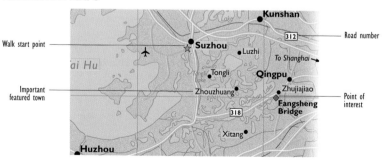

Walk start point

Road number

Important featured town

Point of interest

- Towns and cities described in the Excursions chapters are highlighted in yellow on the map. Other suggested places to visit are shown with a red diamond symbol.

NATIONAL GEOGRAPHIC

TRAVELER
Shanghai

About the authors & photographer

Andrew Forbes earned a degree in Chinese studies from the University of Leeds before completing an M.A. in Islamic Studies and a Ph.D. in Central Asian History. The author of more than a dozen books on East and Southeast Asia, he has also contributed to numerous international publications including *The Guardian, The Asian Wall Street Journal, Strategic Comments,* and *Jane's Defence Weekly.* A Senior Associate Member of St Antony's College, Oxford, he is also editor of CPA Media in Chiang Mai, Thailand, where he works as a writer and lives with his Thai wife, Puangphet.

David Butow is a photojournalist based in Los Angeles. As a contract photographer with *U.S. News & World Report* and Redux photo agency, his assignments have taken him to Asia, Africa, Europe, the Middle East, and South America. His work on Iraq and Kurdistan from a pre-war trip in 2000 was shown at the International Festival of Photojournalism in Perpignan, France. His personal work on the Uighur ethnic group in China has been the subject of solo shows in New York and Los Angeles. He has received awards from World Press Photo, University of Missouri Pictures of the Year, NPPA Best of Photojournalism, Photo District News, The Association of Alternative Weeklies, and American Photography Annual.

Peter Holmshaw, author of the Travelwise, first lived in China in 1988; since then he has traveled extensively throughout the country and now divides his time between Chiang Mai, Thailand, and Yunnan Province in China. He graduated from the University of California at Berkeley, majoring in Middle East studies, and later earned a master's degree in international management. For ten years he managed projects in North Africa before moving to Asia and beginning a new career as a travel writer. He is the author of *The Ramakien and Thai Classical Dance* (Asia Books, 2003) and has contributed to many periodicals and travel books.

History & culture

Detail of Longhua Martyrs Memorial

Shanghai today

SHANGHAI IS A PLACE OF SUPERLATIVES. CHINA'S LARGEST CITY, WITH A population of almost 19 million in the municipal core and more than 10 million in the urban vicinity, it is the nation's richest, most progressive, most stylish, and most modern metropolis. It's also perhaps the least Chinese city in China, having been molded and formed since the mid-19th century by decades of close interaction with other nationalities, most notably Europeans, Americans, and Japanese.

Originally a sleepy fishing port on the west bank of the Huangpu River, Shanghai—which means on sea in Chinese—has always been associated with water. To the east sprawls the South China Sea, while to the north, just 15 miles (24 km) distant, the vast Yangtze River draws a decisive geographic dividing line between north and south China. To the south lie the tidal waters of Hangzhou Bay, and to the west are the scattered canals, lakes, and marshlands surrounding Lake Tai.

Over the centuries, this watery setting has brought Shanghai prosperity as a port, especially after the establishment of the International Settlement in the city following the First Opium War in 1842. Over the same period, its location has also brought the city serious problems in the form of foreign invaders—Western opium dealers and monopoly capitalists to be sure, but, more recently and more disastrously, soldiers of Imperial Japan. Today, after 40 years of communist austerity between 1949 and 1990, the city is once again booming, having surpassed Singapore in 2005 to become the largest cargo port in the world.

Shanghai is still very much on sea, but it is also the driving force behind a massive and increasingly hi-tech industrial complex centered on the city and the neighboring Yangtze River Delta covering a relatively small area—in Chinese terms at least—of 38,650 square miles (100,100 sq km), or just over one percent of the national territory. Yet the delta is also home to over 10 percent of China's population—some 132 million people—and accounts for in excess of 22 percent of China's gross domestic product and around 25 percent of national revenues, while handling a staggering 28.5 percent of the country's import and export volume. Shanghai remains the single major engine driving Chinese economic expansion. The city's own economy has continued to expand each year at double-digit rates since 1992, when Beijing gave the green light to unrestricted economic development. Quite simply, Shanghai today is a Pacific Rim prodigy that rivals, and may soon surpass, Hong Kong and Tokyo. And it shows.

Shanghai has long been China's most fashionable city, even if that stylishness has been tinged with more than a whiff of corruption and decadence, thus earning the city at various times opposing sobriquets: the unforgiving (yet strangely appealing) Whore of Asia and the more flattering Pearl of the Orient.

A CITYWIDE FACELIFT

When Deng Xioapeng, China's leader from 1981 to 1992, permitted the economic opening of Shanghai in 1990, the city responded with alacrity and enthusiasm. In 1988 the city's tallest building was the 275-foot-tall (84 m) Park Hotel, built in 1934; by 1993, the striking 1,535-foot-tall (468 m) Oriental Pearl Tower, a television tower, rose up in Pudong, across the river from The Bund, changing forever the Shanghai skyline and ushering in a new era of construction.

By 1998 Pudong boasted the tallest building in China, the 1,379-foot (420 m) Jinmao Tower, and an estimated one-quarter of all high-rise construction cranes in the world were busy transforming the Shanghai skyline. Today four thousand–plus buildings that stand more than 330 feet (100 m) tall, a statistic matched by no other megalopolis on Earth. To this may be added such engineering marvels as the the sparkling new Pudong International Airport; the German-built Maglev train line, connecting the airport to the city; Nanpu Bridge, which was the first bridge across the Hangzhou River when it opened in 1991; Lupu Bridge, officially the world's longest arched bridge at 5.1 miles (8.3 km; you can climb to the top for breathtaking views); and the massive Hangzhou Bay Bridge, which, when completed in 2008, will be the longest transoceanic bridge in the world at 22 miles (36 km).

Even as Shanghai blazes the way into China's 21st century, the increasingly

Neon-lit buildings on bustling Nanjing Donglu signal Shanghai's ultramodern future.

affluent middle classes appreciate the city's former glories. Buildings that date from colonial times, especially along The Bund and in the Fuxing Park area, are being renovated: Buddhist, Taoist, and even Confucian temples are being painstakingly restored; Nanshi, the center of the Old Town, has been carefully re-created in Ming and Qing dynasty styles; and areas of traditional *shikumen* housing are now also being preserved and restored, or rebuilt as

trendy, upmarket shopping and restaurant areas, such as Xintiandi. Another notable trend in recent years has been the conversion of large, old warehouses in the Zhabei area and along Moganshan Road into art galleries and artist studios. Across town, from Pudong in the east to Xujiahui and Hongqiao in the west, spectacular skyscraper architecture continues to rise on an almost monthly basis, offering Shanghai's citizens access to gigantic, air-conditioned

shopping malls, designer clothing, the latest electronic and computer gadgetry (much of it locally made, even if it bears Japanese or Korean trademarks), international cuisine, and even German microbreweries.

DISTINCTLY SHANGHAI

Shanghai's long history as a city of commerce has created a cosmopolitan culture, one that the rest of China sometimes envies. Many Chinese, whether from the

Partygoers toast the approach of the New Year at a bar on Maoming Road South. This busy street is considered one of Shanghai's top bar venues.

capital or the provinces, will stereotype the Shanghainese as being materialistic, pretentious, parsimonious, and disdainful of people from other provinces. On the other hand, they generally acknowledge that the Shanghainese are also hard workers,

attentive to detail, professional and honest in business matters, and—last but not least—stylish.

Shanghai is the richest and most go-ahead city in China, and its people have more money to spend on everything from fashion to fine arts to theater and opera house tickets.

Shanghai identities

Shanghai is a cultural and ethnic melting pot, drawing in huge numbers of migrant workers from all over China as it has done, almost without interruption, since its rise as a treaty port in the mid-19th century. The indigenous Shanghainese can be more readily identifiable by their dialect.

The Shanghainese speak a variant of Wu, the second largest Chinese language group, which is unintelligible both to the Mandarin speakers of the north and to the Hakka, Cantonese, and other Chinese lan-

guage groups of the south. There are about a hundred million Wu speakers in Zhejiang and Jiangsu Provinces, as well as in parts of Anhui, Jiangxi, Fujian, Taiwan, and Singapore. Wu is widely considered to be softer, lighter, and more flowing than Mandarin. The largest linguistic subgroup within Wu, spoken by about 16 million people, is Shanghainese.

Few foreigners apart from long-term resident expatriates ever learn to speak

Traditional Chinese gardens abound in the Shanghai region, the most famous of which is Yu Gardens. Pavilions, rockeries, ponds, and cloisters occupy this beautifully tranquil space, which was finished in 1577.

Shanghainese, and even in the city itself Mandarin—more commonly referred to nowadays as *putonghua* or common speech—is used as the everyday lingua franca of the many diverse Chinese peo-

ples who have made Shanghai their home.

The central government would like everybody in Shanghai to speak Mandarin, and Shanghainese is not taught in schools, while its use is discouraged in the media and censored in advertisements and entertainment. The government has recently rolled out a campaign urging the populace to "be a modern Shanghai person and speak Mandarin first." A recent edict requires that all service-industry employees must pass a Mandarin-

fluency test by 2010 or enroll in compulsory remedial language classes. Despite these pressures, there has been some resurgence of the use of Shanghainese by Wu speakers who refuse to give up their linguistic heritage, particularly among the youth culture. Vernacular Shanghainese has become a popular medium in the city's vibrant underground music scene, as it both challenges and offers an alternative to the Mandarin and Cantonese music that dominate most of the

Chinese music industry elsewhere in
the country.

Yangjingbang style

Linguistic distinctions aside, Shanghainese
differ from most other Chinese in having
been exposed for so long and so completely to foreign—especially Western—ideas
and influences. Only Hong Kong has experienced a longer and more intense relationship with the West. Even before the advent

**Worshippers burn incense as an offering
to Buddha at Longhua Temple, the largest
temple in Shanghai. It's also Shanghai's
oldest temple, dating back to 242 A.D.**

of colonialism, the seaport of Shanghai welcomed sailors from many nations. This
open face to the outside world was massively reinforced with the establishment of the
International Settlement and French
Concession in the mid-19th century.

Young skateboarders at a skateboard park in Zhubei. Wearing big T-shirts and baggy pants, a new generation of skateboarders has come into fashion in Shanghai.

A willingness to embrace foreign culture—or at least to take from it that which seems good, useful, or attractive—first developed in the late 19th century. It was popularly styled *Yangjingbang*, after the name of the stream that once separated the International Settlement and French Concession from the old Chinese city of Nanshi. (The stream was filled and paved over in 1915; the thoroughfare Yan'an Donglu now follows its course.) Yangjingbang style referred to something uniquely Shanghainese in terms of dress (see pp. 52–53) and, above all, attitude. It also blended Chinese with Western tradition, often in the trendiest of ways, and it was anathema to the hard-line communists who took over Shanghai in 1949.

Yangjingbang also referred to a pidgin especially popular among colonial-era traders that combined elements of Chinese

apparent than among the young and upwardly mobile. Foreign products—especially Western—are considered desirable, and all over the city giant, air-conditioned shopping malls and covered markets feed the consumer rush. The fashionably dressed seek out designer labels: Giorgio Armani and Yves Saint Laurent clothing, Calvin Klein and Givenchy shoes, Gucci sunglasses, Christian Dior and Estée Lauder perfumes, and Burberry handbags.

So what does all this say about modern Shanghai and the new Shanghainese? To be sure, it is a cultured, sophisticated city. The Shanghainese prefer to compare their city with Paris, London, Tokyo, or New York than with other Chinese cities. Quite simply, most Shanghainese like to see themselves as China's cultural trailblazers, the most internationally oriented people in China. As such, they like to stay one step ahead of other Chinese, whom they often refer to as *waidiren* (outsiders) or (in Shanghainese) *xiangwonin* (provincials)—an attitude not always appreciated by those to whom the designation is aimed.

Shanghai is home to about 20 million people, most of whom are most keenly ambitious and anxious to get ahead. It's a financially driven city where people traditionally like to haggle over prices and enjoy the fine skills of bargaining and bartering. The Shanghainese like to get value for money and appreciate quality.

The men by and large are more interested in commerce than in politics. They are said to drink less alcohol than men in other parts of China and to keep their tempers better.

Shanghailander women differ from those in the rest of the country in that, for more than 150 years, they have been at the forefront of Chinese women's development. Whether 19th-century farm girls escaping rural poverty or progressive-thinking socialites rejecting archaic Chinese traditions like foot binding and concubinage, Shanghai's women have been obliged to stand on their own feet and compete to make a living in a great

and English. Today, pidgin English is making a comeback, especially among young people, partly for convenience, partly to show off their educational background, and partly just for fun. Not everyone is happy about this comeback—it's triggered a hot debate about how to maintain the purity of the Chinese language without hindering the drive for openness.

CONSUMER CULTURE

The Shanghainese are great fans of consumer culture, and nowhere is this more industrial city for longer than anywhere else in China—and, of course, it shows in their character. They can be strong-willed and opinionated, and they know what they want.

GROWING PAINS

Clearly, change is sweeping Shanghai perhaps faster than any other city on Earth. The skyline has altered beyond recognition, and the city enjoys a prosperity that could scarcely have been envisaged during the colonial period. But affluence

Chic & fashionable architecture

Blending features of East and West, the *shikumen* style of architecture—literally stone gate—is uniquely Shanghainese. It originally developed in colonial times when Shanghai-based architects adapted Western-style terrace housing to crowded Chinese conditions. Built along narrow alleys, the residences were connected and each boasted a stone gate that led to a small enclosed courtyard. This way, residents could feel they had a peaceful place to go, away from the city's bustle. Traditional shikumen housing once dominated the city, with up to 80 percent of the population residing in these types of houses. Over the years, much of it has been torn down and replaced with high-rise blocks. However, you can still find pockets that are being redeveloped and rebuilt as upmarket holdings. They serve as prized locales for restaurants and bijou shopping streets. Xintiandi has some lovely examples of shikumen architecture. ■

is far from ubiquitous, and for every smartly dressed executive, there are many impoverished but aspiring workers from the provinces seeking employment at one of Shanghai's construction docks or dockyards.

And affluence can induce negative side effects as well as positive. With increased political freedom and spiraling wealth, some of the vices of Old Shanghai—prostitution, drugs, gambling—are reappearing, though updated for the times. Young, relatively affluent *diaomazi*, or fishing girls, of Maoming Lu seeking the wherewithal to purchase the latest mobile phone or some other desirable fashion accessory, are choosing to prostitute themselves, while poor girls from the countryside are again falling victim to predatory brothel keepers. Drugs, more or less banished under Mao Zedong, are also back, although it's much easier to find ecstasy or even cocaine at a downtown disco than it is to find a genuine opium parlor. Gamblers continue to place bets on mahjongg and card games, but more perniciously they participate in online gambling. And many people play on the popular and celebrated Stock Exchange, where the government is concerned that too many locals are racking up serious losses against credit card and other debts.

Having excised the ghosts of its previous immoral reputation, the city is making every effort to prevent a recurrence. Its leaders are cracking down on brothels and informing the populace of the risks of playing the stock market. And the city is certainly much safer now than it was during colonial times. Happily, even the 19th-century expression "to Shanghai" (meaning to seize some unfortunate off the street and press them into service at sea) no longer has any currency—the People's Liberation Army Navy uses only professional sailors.

As Shanghai forges ahead, the city remains a paradigm, displaying much that is best and most impressive, as well as some elements that are less than appealing, about the emerging New China. Despite these obvious contradictions, Shanghai's future looks rosier than it has at any time in its history. Long the nation's most go-ahead metropolis, it is thriving, noisy, polluted, overflowing with humanity—and, above all, a modern, vibrant, and exciting destination. ■

An everyday street scene in Shanghai's old Jewish Quarter in Hongkou District. Much of this residential area is slated for demolition as part of a redevelopment plan.

Food & drink

COSMOPOLITAN SHANGHAI OFFERS A WEALTH OF CHINESE CUISINES. THE Shanghainese have developed *hu cai,* their own style of cuisine, but the melting pot nature of the city means that China's "eight great culinary traditions" feature prominently, too, along with other regional cuisines, including Chinese Islamic and spicy Uighur. In addition, a profusion of establishments serve international cuisine. No visitor to Shanghai, regardless of budget, will ever go away hungry or unsatisfied.

SHANGHAINESE CUISINE

Shanghai hu cai is delicious, homey, down-to-earth, and ubiquitous. Chinese culinary experts consider it a borrowed and refined blend of Jiangsu, or *yang,* and Zhejiang, or *zhe*—two of the eight great culinary traditions that developed in richer and more sophisticated neighboring provinces while Shanghai was still a sleepy fishing port. The fare is most readily identifiable by the use of alcohol, particularly with seafood or chicken, to prepare drunken or *jiaohu* dishes, as well as by an unusually liberal use of sugar in combination with soy sauce to create savory

dishes, most notably sweet and sour pork spare ribs—*tangcu xiaopai* in Shanghai's Wu dialect.

Most forms of meat are available in the city, especially pork, duck, beef, and—in *halal* (Islamic permissable) Muslim establishments—lamb. Poultry is less popular in Shanghai than in some other parts of China, but the dish *jiaohua ji* (beggar's chicken) is an exception. Claimed as a local creation, the chicken is wrapped in lotus leaves before being covered with clay and oven-baked until it is so tender that the flesh literally falls from the bones.

Given the city's seaside location, it's not surprising that the favorite constituent of hu cai is seafood, followed closely by freshwater fare. Fish of all kinds, as well as crabs, lobsters,

mussels, oysters, eels, shrimp, and crayfish, are plentiful (though don't expect them to be inexpensive). Popular fish dishes include *huang yu* (yellow croaker), *lu yu* (Songjiang perch), and *gui yu* (Mandarin fish), all delicious steamed or stir fried, but perhaps best when cooked with corn and pine nuts.

The most celebrated of all local seafood dishes is the Chinese mitten crab or *dazhaxie*, better known as the Shanghai hairy crab. These creatures are at their best when retrieved from the deep, clear waters of Lake Yangcheng. Served steamed with a mixture of raw ginger, soy sauce, and black vinegar, and traditionally accompanied by Shaoxing wine, the crabs are in season in fall.

Dumplings

The locals are great lovers—and dedicated cooks—of a wide variety of dumplings, available from street stalls and small restaurants at just about any hour of the day or night. Dumplings may be filled with pork, beef, chicken, fish, or shrimp (plus lamb in halal Muslim restaurants) that is mixed with cabbage, scallions, chives, and other vegetables and then steamed, pan fried, or boiled. Exclusively vegetarian versions are also widely available or can be made to order; ask for *shu-cai* in Mandarin. Dumplings are served with a soy-based dipping sauce that may be mixed with vinegar, ginger, garlic, rice wine, chili, or sesame oil, depending on style and taste.

The most popular dumplings are small steamed buns, called *xiao long bao* in Mandarin or *sho lonpotsi* in Wu. Steamed in bamboo baskets, these tasty snacks are stuffed with minced meat and soup, with variations including seafood and vegetarian fillings. The soup is actually meat gelatin that has turned to liquid as the dumpling is heated. Careful—the broth can be scalding.

Another favorite dumpling dish is *shengjie mantou*, a pan-fried meat- or vegetable-filled, crescent-shaped *jiaozi* (the Chinese version of Japanese dumpling known as *gyoza*).

Red cooking

Hong shao, or red cooking, is claimed by

A chef prepares food to go at a popular night stall in Xujiahui.

locals as a hu cai invention. This popular Shanghainese style of cooking involves slowly simmering meat and vegetables in a stock flavored with soy sauce, star anise or five spice powder, alcohol (in the form of a local cooking sherry or rice wine), and sugar. The name is derived from the deep red-brown color this sauce imbues to the meat, which more often than not is

The city's famed *xiao long bao* (little basket buns) are a popular part of many Shanghainese feasts.

pork, especially pig's knuckle. Red-cooked pork or *hong shao zhu rou* is an enduringly popular delicacy from Shanghai to Hangzhou and Suzhou.

Other specifically local creations—or at least as the Shanghainese would have it—include lime-and-ginger-flavored one-thousand-year old eggs, and fermented tofu. The Chinese name for the latter, *chou doufu* (stinky tofu), accurately suggests that this snack produces a powerful aroma, beloved of aficionados but less so of most other people. Thousand-year-old eggs and stinky tofu are certainly a taste that once obtained can become very addictive.

OTHER REGIONAL CUISINES

China's eight great culinary traditions—Anhui, Fujian, Guangdong, Hunan, Jiangsu, Shandong, Zhejiang, and the ever popular and ubiquitous Sichuanese—can all be found in Shanghai. Zhejiang cuisine, in particular, stands on its own as outstanding for its fresh and mellow qualities and elegant appearance. Zhejiang specializes in a variety of preparations, including quick-frying, stir-frying, deep-frying, and simmering, to make the food as tender as possible. Of its three sub-cuisines—Hangzhou, Ningbo, and Shaoxing—Hangzhou is the most famous, featuring dishes such as beggar's chicken, Dongpo pork, and West Lake vinegar fish.

Another popular regional cuisine is Jiangsu. Jiangsu Province possesses fertile lands and abundant waterways, so it's natural that its cuisine features only the freshest ingredients, especially seafood. Jiangsu cuisine actually consists of several variations: Nanjing style favors freshwater fish and poultry and traditionally emphasizes an even taste; the most famous dish is Jinling salted dried duck. Suzhou cuisine has a tendancy to be sweet, while Wuxi cuisine focuses on different varieties of congee, or rice porridge, eaten as a savory dish with a selection of pickled vegetables, bamboo shoots, thousand-year-old eggs, beef, pork, fish, or shrimp that is served with ground white pepper, soy sauce, and vinegar as condiments.

Uighur fare

The great western province of Xinjiang, spanning the steppes and deserts of Central Asia, may be a long way from Shanghai, but its indomitable Uighur Muslim entrepreneurs never like to miss a good business opportunity, and over the past six decades of communist rule they have migrated in substantial numbers to Shanghai in search of profit. Many opened *ashkana,* or Uighur restaurants. These establishments serve such spicy and delicious Xinjiang delights as *laghman* (stir-fried noodles with mutton, eggplant, tomatoes, potatoes, and hot green peppers); *poluo* (rice pilaf); *samsa* (samosas with mutton, beef, or vegetables); *chushira* (dumpling soup with spicy peppers); nan (bread with garlic or salt-and-sesame top-

Japanese to Mexican, Moroccan, Indian, and Nepali. Whether you crave British-style fish and chips, New York–style pizza, Spanish tapas, or the latest and tastiest fusion cuisine, you will find it available and served with panache somewhere between The Bund and Hongqiao—and most probably in the Xintiandi–Fuxing Park area. ■

Patrons dine in style at an elegant restaurant in Shanghai's former French Concession.

pings); and, of course, the ubiquitous Central Asian kebab, the aroma of which, grilling over charcoal fires, should help guide the hungry visitor the last few steps to the *ashkana* threshold, most notably in Huangpu's Little Xinjiang.

INTERNATIONAL CUISINE

Shanghai is developing a worldwide and well-deserved reputation as a destination for sophisticated and diverse dining opportunities. The city overflows with bustling restaurants and food malls, and more open every week. Diners may choose cuisines ranging from Italian, German, French, and Russian to Thai, Korean, Vietnamese, and

TEA & OTHER BEVERAGES

The most popular drink in China is, of course, tea, with green tea being the most common. Hangzhou's Longjing tea, which has been produced near Shanghai for nearly a thousand years, is considered one of China's best teas (see sidebar p. 182). Look also for flower tea (jasmine, for example), which mixes green tea with flower petals; black tea; red tea; and the highly prized oolong tea.

Beer is popular with meals; China has taken over as the world's largest brewer, and Shanghai boasts several breweries that produce decent lagers. Chinese spirits, a centuries'-old tradition, can be tame or deadly; be forewarned! ■

History of Shanghai

THE ANNALS OF CHINA'S PAST REVEAL SHANGHAI'S DEVELOPMENT FROM A tiny fishing outpost more than a thousand years ago to China's greatest and most developed city by the start of the 21st century. The intervening millennium saw the port's history of poverty and suffering transform into unprecedented prosperity.

EARLY TIMES TO THE QING

Originally a small fishing village on the west bank of the Huangpu River, Shanghai was generally overshadowed by its larger and more eminent neighbors, Hangzhou and Suzhou. It gradually grew in size and importance, with its status being upgraded first to town, then to market town, and then in 1292 to regional capital of a newly created Shanghai County under Kublai Khan.

In 1404, shortly after the establishment of the Ming dynasty (1368–1644), Shanghai's commercial importance had increased sufficiently for the new government to order the Huangpu dredged and developed into the major waterway of the southern Yangtze River Delta, thus ensuring Shanghai's eventual supremacy as regional port. The emerging port's rising prosperity attracted the unwanted atten-

carefully restored Dajing Tower remains. The area once enclosed is now known as Nanshi, or Southern City; it is more generally referred to in English as Shanghai Old Town.

QING DYNASTY (1644–1912)

Shanghai continued to prosper, and by the time the Qing dynasty began its rule, the city had developed into the most important maritime port in the lower Yangtze region. Its fortunes increased further when the great Qing Emperor Kangxi (1661–1722) lifted a late 14th-century ban on overseas trading, allowing the port to become the main trading port for regional maritime shipping as well as for commerce along the Yangtze River. In 1732 Shanghai was made the headquarters of the Jiangsu Customs Office, and by the middle of the reign of Emperor Qianlong (1735–1796), the city had emerged as the largest port in East Asia.

Qianlong grew disturbed by the rising tide of opium arriving on Western shipping and the corresponding depletion of the national treasury, especially in silver coinage, so in 1760 he restricted all foreign trade to Canton (Guangzhou). Seeing their trading companies' profits sink, the Western powers, especially Britain, pressured Qianlong to rescind this legislation and open China fully to overseas trade. Qianlong famously refused and warned the British that vessels putting ashore at any point other than Guangzhou would be immediately expelled. In reality, the restrictions proved little more than a formality: Shanghai continued to function as a major port and transshipment center, albeit in a more clandestine fashion.

A natural disaster in the mid-1820s reversed Shanghai's official closure to trade. The Huang He (Yellow River) burst its banks, damaging the Grand Canal and disrupting the vital transport of grain from the fertile granaries of Central China to Beijing, forcing Emperor Daoguang

tions of the infamous Japanese pirates—known as *wokou* in Chinese—who had begun raiding the Korean and Chinese coasts around 1350.

By 1550 these raids had increased in frequency to the point where the Zhejiang and Jiangsu coastal regions were being attacked on an annual basis, prompting the citizens of Shanghai to appeal to the government for permission to build a 3-mile-long (4.8 km), 27-foot-tall (8 m) defensive wall around the city. Completed in 1553, a date that is generally accepted as the foundation of the present city, these fortifications would survive until the early 20th century, when they were torn down as part of a modernization program by the Nationalist authorities—only the

(1820–1850) to decree that rice should be shipped by sea from the expanding docks of Shanghai to Beijing. This only enhanced Shanghai's growing wealth and strategic importance.

Opium trade

Meanwhile, the traffic in opium, mostly shipped by the British from their colonies in Bengal (since incorporated into Bangladesh and India), continued to increase at an

In 1799 Emperor Jiaqing (1796–1820) reaffirmed the ban on opium promulgated by his father, Qianlong, but without noticeable effect. In 1810 he further announced that: "Opium is a poison, undermining our good customs and morality. Its use is prohibited by law." His son, Emperor Daoguang, continued to issue edicts after he came to the dragon throne in 1820, but to no avail—the British weren't listening, nor apparently were the opium addicts.

Migrants from all over China came to seek their fortunes in colonial Shanghai.

unchecked rate. At the end of Qianlong's reign, imports had reached around 1,000 chests annually. By the time Daoguang ascended to the imperial throne just 24 years later, this figure had grown to 30,000 chests annually. Each chest held 140 pounds (64 kg) of opium. By the end of the 18th century, there were millions of addicts in China, and the country was paying for its spiraling drug habit with silver specie, disastrously depleting the Qing treasury. Clearly, from a Chinese perspective, something had to be done.

Accordingly, in 1838 Daoguang sent Lin Zexu, the formidable governor-general of Henan and Hubei, as his commissioner to impose Qing anti-opium legislation on the unruly foreign traders in Canton (modern-day Guangzhou). To the fury of the Westerners—at whose head stood the British—Lin confiscated and destroyed more than 20,000 chests of opium and blockaded the port to foreign shipping. Lin also wrote to Queen Victoria, asking why the British prohibited opium imports into their own country but forced it on China. Was this a morally correct position, the commissioner asked?

Lin's letter was never delivered to Queen Victoria, though it was published in *The Times*. And while it may have given liberal anti-opium campaigners in Great Britain pause for thought, it raised no sympathy at all with the opium merchants of India and Canton, who loudly demanded compensation for their lost opium and pressed for military retaliation. This came in 1840, with the arrival of warships and soldiers from India. European military superiority ensured the First Opium War (1840–42) was short, sharp, and one-sided. The British seized control of Canton and sailed up the Yangtze to interdict tax barges carrying grain to the Imperial Court at Beijing. In June 1842, they also sailed up the Huangpu, storming and capturing the walled city of Shanghai in a single night.

Shortly after the fall of Shanghai, the Qing authorities sued for peace and the Treaty of Nanking was signed in August, transferring Hong Kong Island to the British in perpetuity, awarding Britain 21 million ounces (595 million g) of silver in compensation for the seized opium, and opening five Treaty Ports to foreign shipping and residence: Canton (Guangzhou), Xiamen, Fuzhou, Ningbo—and Shanghai. A supplementary agreement, the Treaty of the Bogue (1843), was also forced on the Qing, giving British subjects extraterritorial rights throughout China. From this time until the fall of the dynasty in 1912, Shanghai may have remained notionally a part of the Qing Empire, but in reality it was well on the way to becoming a new kind of international colony.

COLONIAL RULE (1842–1912)

The British forced open Shanghai in 1842, taking possession of a small section of muddy riverbank to the north of the Old Town; this area, centered on The Bund and Suzhou Creek, would soon become the heart of the British Settlement. It wasn't long before other Western nations anxious for a share in the rich China trade made their appearance. China signed similar treaties with France (Treaty of Whampoa, 1844) and the United States (Treaty of Wanghia, 1844), and new concessions were parceled out at Shanghai. France established a French Concession between the British Settlement and the Old Town, and the United States set up an American Settlement north of Suzhou Creek. Over the next 50 years, both the British Settlement and the French Concession would expand substantially to the west; in 1863 the British and American Settlements would voluntarily unite to create the International Settlement. Both the French Concession and the International Settlement were administered by their own municipal governments, and Qing law and authority did not apply there.

Though Qing law did not apply, Shanghai was still very much a Chinese city, packed with tens of thousands of nominal Qing subjects and loosely ruled by a handful of foreigners, less than a hundred of whom had settled in the city by 1848. As a result, Shanghai became an ideal refuge for all those anxious to escape the supervision of the Chinese authorities, from anti-Qing nationalists calling for the restoration of the Ming to common bandits and criminals. In 1851, the great proto-Christian Taiping Rebellion (see pp. 224–25) broke out across central China, bringing a new flood of refugees. And in 1853 Shanghai was briefly occupied by the Small Swords Society, a group opposed to Qing rule. Though the foreign settlements were unscathed by these events, in 1854 the settlement authorities created a joint military force, the Shanghai Volunteer Corps. It strengthened their hold on the city and incidentally created a safe haven for thousands of Chinese refugees fleeing the fierce fighting between the Qing and Taiping armies.

Partly in response to this, in 1854 new regulations were drawn up giving Chinese nationals the right to own property in the foreign settlements. Land values began to rise, and the first *shikumen* housing began to spring up (see sidebar p. 19). This architecture, a mix of Chinese and Western styles, was unique to Shanghai and would, in time, come to exemplify the city.

During the latter half of the 19th century,

as Western colonial power waxed and Qing authority waned, increasing numbers of migrants from Europe and North America settled in the foreign settlements, calling themselves Shanghainese. They prospered from the enforced, unequal system of free trade. The burgeoning city took on a still more international character as these early settlers were followed by their colonial sub-

Sikh policemen were one of the symbols of Old Shanghai. The British recruited them for police services, traffic duties, the riot squad, and the mounted section.

jects from elsewhere in the world. Vietnamese police, together with Moroccan, Algerian, and Senegalese soldiers, strolled and patrolled the streets of the French Concession, while Sikh police, Punjabi soldiers, and Parsee merchants fulfilled a similar role in the International Settlement. Soon they would be joined by Sephardic Jews from India and the Middle East, some of whom would develop into the richest business moguls in the Far East. Meanwhile,

by 1860 an estimated 300,000 Chinese were living in Shanghai, and property values had soared from $74 per acre (0.4 ha) at the beginning of the 1850s to around $12,000 per acre by the end of the decade.

As Shanghai grew increasingly wealthy and more detached from Qing rule, the city's foreign residents gradually began to adopt and adapt the foreign settlements to suit their increasingly sophisticated requirements, eventually transforming Shanghai into the least Chinese but most progressive city in China. The Western residents built a range of sports and entertainment venues for their amusement. Numerous clubs and societies came into existence; in 1866 the Amateur Dramatic Club was formed and the Lyceum Theater was opened in 1871. (It later burned down and the current Lyceum Theater on Maoming Nanlu dates from 1931.) The upper echelons of Shanghai society grew increasingly sophisticated, and when the Duke of Edinburgh, Queen Victoria's second son, visited the International Settlement in 1869, the city earned its first royal seal of approval.

During the latter half of the 19th century, Shanghai continued to prosper as a unique hybrid Sino-Western city, introducing a series of "firsts" in China that would later spread elsewhere in the country: gas lighting (1865); modern fire brigade (1866); railway (1876), which linked Shanghai with Wusong Fort, where the Huangpu enters the Yangtze; telephone system (1881); electricity (1882); tap water (1883); postal system (1896); motor cars (1901); city trams (1908); and the first airplane flight (1909).

Rising Japanese threat

While Shanghai and its Western colonial overseers were enjoying these successes, a new power, Imperial Japan, was rising in the east. After the Meiji Restoration of 1868, the emerging Japanese military began to cast covetous eyes on neighboring Korea and China, anxious to enjoy the same special rights and privileges the European colonial powers had forced from the Qing. In 1875 Tokyo made its first move, forcing Korea to open itself to Japanese trade and to declare itself independent of China in foreign policy.

The Qing authorities refused to countenance this, ushering in a period of competition between Japan and China for control over the "hermit kingdom" of Korea.

In 1894 this conflagration erupted into a full-scale war, which the Japanese with their modernized military swiftly won, sinking the Chinese fleet off the Yalu River, as well as occupying all of Korea and part of Manchuria, including the strategic port of Dalian (also known as Port Arthur). In 1895 the humiliated Qing were forced to sign the Treaty of Shimonoseki. In addition to control over Korea, Formosa (modern-day Taiwan), and other territories in perpetuity, Japan won substantial reparations and the right to settle and open factories in Shanghai. Before 1895 only a small handful of Japanese resided in Shanghai; by the fall of the Qing dynasty in 1912, the Japanese formed the largest non-Chinese element in the city, numbering more than 5,000. Most of them settled and lived in the northern district of Zhabei, which would soon acquire the sobriquet Little Tokyo.

Early 20th-century Shanghai

By the beginning of the 20th century, Shanghai was effectively detached from China and the declining Qing government. During the anti-Qing and anti-foreign Boxer Uprising (1899–1901), the foreign legations in Beijing came under siege, but the Boxers (The Group of Righteous Harmony) made no move against the foreign settlements in Shanghai. Nevertheless, the British dispatched a force of 3,000 Indian Army troops to the city from Hong Kong, and the French sent 350 Vietnamese riflemen. A military parade held in the foreign settlements at this time gives a clear idea of the polyglot, multiethnic nature of Shanghai society at the turn of the 20th century: The force reportedly was composed of Rajputs, Sikhs, Baluchis, Gurkhas, Japanese, and Vietnamese, as well as British, French, and German regulars, together with assorted European volunteers.

During the first decade of the 20th century, the nature of Shanghai began to change as a result of the Japanese establishment of factories in Zhabei, a move that

China's dynasties

Xia ca 2205–1766 B.C.

Shang ca 1766–1122 B.C.

Zhou
Western ca 1122–771 B.C.
Eastern ca 771–256 B.C.

Qin 221–206 B.C.

Han
Western 206 B.C.–A.D. 9
Xin (Wang Mang) A.D. a 9–23
Eastern A.D. 25–220

Three Kingdoms period 220–265

Jin
Western Jin 265–316
Eastern Jin 317–420

Northern
Northern Wei 386–534
Eastern Wei 534–550
Western Wei 535–557
Northern Qi 550–577
Northern Zhou 557–581

Southern
Song 420–479
Qi 479–502
Liang 502–557
Chen 557–589

Sui 581–618

Tang 618–907

Five Dynasties
Later Liang 907–923
Later Tang 923–936
Later Jin 936–947
Later Han 947–950
Later Zhou 951–960

Song
Northern 960–1127
Southern 1127–1279

Yuan 1279–1368

Ming 1368–1644

Qing 1644–1911

Republic of China
1911–1949 (maintained in Taiwan)

People's Republic of China
1949–present

A dangerous beauty

The lovely, delicate opium poppy flourishes in the cool, nutrient-poor hills of southwest China. A plant of eastern Mediterranean origin, it was probably introduced about a thousand years ago to both China and India by Arab traders. At first the Chinese prized the plant for its medicinal values—in the raw state it acts as an antidote for pain, diarrhea, and coughing, and it was widely used as an anaesthetic.

But the situation changed in the 18th century, when Great Britain began to pay for Chinese tea shipments with opium from India, rather than with silver. With the added increase in supply, thousands grew addicted to the narcotic, creating an unprecedented social problem in China. Shanghai played a pivotal role in the drug's distribution.

The Qing emperors recognized the substance's rising use and the effect it was having on their people. They made it illegal to import opium. However, after the Second Opium War (1856–1860)—fought against France and Britain—they were forced to sign unequal treaties, including opening China to the opium trade. In 1870 opium accounted for 43 percent of China's total imports. By 1890, about 10 percent of China's total population were opium smokers.

During this time, there were literally hundreds of dens in Shanghai where people would go to smoke opium, or *tu* (earth), as it was usually called. Most opium dens were clustered in Nanshi and Zhubei, along the waterfront and Fuzhou Road, as well as in the Great World. The dens were generally very basic: Patrons were given a hard, wooden bunk or board to lie on, a wooden pillow, and a pipe. The smoke-filled dens tended to be quiet since users were more likely to doze while under the influence than to shout. The experienced smokers would have half a dozen or more pipes in one sitting.

The Europeans didn't seem overly concerned about their contribution to the growing addiction problem. The Jardine, Matheson Co. made the following statement in the 1800s in response to the opium question: "The use of opium is not a curse but a comfort to the hard-working Chinese; to many scores of thousands it has been productive of healthful sustention and enjoyment."

Due to fierce competition, compounded

Opium smokers at an upscale Shanghai opium den, circa 1905. Shanghai's fortunes were founded on such illicit operations as drug trafficking.

of the Pearl of the Orient that had illuminated the city through decades of civil war, Japanese invasion, and freewheeling capitalism were turned off, and at night the streets were dark, lit here and there only by a guttering candle or flashlight.

Today, Shanghai is vibrant, throbbing with life and commerce of all kinds. The only candles to be seen grace the tables of fine restaurants, and the entire city is vividly illuminated, from the neon signs of Nanjing Donglu to the bright laser beams that wheel above the city, piercing the night from the tops of newly constructed skyscrapers in Pudong and around Remin

Park, as well as along the historic Bund. Shanghai, the Pearl of the Orient, is back, and not as the Whore of the Asia. To be sure, social inequalities have re-emerged, and Beijing is seriously concerned at rising income disparities. Yet during the years of communist austerity, the only equality achieved was that of poverty. For all their continuing problems, Shanghai and its people have never had it so good at any time in their history. ■

Pudong's skyline illustrates the nation's new dynamically changing economic powerbase.

44

Arts & culture

IT WOULD BE DIFFICULT, IF NOT IMPOSSIBLE, TO FIND A MORE SOPHISTICATED and cosmopolitan center of the arts in China than Shanghai. Shanghai's long exposure to the Western world—and, indeed, Japan—have made the city's intellectual and artistic outlook the most forward and progressive in the country, embracing with readiness overseas cultural concepts and traits that would seem strangely foreign farther inland even today. Long the richest city in China, 21st-century Shanghai prides itself on its past cultural achievements and current sophistication, and now it can afford to build more opera houses, theaters, and galleries than anywhere else in China.

CHINESE OPERA

Chinese opera traces its roots back to the Pear Garden opera troupe of Emperor Xuanzong of the Tang dynasty (618–907). Today's performers of Chinese opera are still sometimes referred to as "adepts of the Pear Garden." The dramatic art form grew increasingly complex and sophisticated through the Yuan, Ming, and Qing dynasties, diversifying into no fewer than 368 different forms. The most popular and best known, by far, is Beijing opera, which had developed into its present form by the mid-19th century. Most Chinese opera performances staged in China are of this genre.

Beijing opera

In Chinese, Beijing opera is styled *jingxi*, or opera of the capital. It incorporates elements of traditional Chinese opera from the Anhui and Hubei Provinces and is sung in Mandarin. Traditional percussion and string instruments provide a powerful rhythmic background to the singing and acting. The entire process is allusive. Hand gestures, footwork, general body movements, and posture all play a significant role; acrobatic movements indicate violent action, usually accompanied by loud use of clapper drums and cymbals; heavy makeup indicates mood, personality, and even morality. Costumes are invariably colorful and richly lavish. Traditionally, all jingxi roles, regardless of gender, have been played by males; only in the latter part of the 20th century were female actors introduced.

Beijing opera has a vast repertoire of more than a thousand operas, mainly derived from historical events and novels concerning political intrigues and military struggles. A very popular form of entertainment, opera is enjoyed by viewers both live in theaters (often open air) and on television. A good place to see Beijing opera performed live is at downtown Shanghai's Yifu Theater.

Kunqu, Shaoxing, & Huju opera

Shanghai stages also feature, although to a lesser extent, three local or regional schools of opera: Kunqu, Shaoxing, and Huju. Kunqu opera, named after Kunshan in nearby Suzhou Prefecture, reached its peak in the Ming and Qing periods, but virtually disappeared by the beginning of the 20th century. Predating Beijing opera, Kunqu draws on southern traditions and is generally performed in Wu rather than Mandarin. Today it has made something of a comeback and is performed in Shanghai, Suzhou, and Nanjing, as well as in Beijing and Taipei. Two famous Kunqu operas are *The Peony Pavilion* and *The Peach Blossom Fan;* some of China's best-known classical novels have also been adapted to Kunqu performances, including *Romance of the Three Kingdoms* and *Journey to the West.* The Kunqu Museum in Suzhou is an excellent place to listen to this genre of Chinese opera.

Shaoxing opera originated in Shengxian County, Zhejiang Province. Also known as Yue opera, it derives from a style of storysinging accompanied by a drum, clappers, and a small orchestra. The homegrown Huju opera has a distinct repertoire all of its own. It is sung in the Shanghai dialect and is performed at outdoor venues and religious locations such as the Temple of the Town

A performer acts in a Beijing opera staged at Shanghai's popular Yifu Theater.

God or Chenghuang Miao in Shanghai Old Town.

TRADITIONAL & CONTEMPORARY DANCE

Shanghai has a rather modern and international tradition of dancing, encompassing dance styles dating from the 1920s, when jazz was the rage and the city dance halls swung to the sound of visiting Filipino bands. All this was swept away by the communists in 1949 but has made a return since the liberalizing 1990s. Ballroom dancing remains popular, and not just in dance halls but in parks and public places across the city.

Western-style classical ballet was introduced to the city by colonial Shanghainese in the 19th century, but still more so by the White Russian refugees of the early 20th century, who opened a ballet school in 1935. After the communist revolution in 1949, Soviet ballet teachers came to Shanghai and helped develop the Shanghai Ballet, only for this admirable institution to be culturally and artistically crippled during the Cultural Revolution. Today the Shanghai Grand Theater in People's Square is home to the Shanghai Ballet and puts on regular performances of both classical Western and revolutionary Chinese ballet.

Modern dance enthusiasts should try to catch a performance by the Jin Xing Modern Dance Company. This renowned troupe has performed in Australia, Europe, and North America. But Shanghai's modern dance scene isn't limited to classical and traditional forms. Inevitably, in a city that sees itself on the cutting edge of interaction between China and the West, hip-hop appeared in the city's discos and dance studios by about 2000. But this hip-hop came via the culturally distorting route of Japan, Taiwan, and South Korea. The result is still recognizably hip-hop, but in a sanitized, moderated form that better suits both the locals and their political masters in Beijing. In a city once dominated by triads, celebration of gang culture would scarcely be welcomed as cool by the Communist Party. Chinese hip-hoppers rap about getting ahead, not about guns. For Shanghai hip-hop at its most authentic, check out the Dragon Dance Studio, just off The Bund, or the Pegasus Club on Huaihai Zhonglu, where U.S. rapper Ice-T performed in 2005.

MUSIC
Traditional
Shanghai and the surrounding region—perhaps most especially in Suzhou—is noted for *pingtan*, a form of *shuochang* (spoken song) associated particularly with Jiangsu Province. Two people—usually a man and a woman—tell stories to music played on string instruments like the *pipa*, accompanied by bursts of song and lively facial expressions. Good places to hear authentic Suzhou pingtan are the Shen Residence in the town of Luzhi and the Pingtan Museum in Suzhou.

Classical
As a cultured and affluent city, Shanghai takes pride in its Western-style orchestras, most notably the Shanghai Symphony Orchestra, based at the stunning Shanghai Grand Theater on People's Square. Established in 1879, it originally was called the Shanghai Municipal Band. Since those early days, it has gone from strength to strength, and today it puts on regular world-class performances and is generally judged the best in China.

Visiting orchestras (including the Hong Kong Philharmonic and Philadelphia Chamber Orchestra) frequently perform at Shanghai Concert Hall on Yan'an Donglu, while farther to the west, in the Fuxing area, the Shanghai Conservatory of Music holds classical music concerts each Sunday night.

Pop & rock
Shanghai is at the forefront of China's still nascent but increasingly sophisticated pop and rock scene. Over the past six or seven years, the authorities have quietly relaxed their opposition to the open performance of musical forms once considered decadent and subversive manifestations of Western cultural imperialism. Shanghai's rockers have been mainly influenced by groups like U2, Blur, Suede, and, more recently, Coldplay and Arctic Monkeys, as well as Goth bands such as The Cure and punk

bands such as The Clash. American funk-rock, too, is increasingly popular, especially the Red Hot Chili Peppers. These Western influences, however, have been tempered by Taiwanese and other East Asian influences to become more suited to the mores and sentiments of modern Shanghai.

A deliberately self-styled underground alternative rock movement parallels but doesn't exactly duplicate its Western roots, embracing elements of grunge, heavy metal, and punk, together with moderated forms of dress to suit the genre. The authorities seem to be turning a relatively blind eye to such manifestations of individualism and opting out.

Most Chinese pop/rock bands have yet to find success outside China, but there are a few of note: The band Banana Monkey produces a danceable funk sound. As lead singer, Miss Tan provides the sweet, sad vocals of Booji, a Shanghai rock band. Xiao Yao sings lead for the eponymous band that plays hard beat electronics.

A group of young acrobats perform at Shanghai Center Theater on Nanjing Road West.

A scene from 1995's *Shanghai Triad (Zhang Yimou)*, starring Chinese actress Gong Li (center)

Widely popular groups are booked into the Shanghai Stadium on Xaoxi Road North, which can seat 80,000. The Rolling Stones performed here in 2006, although the authorities banned songs with sexually suggestive lyrics, including "Beast of Burden," and "Let's Spend the Night Together." Other rock and pop concert venues include Hongkou Stadium in the north of the city and Changning Stadium in the west. The popularity of smaller venues is changeable, and the city has many discos and dance clubs—currently Ark Live House, Yuyintang, and Bandu Music lead the scene—with more opening every year.

FILM

Shanghai was the birthplace of Chinese cinema. The country's first short film, *The Difficult Couple (Nanfu nanqi),* was made here in 1913, and the first full-length feature film, *Orphan Rescues Grandfather (Gu'er jiu zuji),* was similarly made here in 1923. By the 1930s, Shanghai was firmly established as the center of China's filmmaking industry, generating such famous stars as the

tragic Ruan Lingyu (1910–1935). China's first silent movie goddess, she made more than 15 movies—including *White Cloud Pagoda (Baiyun Ta,* 1928), *Goddess (Shennu,* 1934), and *New Woman (Xin nuxing,* 1934), before committing suicide at age 24. Another famous movie star was the lovely Zhou Xuan (1918–1957), who achieved stardom in *Street Angel* (1937) but died tragically of encephalitis at the young age of 39. The most infamous film actress to come out of Shanghai was Jiang Qing who, later as wife to Mao Zedong and leader of the Gang of Four, dealt a virtual deathblow to all aspects of art and culture in China during the Cultural Revolution (1966–1976).

Inevitably, Shanghai cinema suffered under the austere regime of hard-line communism, but the city has gradually been reclaiming its cinematic birthright since the mid-1980s. Stephen Spielberg shot *Empire of the Sun* here in 1987, and more recently, Merchant Ivory Productions shot *The White Countess,* a 2005 feature about a White Russian countess fallen on hard times in 1930s Shanghai. Locally made movies are making a long overdue comeback, too, including Zhang Yimou's 1995 *Shanghai Triad,* set in the 1930s and starring the actress Gong Li, and Lou Ye's 2002 *Suzhou River,* a difficult love story set by the banks of Suzhou Creek in the north of the city. In 2004 the Shanghai Film Academy opened, perhaps heralding a return to the city's film-making glory days of some 80 years ago.

LITERATURE

Shanghai is not closely associated with traditional Chinese literature, but it certainly emerged as a center of literary excellence during the first half of the 20th century. The city's vibrancy provided inspiration for both revolutionary socialist writers, like Lu Xun, whose most celebrated work is *The True Story of Ah Q* from the 1920s, and Mao Dun, author of *Midnight,* and more romantic bourgeois writers, like Eileen Chang and Shao Xunmei. The northern district of Hongkou, in particular, is associated with Lu Xun, the father of modern Chinese literature, and his League of Left-wing Writers. Today considerable space is devoted to Lu Xun in and around the area's Duolun Road walking street. See pp. 239–40 for a run-down of Shanghai's writers past and present.

Besides being associated with such famous Chinese writers, Shanghai is also linked with the names of several well-known foreign writers and playwrights. Noel Coward (1899–1973) wrote his novel *Private Lives* (1930) while staying at the Cathay Hotel. The French novelist André Malraux set his 1933 novel *La Condition Humaine (Man's Fate)* in the city, examining the White Terror launched against the communists by Chiang Kai-shek and his Green Gang associates in 1927. More recently, Japanese novelist Kazuo Ishiguro set the first part of his novel *When We Were Orphans* (2000) against a backdrop of Shanghai.

PAINTING & VISUAL ARTS

In traditional China, painting and its more exalted corollary, calligraphy, were the most highly valued arts in court and intellectual circles. They were produced mainly by scholars and Mandarins, who had sufficient artistic training and leisure time to produce

Chinese writer, thinker, and revolutionary Lu Xun (above) and French writer and leftist André Malraux (below) both feature prominently in Shanghai literature.

the high quality brushwork. Original texts by famous calligraphers have been greatly valued throughout China's history and are mounted on silk or paper scrolls and hung on walls in the same way that paintings are. Since the Tang dynasty, most traditional paintings have emphasized the sparse and simple qualities of nature, as well as the complex relationship between natural scenes and the inner harmony of man.

The area around Shanghai, including Hangzhou and Suzhou, has a long and distinguished history in the field of painting and other visual arts. The Songjiang School of Painting dates back to the Ming dynasty, when it was centered on Suzhou. It emphasized traditional Chinese painting techniques, as well as calligraphy and poetry, examples of which may be seen today on the walls of Suzhou Museum.

The Shanghai School of Painting is also traditional in style, but it dates from the late

Young artists gather to admire an exhibition at a Moganshan Road gallery.

criticism is that Shanghai painting and sculpture is commercially driven, creating little that is genuinely original and driving up prices in a status-conscious, nouveau riche society that tends to value image over substance. This may be so, but compared with just a decade ago, the Shanghai art scene is freer and more original, as well as involving a broader spectrum of the city's populace, than it has ever been in the city's history.

The best places to visit and learn about the Shanghai art scene, both traditional and contemporary, are the Shanghai Art Museum and the Old Shanghai Art Museum, both in the People's Park area; and the Bund Center, where a Museum of Public Art features thousands of Chinese and Western masterpieces. ■

Festivals

CHINA, LIKE MUCH OF EAST ASIA, FOLLOWS TWIN CALENDRICAL SYSTEMS when it comes to marking and celebrating festivals. Traditional Chinese holidays and indigenous religious festivals follow the Chinese lunar calendar, in line with neighboring Korea, Vietnam, Singapore, and Malaysia, while modern secular holidays and imported Christian religious holidays follow the Gregorian calendar. Muslim religious holidays, marked by Shanghai's Hui and Uighur minorities, follow the Islamic lunar calendar but are not officially celebrated by the city authorities. Notable festivals and holidays are divided below into traditional/indigenous and secular, then listed in chronological order.

TRADITIONAL CHINESE & INDIGENOUS RELIGIOUS HOLIDAYS

Chinese New Year

The single most important event in the Chinese calendar, the three-day Chunjie, or Spring Festival, begins on the first day of the first lunar month, which generally occurs in late January or early February. On the first day, families gather together at home for special feasts. Debts are paid off, the household is put in good order, new clothes are worn, and children receive red envelopes, called *hong bao,* containing monetary gifts. In Shanghai, the Longhua Temple plays host to special celebrations and a traditional Buddhist temple fair.

Lantern Festival

Celebrated on the 15th day of the first lunar month, Yuanxiao Jie, or Lantern Festival, marks the official end of winter and the coming of spring. People traditionally hang red lanterns outside their homes as tribute to the Taoist Lord of Heaven, or Jade Emperor. In Shanghai, much of the festivities center on Yu Gardens, where traditional delicacies, including *tangyuan* (sweet rice dumplings), are for sale. A wealth of red lanterns line the nearby walking street.

Birthday of the Goddess of Mercy

Guanshiyin Shengri, the Birthday of Guanyin, Goddess of Mercy, feminine aspect of the Bodhisattva Avalokitesvara, falls on the 19th day of the second lunar month. Pious Buddhists make offerings to the goddess at temples and ask for her blessing. The most interesting and active celebrations take place on the island of Putuoshan in Hangzhou Bay, the supposed *bohimanda,* or place of enlightenment, and spiritual home of Guanyin.

Tomb-Sweeping Festival of Qingming

This traditional festival honors the dead and is now held annually on April 4 or 5. Relatives tidy and clean the tombs of their deceased ancestors and lay out offerings of flowers and incense. Various symbolic paper gifts are burned for the use of the deceased in the hereafter, including hell money, domestic items such as televisions and refrigerators, and consumer desirables such as cars and motor bikes. Qingming is celebrated with some enthusiasm in Shanghai, where as many as eight million Shanghainese visit the tombs of their relatives.

Longhua Temple Fair

The Longhua Temple Fair, the largest and oldest temple fair in Shanghai, dates back to Ming dynasty times and is held on the third day of the third lunar month, which usually falls in April or May. Local belief holds that a dragon capable of granting people's wishes visits the temple on this day, normally coinciding with the blossoming of the peach trees in Longhua Park. The Buddha Maitreya is honored, and a street fair featuring Chinese opera, street theater, a vegetarian food fair, and displays of traditional arts is held.

Birthday of Mazu

On the 23rd day of the third lunar month, which usually falls in late April or early May,

A canopy of red lanterns hangs in Shanghai's Yu Gardens for the Spring Festival.

Shanghainese join devotees along the China coast, in Taiwan, and in Vietnam to honor Mazu, the Queen of Heaven and a sea goddess who has become the patron saint of sailors. Mazu is particularly venerated in Fujian. In Shanghai, the celebrations center on Longhua Temple, where visitors offer flowers and incense and gifts of money. Special traditional theatrical performances honor the goddess.

Birthday of Sakyamuni Buddha

On the eighth day of the fourth lunar month, usually falling in May, Mahayana Buddhists celebrate the Birthday of Sakyamuni Buddha (Gautama, the historic Buddha). In Shanghai, the best and most elaborate celebrations occur at Jingan Temple, which is dedicated to Sakyamuni. Buddhist monks chant prayers and play clappers and other temple instruments while the faithful clean images of the Buddha and make offerings.

Dragon Boat Festival

Generally held each June, Shanghai's Dragon Boat Festival—known in Chinese as Duan Wu—is centered around Suzhou Creek. The festival commemorates the death of Qu Yuan, a third-century B.C. poet-official who drowned himself to protest against government corruption during the Warring States Period. The dragon boat races are held on both Suzhou

Creek and the Huangpu River. Special delicacies served for the occasion include rice cakes called *zhongzi* that are stuffed with egg, pork, or bean paste.

Mid-Autumn Festival
The Mid-Autumn Festival of Zhongqiu Jie, also known as the Moon Festival, is celebrated on the 15th day of the eighth lunar month, which generally falls in September or October. This is a family-oriented celebration, when children listen to age-old tales of a mythical fairy that lives on the moon together with a jade rabbit, eat moon cakes (and all other kinds of delicious foods), watch firework displays, and stay up late.

SECULAR HOLIDAYS
Western New Year
Although a relatively new addition to the Chinese festival calendar, Yuandan—International, or Western, New Year, falling on January 1—is celebrated with some enthusiasm in Shanghai, as it is increasingly across China. Unlike Chinese New Year, which is a time for home and family, Shanghainese stay up late and celebrate the Western New Year with meals in restaurants, drinks in bars, and fireworks displays, much as other parts of the world do. In Shanghai, the event signals a three-day holiday. A bell-ringing service is held at Longhua Temple to pray for good fortune and prosperity in the coming year.

St. Valentine's Day
There is nothing traditional—in China, at least—about this secular Western celebration that falls on February 14. Purists might object to its growing popularity in China, but nowhere is St. Valentine's Day more popular than in outward-looking, Western-influenced Shanghai.

Shanghai International Literary Festival
Held each March or April, this two-week-long festival showcases local literary talent and provides an opportunity for internationally known writers to visit Shanghai and interact with each other and with Chinese writers. Booker Prize winners feature high on the list of celebrity names, with Kiran Desai, Amy Tan, and Simon Winchester attending in 2007. The event is generally held at the Glamour Bar at No. 5 The Bund.

Anting Kite Festival
This kite-flying festival and competition is held at Anting, in Jiading District in the northwestern suburbs of Shanghai, in the middle of April. Kite flying is an enduring popular pastime in the city, and any given evening enthusiasts fly their kites along the banks of Suzhou Creek. At the festival,

The Dragon Boat Festival commemorates the patriotic poet Qu Yuan.

Young girls dress in traditional costume for Shanghai's Dragon Boat Festival.

competitors strive to see who can reach the greatest heights.

Nanhui Peach Blossom Festival

Held each April at Nanhui in southeastern Pudong, this ten-day-long festival celebrates the gorgeous peach blossoms that bloom here each spring. Thousands of Shanghainese come year after year to enjoy the blossoms and partake in a variety of activities, including fruit-picking—Nanhui is home to thousands of acres of peach groves and is famous for the quality of its fruit. Festivalgoers can take in performances of lion dancing, stilt dancing, and ethnic dancing and sample some of the celebrated local rustic fare.

International Tea Festival

Taking place every April near the Shanghai Train Station in Zhabei District, the International Tea Festival celebrates the region's long association with tea production. Tea aficionados and experts from all over China and farther afield attend the festivities. Visitors can partake in tea ceremonies and tea tastings, wander through exhibits on tea culture, and join organized visits to out-of-town tea estates, notably at Hangzhou and Moganshan.

May Day

This secular holiday marking International Labor Day has now been extended to a seven-day break known as Golden Week. As at the Chinese New Year, people travel home in vast numbers at this time, clogging the transport system and making this week a good time to stay home. In Shanghai, a major fireworks display is staged at Daning Lingshi Park.

National Day

This secular event honors the founding of the People's Republic of China on October 1, 1949. It kicks off a weeklong holiday, so hundreds of thousands of people use the opportunity to return home, making transportation means impossibly crowded during this period.

Christmas

Christmas is now unofficially but widely celebrated in Shanghai, and not just by Christians. People go out for meals in restaurants, hold Christmas parties in offices and homes, and generally make the Christian religious festival an occasion for the exchange of presents, simple indulgence, and listening to Christmas jingles and other music. ■

Home to the elegant buildings that graced Shanghai's colonial-era International Settlement, the commercial district between The Bund and People's Park remains the vibrant, bustling heart of downtown Shanghai.

Waitan to Renmin Gongyuan

A unicycling pensioner on The Bund

Waitan to Renmin Gongyuan

WAITAN (THE BUND) TO RENMIN GONGYUAN (PEOPLE'S PARK) TAKES IN the nucleus of downtown Shanghai. It encompasses a famous stretch of the city's riverfront, featuring some of its grandest buildings, as well as Nanjing Donglu, Shanghai's busiest shopping thoroughfare. Not to be missed in this corner of the city is Renmin Guangchang (People's Square). Packed with civic buildings, a theater, and the city's best museum, the square forms the glittering cultural heart of Shanghai.

When Shanghai emerged from the Sino-British First Opium War of 1842 as a major international port, the riverfront area on the west bank of the Huangpu River just south of Suzhou Creek seemed destined to become the commercial heart of the newly minted city. Though the docks were farther downstream, closer to the

Huangpu's junction with the great Yangtze River at Wusong, the triumphant British decreed that this undistinguished stretch of riverside—the best real estate available to them at the time—would front the new British settlement.

The British named the waterfront road The Bund, after the Persian term

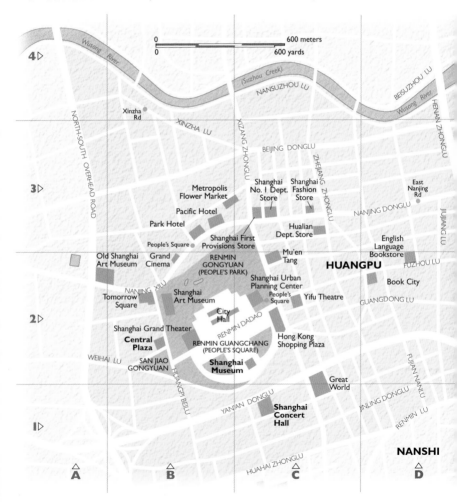

for embankment. Threading the heart of the British Concession was Nanjing Lu. Today this artery extends west from The Bund as far as the racecourse, which was decommissioned in the wake of the communist victory in 1949 and now forms the center of People's Square. Although the communist takeover largely purged The

Bund (and indeed the city in general) of its shocking social and racial inequalities, it likewise sapped the avenue's commercial prosperity and joie de vivre.

Since Shanghai reopened to foreign commerce in 1990, however, The Bund—ever the microcosm of the metropolis itself—has staged an astonishing comeback. Renamed Waitan and now part of Zhongshan Donglu, The Bund is once again the pulsing heart of modern Shanghai.

About midway along its length The Bund intersects Nanjing Donglu, a bustling pedestrian thoroughfare thronged with shoppers, street sculptures, toy trains, and street entertainers performing Chinese opera.

West of Nanjing Donglu the rehabilitated racecourse is now divided between Renmin Gongyuan (People's Park) to the north and Renmin Guangchang (People's Square) to the south. Like Nanjing Road, this extraordinarily prosperous area is ringed by fine civic buildings and suffused with a relaxed atmosphere. Early in the morning, before shoppers fill the new airconditioned malls and older markets, this is a popular site for people to practice tai chi. And it is not unusual to glimpse couples dancing.

Home to the best museums and theater in Shanghai, the Renmin Gongyuan area constitutes a cultural magnet that pulls in residents and visitors alike. Here it is possible to trace the origins and evolution of a booming international metropolis. Dignified civic buildings dating from the colonial period huddle in the shadow of futuristic towers of steel and glass that have soared into the sky during the last 15 years.

Beyond Renmin Gongyuan to the immediate west lies the small recreational area of Sanjiao Gongyuan, or Triangle Park. Quieter and less crowded than Renmin Gongyuan, the park attracts older city denizens who congregate here to chat, read newspapers, play chess or mahjong, exercise, or admire one another's caged pet birds. It's a pleasantly laid-back conclusion to any exploration of busy downtown Shanghai. ■

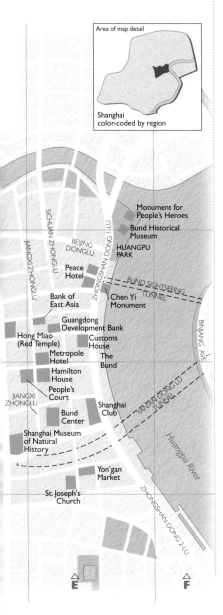

Area of map detail

Shanghai color-coded by region

Waitan—The Bund

The Bund

🅰 Map p. 63 E2–E4
& p. 69

THE BUND COMPRISES A COLLECTION OF BUILDINGS that developed along the Huangpu River (Shanghai's celebrated Yellow Creek) in the aftermath of the 1842 Treaty of Nanjing. The pact, signed aboard the HMS *Cornwallis* on the nearby Yangtze River by representatives of the Qing Emperor Daoguang and Queen Victoria's representative Sir Henry Pottinger, was one of many unfair treaties forced upon China by the West (and later Japan). Its provisions threw open five ports—Fuzhou, Guangzhou, Ningbo, Xiamen, and Shanghai—to foreign trade, residence, and consulates. (The Treaty of Nanjing also ceded Hong Kong Island to Great Britain in theoretical perpetuity.)

A smattering of Shanghai's increasingly prosperous citizens enjoy a stroll along The Bund.

AFTER THE TREATY

Within months of the treaty's signing, British merchants and seamen, together with their South Asian associates—soldiers, servants, and camp followers—began pouring into the most important of the five treaty ports: Shanghai. They landed at The Bund and established a toehold south and west of Suzhou Creek, on whose banks the British Consulate was later built. Landing stacks, or floating platforms, were erected along The Bund, project-

ing into the river to facilitate loading and unloading. (They have long since been dismantled.)

The British settlement in Shanghai more than doubled in size from 1843 to 1848, spurring other Western nations covetous of the rich China trade to follow suit. Both the United States and France used similar unequal treaties to wrest concessions of their own elsewhere in Shanghai.

Yet The Bund remained paramount, an emblem of Shanghai's ascendance, and it was trade that paid for it. Ships carrying silk, ceramics, and tea plied the Pacific to America, then returned via India with their holds full of opium. The British controlled most of the narcotics trade (which lasted well into the 20th century), and while Britons and other Westerners profited, China and the people of Shanghai decidedly did not.

The China trade soon outgrew its drug-soaked roots. Great financial houses, though founded largely on opium wealth, were eager to move into more legitimate spheres: banking, insurance, shipping, and real estate. To do so, they needed local bases in China. In Shanghai, the preferred location was the prestigious Bund.

In 1863 the British Concession merged voluntarily with the American Concession on the northern side of Suzhou Creek, and the International Settlement was born. By the early 20th century, the banks and trading houses dotting The Bund represented many nations, including

Great Britain, the United States, Russia, Germany, Japan, Holland, and Belgium. The French kept to their own exclusive preserve.

The citadels of commerce set up by British banking giants such as Jardine Matheson and Butterfield & Swire slowly transformed The Bund into a smaller (and uniquely Chinese) version of London's financial hub. Against all odds, these stone-and-marble edifices have survived years of communist austerity to reclaim their former splendor.

Visitors absorb the colossal scale of the Monument to the People's Heroes in Huangpu Park.

What's in a number?

The Chinese have traditionally regarded certain numbers as lucky and others—such as No. 4 on The Bund—as unlucky. This belief—frowned on under hard-line communism, but staging a comeback today—hinges on the tonal nature of the Chinese language, which decrees that one-syllable Chinese words have wildly different meanings depending on the tone with which they are pronounced.

Lucky numbers include 2 or *èr,* because good things generally come in twos (double happiness and so on). The number 6 is also lucky because *liù* or "six" sounds very similar to *liú,* or "flowing easily." Whereas 666 is considered unlucky

or even Satanic in some Western cultures, in China it is highly auspicious. The number 8, too, is considered lucky because it is pronounced *bā,* which sounds similar to *fā,* meaning wealth or prosperity. Finally, 9 is also considered fortuitous, as its pronunciation, *jiǔ,* sounds like *jiǔ* or "long-lasting." On the other hand, the number 4 is definitely bad news. Its Mandarin pronunciation, *sì,* sounds similar to the word *sǐ* or "death." For this reason, many streets—The Bund included—skip house No. 4. Likewise, many hotel and apartment blocks lack a 4th floor. The superstition has even gone high-tech: Nokia phones have no exchanges beginning with a 4. ∎

VISITING THE BUND

Foreign visitors to Shanghai once approached the city by water, disembarking at Wusong (where the Yangtze meets the Huangpu) or sailing up the Huangpu to The Bund. In a China chronically impoverished, exploited, or at war, such an arrival must have impressed travelers with visions of Shanghai's sophistication and wealth. Nowadays the visitor's first impressions are no less vivid, but they are forged by the new and massively impressive Pudong International Airport, whence travelers are whisked into Pudong on the Maglev railway before being shunted onto the metro or the freeway. The Bund's storied grandeur is less visible than it was before, and some might consider it eclipsed by the towers of downtown Pudong.

It's still easy to appreciate The Bund, however, and not just by day. Magic infuses an early morning stroll along this fabled section of the Huangpu River, especially when the air is chill and ships' sirens sound eerily out of the mist. The evenings can be equally enchanting, as hundreds of people gather on the west side of the Huangpu, by the reinforced and restored Bund embankment, to watch the evening sun light the great skyscrapers and other futuristic structures of Pudong.

As darkness falls, the lights on both sides of the river illuminate the city—literally and figuratively. It's fascinating to contemplate the two halves of downtown Shanghai: the silhouette of Pudong, constantly changing as new towers of modernity spring up, and the skyline of Puxi, now restored to—and quite possibly surpassing—its erstwhile glory. These twin spectacles jointly symbolize modern China's most affluent and progressive city. ∎

Bank of Communications

Customs House

Hong Kong & Shanghai Bank

Walk The Bund

With the Huangpu River on one side and a string of historic buildings on the other, The Bund is a great place for a gentle north-to-south walk. There's some greenery at the northern end in Huangpu Park (Huangpu Gongyuan), and streetside stalls sell tempting snacks such as roast chestnuts—the ideal restorative on a cold winter day.

Start to the north, by Suzhou Creek and the **Waibadu Bridge** ❶. This venerable structure, once made of wood but replaced by a steel span in 1907, sits so low above Suzhou Creek that you wonder how even the low flat-bottomed sampans once managed to sail beneath the bridge. Today the once polluted creek has been cleaned up enough that the area is popular for kite-flying enthusiasts.

Heading south, on the left you'll come across **Huangpu Park.** Just beyond, where Suzhou Creek meets the Huangpu River, stands the massive **Monument to the People's Heroes.** The park is also home to the **Bund History Museum** ❷ (Waitan Lishi Jinianguan, *9 a.m.–4:15 p.m.*), which displays historical photographs of The Bund. Opposite, on the west side of the road (where most of the action is) you'll find the **former British Consulate.** It dates from 1873, making it the oldest surviving building on The Bund; today it's a municipal government building and usually closed to the public.

There follows a long stretch of fine neoclassic buildings running south along the west side of The Bund. Especially at night,

these structures are best admired from the promenade along the Huangpu River. Bear in mind, however, that from this removed vantage point a closer look at any of the facades will require a crossing of busy Zhongshan Donglu—typically a hectic experience. At No. 29 is the old building of the evocatively named **French Banque de l'Indochine** (now the Everbright Bank), and at No. 28 you'll find the former **Glen Line Steamship Building** (currently a broadcasting station). Next, at No. 27, is the former **Jardine Matheson Building** ❸, today the Shanghai Foreign Trade Corporation. Corinthian pillars still grace the edifice, a reminder of Jardine's former wealth.

No. 26 once housed the Danish Consulate and the Italian Chamber of Commerce, but it is now the **Agricultural Bank of China.** The upswept eaves and repeated

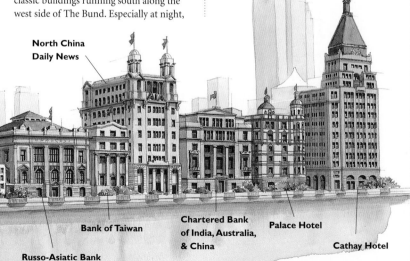

North China Daily News

Russo-Asiatic Bank

Bank of Taiwan

Chartered Bank of India, Australia, & China

Palace Hotel

Cathay Hotel

THE BUND AND ITS EARLY TENANTS

geometric motifs lining the facade of No. 23 **(Bank of China Building)** distinguish the address as the only Chinese-influenced building of any significance on The Bund.

Though Nos. 20 and 19 were once, the Cathay Hotel and the Palace Hotel, they were subsequently merged to form the celebrated art deco **Peace Hotel,** once stayed in by such distinguished guests as Charlie Chaplin, George Bernard Shaw, and Noël Coward—not to mention Sun Yat-sen's wife, Song Qingling. This venerable building is currently undergoing complete renovation and is due to reopen by 2009 as the Fairmont Shanghai. On the outer wall of the former Palace Hotel (if not covered by construction) there is an interesting brass plaque commemorating the International

Victor Sassoon built, designed, and lived in the original Cathay Hotel.

Opium Commission, held here in 1909, which marked the first truly rigorous concerted effort to halt international trafficking in the substance.

Opposite the Peace Hotel and the eastern end of Nanjing Donglu (Nanjing Road East), close by the embankment, stands a large **statue of Marshal Chen Yi** ❹ (1901–1972), commander of the communist New Fourth Army and later the mayor of Shanghai. Purged in 1967 during the so-called Great Proletarian Cultural Revolution, Marshal Chen Yi was initially offered protection by his old comrade Zhou Enlai, only to die at the hands of Red Guards in 1972.

South of Nanjing Donglu at No. 18 rises the **Chun Jiang Building,** now famously known as 18 The Bund. Formerly the Chartered Bank of India, Australia, and China, the structure today hosts various Western designer-label companies. On the seventh floor, the Bar Rouge offers cold drinks and inspiring views across The Bund and the Huangpu River to Pudong.

Just next door, No. 17 once housed the **North China Daily News,** the English-language newspaper that closed its doors in 1951. A lengthy tenancy by an austere communist bureaucracy ensued, but today the building houses the American International Assurance Company—another sign of Shanghai's headlong reversion to capitalism.

More famous buildings follow in profusion. At No. 16, the former Bank of Taiwan is now the **China Merchants Bank** ❺, while No. 15 (the former Russo–Asiatic Bank) today houses the **Shanghai Gold Exchange.** Once the Bank of Communications, No. 14 these days is the **Shanghai Trade Union Building.** At No. 13 note the venerable **Customs House.** Built in neoclassic style in 1925, it is dominated by a clock tower reminiscent of the tower of Big Ben and known locally to some as Big Ching.

At No. 12 you'll find The Bund's most celebrated building: the imposing **Shanghai Pudong Development Bank** ❻, formerly the Hong Kong and Shanghai Bank Building. More than any other icon, perhaps, the paired bronze lions guarding the main entrance have come to symbolize The Bund. Removed as totems of decadent capitalism

frequent, even if shopping is not your bag. Exploring the area is a tutorial of the changes that have taken place in China over the past 20 years and continue to take place at an exponential rate. That city leaders have joined forces with local businesspeople to restore much of the area to its colonial glory is a testament to the growing local fascination with Shanghai's rich past.

BEYOND NANJING DONGLU

To continue browsing turn south (left) at the Xizang Zhonglu (Tibet Road Central) the western end of Nanjing Donglu. In about 80 yards (75 m) you will reach the **Mu'en Tang** (Moore Memorial Church, *316 Xizang Zhonglu*), named after the American benefactor who funded its construction in the 1920s. The church became a school after the revolution, but it reopened in 1979 and continues to function as a house of worship today.

To the south (and closely paralleling Nanjing Donglu) runs Fuzhou Lu. This street lies in the heart of Huangpu District, noted more for its historical attractions than shopping options, but head here if you are looking for books. Two of the biggest and best bookshops in the city, both stocking English-language selections, are the more modern **City of Books** (*465 Fuzhou Lu*) and the **Foreign Languages Bookstore** (*390 Fuzhou Lu*). Both are exceedingly tolerant of browsers. It's not uncommon to see dozens of people—most apparently students—sitting or lying quietly around the stores, reading whatever takes their fancy for hours at a time. ∎

business as the Sun Sun in 1925.

Although the four restored colonial department stores are essentially similar, they are fun to visit for their evocations of Shanghai during the 1920s and 1930s. All four stock a wide variety of modern imported and locally made goods. Each has its adherents, but the best of the four is probably the Hualian.

Nanjing Donglu becomes Nanjing Xilu (Nanjing Road West) just west of the Shanghai No.1 Department Store, where the avenue passes north of Renmin Gongyuan and takes on a less commercial character.

Viewed in its totality, Nanjing Donglu is a fascinating place to

Shanghai's "Yellow Creek"

The Huangpu River is and always has been Shanghai's commercial lifeline. Neither the largest nor the longest river in the world—British spy James Davidson-Houston dubbed it Shanghai's Yellow Creek—the Huangpu is nonetheless both commercially significant and historically fascinating.

Although Huangpu means yellow-shored river, the name may in fact derive from the perennially yellow color of its waters. Just over 70 miles (114 km) long, the river rises in Lake Dianshan, close to the water town of Zhouzhuang (see pp. 198–199) west of Shanghai. It flows southeast and then north through the heart of the city of Shanghai to join the mighty Yangtze at Wusong. After flowing through Shanghai's outlying districts of Qingpu, Songjiang, and Minhang, the waterway courses through the city proper via the Baoshan District, then melds with its more powerful sibling near Changxing Island.

A statistical snapshot would show the Huangpu to average 1,312 feet (400 m) wide

modernistic, and (some would say) menacing bulk of **Tomorrow Square** (Mingtian Guangchang, *399 Nanjing Xilu);* it fairly dominates the western side of Renmin Gongyuan. Soaring 934 feet (285 m) high—good enough to qualify as only the fourth tallest building in Shanghai—it houses the Marriott Hotel and numerous private apartments. Depending on your approach to life—is it literal or is it figurative?—Tomorrow Square resembles a futuristic fountain pen or a nightmarishly gigantic dental instrument.

West of Tomorrow Square at 456 Nanjing Xilu is the **Old Shanghai Art Museum** (easy to confuse with the newer Shanghai Art Museum at 325 Nanjing Xilu). The designation "Old" is doubly addling because the displays are housed in what is clearly a new building. The explanation lies in the fact that the exhibits feature primarily traditional Chinese art. ■

Old Shanghai Art Museum
(Lao Shanghai Meishuguan)
✉ 456 Nanjing Xilu
🕐 9 a.m.–5 p.m.
💲 $

**Serenity suffuses
this painted
and gilt wooden
Bodhisattva from
the Song dynasty
(960–1279).**

Shanghai Museum

Shanghai Museum
(Shanghai Bowuguan)
🅰 Map p. 62 2B
www.shanghaimuseum.net/
en/

✉ 201 Renmin Dadao

☎ 6372 3500

🕐 9 a.m.–5 p.m.
Mon.–Fri.; 9 a.m.–8
p.m. Sat.

💲 $

PARTLY FOR THE INTRINSIC ELEGANCE OF ITS DESIGN
but mainly for its stupendous contents and state-of-the-art displays, the Shanghai Museum (Shanghai Bowuguan) south of
Renmin Dadao is the single most impressive building in People's
Square. The site is a treasure trove of Chinese art, culture, and history. It holds more than 120,000 artifacts, representing almost five
millennia of continuous civilization.

Inspired by the *da ke ding*—an
ancient, three-legged bronze
cooking vessel—on exhibit in the
museum, Shanghai architect Xing
Tonghe designed the building to
represent one. The museum also
incorporates the sacred geometry
of Yuanqiu, the circular altar at
the Temple of Heaven (Tiantan)
in Beijing. Its square base, representing the Earth, is surmounted
by a circular superstructure, representing heaven. Although
founded in 1952, this building
was completed in 1996 after three
years of construction. With its

four display floors covering more
than 420,000 square feet (39,200
sq m), there is plenty to see.
    Fronting the museum is a par-
ticularly elegant plaza. It features
a circular pool and elaborate
fountains, which—like so much
of the Renmin Gongyuan area—
are illuminated at night. This attracts playful children, young
lovers, and older people alike.
    The real attraction, of course,
is the museum itself, which
houses ten permanent galleries
and three temporary exhibition
halls. Before launching your own

actual tour, you can take the virtual tour offered at www.shanghaimuseum.net/en/.

The Shanghai Museum allows flash photos except where it might damage artifacts, such as in the painting and calligraphy halls. (If you plan to use a tripod, you'll need to request a permit in advance from the information counter.) Unless you speak fluent Chinese, you'll want to rent an audio guide, which is available in eight languages and requires a deposit (or passport). For souvenir

vessels, weapons, instruments, and burial objects abound; often these are elaborately decorated with people, animals, and pastoral scenes, including perhaps the earliest representations of housing in China. Chinese bronze-casting technology reached its apex in the late Shang and early Western Zhou periods (circa 1700–771 B.C.), when artifacts were adorned with complex patterns, animals, or religious motifs. Of special note are the impressively preserved racks of musical bells.

seekers, the excellent museum shop sells related literature and faithful reproductions of some of the facility's most famous pieces. There's also a good coffee shop and restaurant.

FIRST FLOOR

The most celebrated display in the museum is the **Gallery of Chinese Ancient Bronze,** where you can see more than 400 bronzes—some dating back more than four millennia to the Late Xia dynasty in the 21st century B.C. Marvelous examples of early

Also on this floor is the **Gallery of Chinese Ancient Sculpture,** which displays Buddhist statuary and iconography from across China and beyond. You'll find artifacts recovered from ancient cities along the Silk Road in Tibet, Mongolia, and Chinese Central Asia (now Xinjiang). There are Confucian stelae—some borne on the backs of turtles—imperial decrees, and records of battle triumphs that would have remained forgotten had they not been incised on these ancient stones. The eras covered

The museum's distinctive architecture evokes classical representations of the Temple of Heaven in Beijing.

SHANGHAI MUSEUM

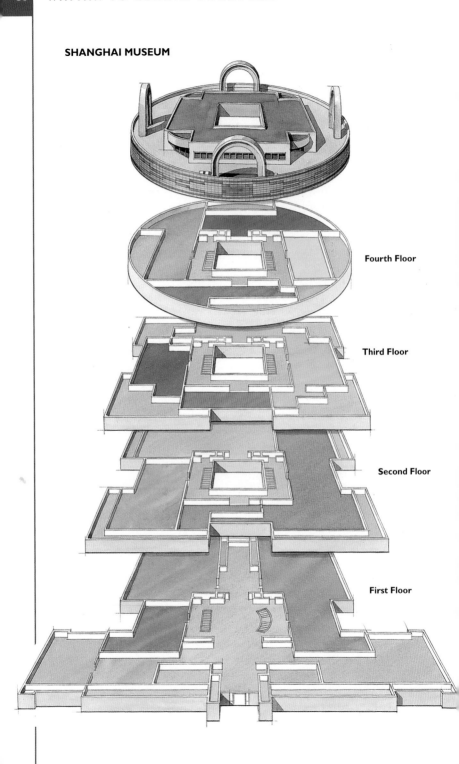

Fourth Floor

Third Floor

Second Floor

First Floor

extend from the Warring States Period (475–221 B.C.) to the Ming dynasty (1368–1644). The museum shop is also on this floor.

Temporary

Ceramic

Bronze

Sculpture

Calligraphy

Paintings

Ethnic

Furniture

Jade

Coins

Seals

Non-exhibition space

SECOND FLOOR

Dominating this floor is the **Gallery of Chinese Ancient Ceramics,** arranged from Neolithic times to the late Qing dynasty (1644–1911)—which seems like yesterday compared with some of the earliest pieces. More than 500 artifacts are on display, from early proto-celadon to the painstakingly finished polychrome-glazed ware of the T'ang dynasty (618–906). You'll learn about the famous ceramic kilns of Jingdezhen in northeastern Jiangsi, China's center of porcelain production from 1279 to 1911. The world-famous Jingdezhen cobalt blue-and-white porcelain, which reached its zenith in the Ming and Qing periods, is especially well represented.

THIRD FLOOR

There are three galleries on this floor, including the superbly lit **Gallery of Chinese Paintings.** Here each exhibit illuminates automatically as you approach, only to fade into darkness as you move on. It's not a tourist gimick but

A visitor takes in the games people played in this painting on display on the third floor.

The art of the state: Visitors feast on the treasures offered in a gallery devoted to ancient landscape painting.

a state-of-the-art technique designed to keep the antique displays from fading. Many of the paintings are landscapes, though exquisite portraits await here as well. More than 120 masterpieces are on display; they date from the early T'ang period onward.

Also on this floor is the **Gallery of Chinese Calligraphy,** similarly protected by the momentary-illumination technique. On parchments and manuscripts dating as far back as the T'ang period, you'll see examples of seal script *(zhuanshu),* official

script *(lishu),* running script *(xingshu),* grass script *(caoshu),* and regular script *(kaishu).* Even with the ability to read modern standard Chinese characters, most people are hard pressed to decipher much of this calligraphy—notably the fast-flowing, imaginative caoshu. Still, you needn't be a scholar of classical antiquities to appreciate the extraordinary elegance and sophistication with which cursive Chinese has evolved over the centuries.

Finally on this floor is the

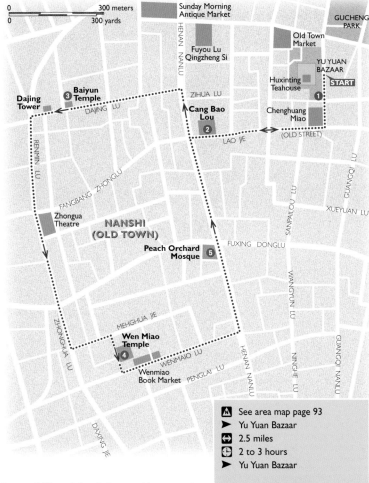

See area map page 93

► Yu Yuan Bazaar

↔ 2.5 miles

⏱ 2 to 3 hours

► Yu Yuan Bazaar

NOT TO BE MISSED
- Lao Jie
- Baiyun Temple
- Wen Miao

9 a.m.– 4:30 p.m.), the city's venerable Confucius Temple. Enter the temple via the back entrance along Menghua Jie (Menghua Street). As you do, you'll have to thread your way among the stalls of **Wenmiao Book Market,** where all manner of printed literature is for sale.

From the temple, continue east along Wen Miao Lu as far as the junction with Henan Nanlu, then turn left (or north) past No. 52, the **Peach Orchard Mosque 5,** or Xiaotaoyuan Qingzhen Si. Anyone can enter if it's not prayer time. You'll know the latter from the muezzin's Arabic call to prayer and from the orderly ranks of Hui Muslim men prostrating themselves west, toward Mecca.

Continue north along Henan Nanlu until you reach the now familiar junction with Fangbang Zhonglu. Turn right and re-trace your steps along Lao Jie, stopping for some delicious *xiao long bao.* These pork dumplings are a local specialty, and they can be seen (and, long before that, smelled) cooking in the doorways of a number of small Nanshi restaurants. Most notable among these is Shanghai Lao Fandian (Old Shanghai Restaurant) at 242 Fuyou Lu. ■

Hopeful visitors
to Yu Gardens toss
wishes wrapped
in red cloth into
a famous wishing
tree.

Yu Gardens

EAST OF THE HUXINTING TEAHOUSE, ABUTTING YU YUAN
Bazaar but not part of it, are the Yu Gardens (Yu Yuan), a sterling
specimen of a traditional Suzhou garden (see pp. 212–213).

Yu Gardens
(Yu Yuan)

🅰 Map p. 93 B3

✉ 218 Anren Jie

🕐 8 a.m.–5:30 p.m.

💲 $

Established by a Ming dynasty official in 1559, the Yu Yuan (Ease-Taking Gardens) took two decades to create. They have weathered multiple desecrations, including damage at the hands of British (1842), French (1853), and Japanese (1942) troops. Restored between 1956 and 1961, the Yu Gardens are once again at their best today.

Like most Suzhou-style gardens, the Yu Yuan are traditional and formal. They create the illusion of size but are in fact quite small—and, on weekends and public holidays, crowded. Spread over 5 acres (2 ha) and surrounded by a wall topped by an undulating, four-clawed dragon (five-clawed dragons being reserved for imperial use), they feature six main scenic areas and 30 pavilions, all linked by fanciful bridges and causeways.

The classical intent was to recreate a world in microcosm, with mountains and ridges, lakes, forests, and caves. These gardens had a more practical aim, too: to create

an idyllic retreat from the outside world and its problems, where the owners—founder Pan Yunduan, his aged father, and other family members—could relax apparently far from, but in reality close to, the travails of local government.

The **Grand Rockery** (Dajia-shan)—a 40-foot-high (12 m) "mountain range" made of Huangshi stone transported from Hubei during Ming times—is intended to resemble the limestone peaks of southern China. The **Exquisite Jade Rock** (Yuling-long) is said to have been acquired by the Pan family when the boat carrying it to the Imperial Court in Beijing sank nearby. Also worth inspection is the **Ten Thousand Flower Tower** (Wanhua Lou) and the **Heralding Spring Hall** (Dianchun Tang). From 1853 to 1855, during the great Taiping Rebellion, the Heralding Spring Hall was reputedly used as a headquarters by the revolutionary Small Swords Society, which sought to overthrow the Qing dynasty emperor. ■

Nanshi temples

AS THE OLDEST AND MOST TRADITIONAL QUARTER OF Shanghai, Nanshi has it fair share of temples. Within the bounds of the former Old Town, China's three main religious traditions—Buddhism, Taoism, and Confucianism—are amply represented.

In northwest Nanshi, **Baiyun Temple** is headquarters to the Shanghai Taoist Association. Taoist monk Xi Zicheng left Beijing's White Cloud Temple (Baiyun Guan), the spiritual center of Taoism in China, and made his way to Nanshi's Ancestor of Thunder Temple (Leizu Guan) in 1882. Six years later he transferred 8,000 Taoist scriptures from the mother temple in Beijing to Shanghai; to honor the event, Leizu was renamed Baiyun.

Centered on three halls, Shanghai's Baiyun Temple is dedicated to seven Taoist deities, the most important being Yuhuang Dadi (the Jade Emperor). Red Guards ravaged the temple during the Cultural Revolution, but it has since been beautifully restored.

The heart of Buddhism in Nanshi is located farther east, near the Yu Yuan Bazaar, at the **Eaglewood Nunnery** (Chenxiangge An, *29 Chenxiangge Lu, $*). This small, ocher temple houses several impressive images of the Buddha, 348 smaller figurines representing his disciples, and a community of 40 nuns clad in dark brown robes.

Taoism and Buddhism dovetail in the nearby **Temple of the Town God** (Chenghuang Miao), devoted to Han dynasty Gen. Huo Guang and Qin Yubo, the patron deity of Shanghai. Established at its present location during the reign of emperor Yongle (1403–1425), this venerable building was turned into a factory during the Cultural Revolution. It, too, has

since been restored.

Confucianism, the third of China's enduring *san jiao* (three teachings), is represented at the **Temple of Literature** (Wen

Baiyun Temple
(Baiyun Guan)
🅰 Map p. 93 A2 & p. 97
✉ 239 Dajing Lu
🕐 9 a.m.–5 p.m.
💲 $

A Confucius statue resides beneath the restored eaves of Nanshi's Wen Miao.

Miao) in southwest Old Town. Girt by a bright yellow wall, Wen Miao—like many Confucian temples elsewhere in China—remains relatively quiet and free of visitors; Confucianism has not enjoyed the same spiritual rebirth experienced by Buddhism and Taoism in the last three decades. The exception is July, the month for annual college-entrance exams, when anxious parents and students gather here to importune Master Kong (Confucius) for academic success. ∎

Temple of the Town God
🅰 Map p. 93 B3
✉ 249 Fangbang Zhonglu
🕐 8:30 a.m.–5 p.m.
💲 $

Temple of Literature
🅰 Map p. 93 B2
✉ 215 Wenmiao Lu
🕐 9 a.m.–4:30 p.m.
💲 $

Shikumen architecture: Twilight of a tradition

Not long ago, traditional Shanghai arch- itecture was distinguished by a style known locally as *shikumen,* or stone gate tenement housing. Once as unique to Shanghai as *hutong* lanes and courtyards were to Beijing, such housing is threatened today. Indeed, it may soon disappear alto- gether except in such restored, upmarket areas as Xintiandi (see pp. 116–117).

Shikumen owes its development to the city's unusual and close association with Western- ers through the Foreign Concessions. Essentially a blend of Chinese and Western styles, shikumen housing is aligned along straight, narrow alleyways called *longtang,* with each alley accessed via a stylized stone gateway in the form of an arch. First intro- duced to the city in the 1860s, houses of this type held as much as 80 percent of the pop- ulation by the 1930s. Today that percentage is far lower—and, as land values skyrocket and an increasingly affluent population demands more comfortable, more conve- nient, and, above all, more modern accom- modations, it continues to fall lower still.

In traditional Chinese domestic archi- tectural design, a central courtyard (the Beijing hutong is the exemplar) offered families an inner sanctum in which to relax, tend small gardens of herbs or flowers, and perhaps keep caged songbirds. Shikumen housing can be seen as a compromise between that model and the space con- straints of cheek-by-jowl 19th-century Shanghai. The tiny, almost vestigial courtyards of shikumen houses permit some fresh air to enter the building and allow a few potted plants to grow.

During the early 20th century, regret- tably, the population of the city swelled still further, making even this style of low-rise, densely packed housing no longer feasible. Shikumen houses were divided and then subdivided, until the only way out was up. (Some Chinese would argue that the shiku- men style was done in by the Shanghainese

love of change for change's sake, and it's undeniable that new styles and ideas are embraced here with an ardor unmatched in the rest of the country.) Whatever the precise forces, the introduction of free- market economics in the 1990s was the writing on the wall: The days of shikumen living were drawing to an end.

Few Shanghainese live in shikumen today. The narrow longtang alleys have all but disappeared, giving way to high-rise tower apartments for most ordinary people. The seriously affluent, for their part, have moved out to mock-Tudor housing estates and French château–style residences in the suburbs. A few traditional shikumen blocks survive, notably at Xintiandi and Huaihai, but the value of these restored or completely rebuilt buildings is astronomical. Most now serve as clubs, restaurants, or shopping complexes for the city's nouveau riche.

It's all very cyclical. In Shanghai (as in Singapore and Beijing), buildings once deemed archaic and fit only for demolition are newly chic—and preservation worthy. This dynamic will keep the last authentic shikumen houses alive. It may even spur modern architects to incorporate elements of this uniquely Shanghai style in contemporary designs. ∎

Residents of a typical shikumen housing arrangement gather in a longtang, or narrow alley, to gossip and play cards.

Nanshi mosques

Fuyou Lu Qingzhen Si

⛰ Map p. 93 B3 & p. 97

✉ 378 Fuyou Lu

🕐 8 a.m.–7 p.m.

IT'S PERHAPS NOT WIDELY KNOWN OUTSIDE CHINA, BUT Muslims have maintained a strong presence in the Middle Kingdom since their arrival by sea (as well as later along the Silk Road) in the 7th century A.D. Because Islam came to China as a religion of trade rather than conquest, its followers have tended to gather in the great mercantile centers—a status Shanghai did not fully achieve until the mid-19th century. For this reason, Islam came later to this city than it did to Xian, Guangzhou, and Beijing. But come it did, and its adherents continue to thrive today—particularly in Nanshi, site of the city's two oldest mosques.

Hui Muslim men in Nanshi gather to exchange a few words after prayers.

Peach Orchard Mosque
(Xiaotaoyuan Qingzhen Si)

⛰ Map p. 93 B3 & p. 97

✉ 2 Xiaotaoyuan Lu

🕐 8 a.m.–7 p.m.

Shanghai's Hui Muslims

Of China's 55 officially recognized national minorities, no fewer than 10 are Muslim, but only one sect, the Hui, speak Chinese. The last national census, conducted in the year 2000, counted 9.8 million Hui scattered throughout every province in China.

Shanghai's Hui Muslims form a small but clearly defined minority. They are chiefly distinguished by their dress (prayer caps and beards for men, but the women do not wear veils); by their places of worship (the mosques known as *Qingzhen Si*, or pure truth temples); and by their seemingly ubiquitous and undeniably popular *qingzhen* (halal) restaurants. ∎

The oldest, dating from 1853, is the **Fuyou Lu Qingzhen Si,** built by Hui (see sidebar this page) merchants who moved to Nanshi soon after the establishment of the Foreign Concessions. A welcoming and friendly people, China's Hui have lived peaceably amid a sea of Buddhists and Taoists for more than a millennium. They are renowned for their business acumen and distinctive cuisine.

There's no admission charge to visit a mosque, but it is essential to dress appropriately (no shorts or short dresses, no sleeveless shirts or blouses, and no shoes), and it is polite to stay away during the five daily prayer times. That said, the Fuyou Lu Mosque is remarkable for its hybrid Middle Eastern–European architecture and the unexpected sight of white-capped, bearded followers of the Prophet Muhammad strolling the grounds thousands of miles from Mecca.

Nanshi's second mosque, the delightfully named **Peach Orchard Mosque** (Xiaotaoyuan Qingzhen Si), was established in 1917 by the Shanghai Board of Muslims. Eight years later, it was reconstructed in a style that fuses Western, Islamic, and Chinese traditions—including circular art deco windows. ∎

and Fuxing parks; the restored dining and shopping district of Xintiandi; and the burgeoning nightlife area around Maoming Lu. Beyond its intersection with Changshu Lu, Huaihai Zhonglu continues past the Song

Qingling residence to Jiaotong University, while Hengshan Lu runs southwest to Xujiahui and southern Shanghai, continuing along Caoxi Beilu to Longhua Temple and Pagoda, the largest Buddhist monastery in the city. ■

A typically up-market teashop on Huaihai Road

Fuxing Park & surrounds

Fuxing Park
(Fuxing Gongyuan)
🅰 Map p. 107 E4
🕐 6 a.m.–6 p.m.

THE FRENCH ESTABLISHED FUXING PARK IN 1909 TO SERVE
as a tree-lined retreat where residents of the French Concession could
stroll and relax far from the city's busy—and often malodorous—
areas. That use prevails today, as locals of all ages and from all walks
of life flock to the park. Young lovers sit side by side on benches.
Pairs of men study games-in-progress of checkers or chess. And clus-
ters of fitness enthusiasts engage in tai chi, gentle jogging, and even
ballroom dancing.

**The onion dome
of St. Nicholas
Church, now a
restaurant, rises
over Fuxing Park.**

As in many public parks in China,
there's a special play area for children. In recent years Fuxing has

also become a popular venue for
music concerts and laser light
shows. The founding fathers of
communism might frown upon
such rock extravaganzas, but the
presence of those fathers still per-
vades the park in the form of two
massive statues, one of Karl Marx
and the other of Friedrich Engels.

As the epicenter of Shanghai's
most elegant and affluent district,
Fuxing Park is surrounded by
numerous points of interest, all
within easy walking distance. Sym-
bolizing the thawing trend in this
unabashedly capitalist enclave, **St.
Nicholas Church** *(16 Gaolan Lu)*
has been converted into an expensive restaurant specializing in haute
cuisine. Once upon a time, however, the church served the city's siz-
able White Russian population (see
sidebar p. 120). Built in 1932 by the
exiled White Russian General
Sergei Glebov to honor "Tsar-
Martyr" Nicholas II (1868–1918),
the church boasts an unmistakably
Russian Orthodox style, as it rises
through several buttresses to cul-
minate in a small onion dome.

Most White Russians fled
Shanghai in the last days of the
civil war between the communists
and the Nationalists, ceding the
church to a long and ignominious
string of secular purposes. During
one stint as a storage depot, for
example, a portrait of Chairman
Mao was painted over the main
portico. It remains intact.

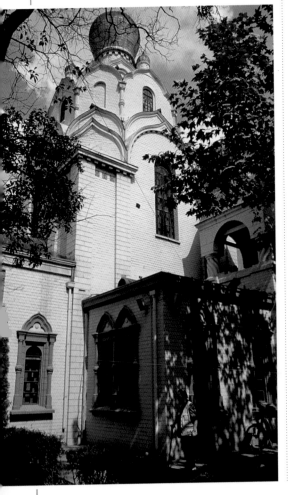

EAST & SOUTH OF THE PARK

To the east of Fuxing Park, beyond busy Chongqing Nanlu, stands a building of considerable historic significance to the People's Republic of China—the **Site of the 1st** **National Congress of the Chinese Communist Party.** In this typical gray shikumen building, the Chinese Communist Party (CCP) was formally established on July 23, 1921. Present at this founding congress were 13 delegates,

Early members of the Communist Party gaze down from the walls— and back from the past—at the Site of the 1st National Congress of the CCP Building.

Site of the First National Congress of the Chinese Communist Party

(Zhonggong Yidahuizhi Jinianguan)

Map p. 107 F4

76 Xingye Lu

9 a.m.–5 p.m.

$

The siren Songs

If there was a "first family" of 20th-century China, it had to be the remarkable Songs. Charlie Song (ca. 1863–1918), born to poor Hainan Island traders in the South China Sea, converted to Christianity at age 15. After graduating from the divinity school of prestigious Vanderbilt University in Nashville, Tennessee, Song returned to China and settled in Shanghai, where he distinguished himself as a printer of Bibles, an importer, and a businessman.

With his wife, Ni Guizhen, Song also sired a remarkable family. The oldest of Song's three daughters, Song Ailing (1889–1973) married H. H. Kung in 1914, then the richest man in China. Kung would go on to serve as President of the Republic of China from 1938 to 1939.

Song's second daughter, Qingling, married Sun Yat-sen in 1915; more than four decades later, she was named Vice President of the People's Republic of China (1949).

The youngest daughter, Song Meiling, married Nationalist leader Chiang Kai-shek in 1927 and followed him into exile on Formosa in 1949, where she remained First Lady of the Republic of China until her husband's death in 1975.

There was a famous son, too. T. V. Song (1894–1971) served as Minister of Finance, Minister of Foreign Affairs, and finally Premier of the Republic of China. ∎

The Shanghai Arts & Crafts Museum bears an eerie resemblance to the White House.

Former Residence of Sun Yat-sen
(Sun Zhongshan Guju)

Map p. 107 E4

7 Xiangshan Lu

9 a.m.–4:30 p.m.

$

including a young representative from Hunan named Mao Zedong. Now something of a shrine for the CCP, the building houses pictures and documents from the early days of the communist struggle. A diorama of the congress strategically positions Mao at center stage.

Less well-known, but still worth at least a glance from the southeast corner of Fuxing Park, is the **Former Home of Agnes Smedley** (185 Fuxing Zhonglu). Smedley (1892–1950) was born into a farming family in Osgood, Missouri, but in 1918 she divorced her husband and moved from California to New York, where she became a reporter for Birth Control Review. In 1929, Smedley moved to

Shanghai to cover the Chinese Civil War for the Manchester Guardian and the Frankfurter Zeitung. In this capacity she traveled with both the Eighth Route Army and the New Fourth Army, becoming a passionate supporter of the CCP in the process. Smedley went on to author six books that chronicle the rise of Chinese communism; these include not only the classic Battle Hymn of China but also a biography of the Red Army commander Zhu De. Agnes Smedley's ashes are buried at the Babaoshan Revolutionary Martyrs Cemetery in Beijing.

To the west of Fuxing Park, just a short distance south of St. Nicholas Church, stands the **Former Residence of Sun Yat-sen.** The

here that the Nationalist generalissimo first met Qingling's younger sister, Meiling (1897–2003), the future Madame Chiang Kai-shek.

Yet another building of historic and symbolic significance to the CCP may be found a short distance south of Fuxing Park. This is the **Former Residence of Zhou Enlai.** Mao Zedong's charmingly sophisticated—and, when necessary, utterly ruthless—deputy, Zhou Enlai (1898–1976) lived here in 1946–47 as head of the Shanghai

Former Residence of Zhou Enlai

(Zhou Enlai Gongguan)

⊠ Map p. 107 E4
✉ 173 Sinan Lu
🕐 9 a.m.–4 p.m.
💲 $

Party street

Just west of Ruijin Er Lu (and therefore within easy walking distance of Fuxing Park) runs a landmark street that has left its quiet, bourgeois origins far behind. Known in the 1930s as Rue Cardinal Mercier, when it was distinguished by the Cathay Theater and the Cercle Sportif Français, Maoming Nanlu is remarkable in the modern era primarily for its pubs, clubs, and unfettered nightlife.

It's here that Shanghai's affluent and often rebellious youth come to indulge in all-night partying that centers around loud disco and techno music, heavy drinking, and—increasingly—substance abuse. The ravers' apparent drug of choice is ecstasy.

It's not hard on a Maoming party night to spot the "head shakers"—that is, those who may have been taking ecstasy or methamphetamines. Evidently the Shanghai police have no trouble making that distinction either, for they have recently undertaken a crackdown. Bars known to tolerate drug use have been shuttered for six months and slapped with stiff fines of 100,000 yuan (about $13,000). ∎

celebrated Father of Modern China lived here with his wife, Song Qingling (see p. 109) from 1918 until his death in 1925. The house is an unassuming, gray stone structure notable chiefly for the memorabilia displayed within. The furniture, decorations, and library are all as Sun Yat-sen left them. In the garden stands a statue of the great man, his hands shoved informally in his pockets.

Under the gimlet eye of French Concession constables and Nationalist, or Kuomintang (KMT), agents, Sun's widow, Song Qingling, lived on in the house until Japan invaded China in 1937. The house was terra cognita to KMT leader Chiang Kai-shek, for it was

Ruijin Guest-house

(Ruijin Bingguan)

🗺 Map p. 107 E4

✉ 118 Ruijin Erlu

Conservatory of Music

(Yinyue Xueyuan)

🗺 Map p. 107 D4

✉ 20 Fenyang Lu

☎ 6431 0334

Shanghai Arts & Crafts Museum

(Shanghai Gongyi Meishu Bowuguan)

🗺 Map p. 107 D4

✉ 79 Fenyang Lu

☎ 6437 3454

🕓 9 a.m.–5 p.m.

💲 $

Taiyuan Villa

(Taiyuan Bieshu)

🗺 Map p. 107 D4

✉ 160 Taiyuan Lu

☎ 6471 6688

branch of the CCP. Zhou's simple but elegant office has been preserved. A separate building has been converted into a small museum dedicated to his life. Outside, fresh flowers bedeck a statue of the man, a tribute to the esteem in which he is still held.

Also not far from Fuxing Park, just a short distance west of the Former Residence of Zhou Enlai, stands the **Ruijin Guesthouse.** In its earlier guise as the Morriss Estate, the manor house and five villas (all built in 1928) were home to H. E. Morriss, Jr., son of the founder and owner of the prestigious *North China Daily News.* Today the complex houses one of Shanghai's more exclusive lodgings, as well as upmarket bars and restaurants. It's a relaxing place to sip a cool drink and ponder the wealth and influence that Western tycoons once wielded in colonial Shanghai.

FARTHER AFIELD

Slightly farther afield, but still in the Fuxing area, Fenyang Lu (Fenyang Road) branches southwest from Huaihai Zhonglu, past the **Conservatory of Music,** which holds classical music concerts each Sunday at 7 p.m., to the **Shanghai Arts & Crafts Museum.** Set in another building designed by the distinguished Hungarian architect Ladislau Hudec, the museum suggests a smaller version of the White House in Washington, D.C. The institution also comprises a research institute for arts and crafts; here visitors can witness creative activities such as embroidery, kite manufacturing, carving in various materials, and painting. Many of the goods produced on site are for sale in the gift shop. In addition, you may want to browse the antique shop in the basement.

Just southwest of the museum, at the junction of Fenyang Lu and

Yueyang Lu, stands a small bust of Russian poet **Alexander Pushkin** (1799–1837, rendered in Chinese as Puxijin). Although the memorial was damaged during the Cultural Revolution—perhaps the Red Guards were unaware that Pushkin's anti-establishment views brought him internal exile at the hands of Tsar Alexander II?—the bust has since been restored. Today the statue pays quiet homage to the former White Russian association with Shanghai, as well as to the city's sophisticated multicultural tradition.

Southeast of the Pushkin Monument, past the Former Shanghai Jewish Hospital (now the Eye, Ear, Nose, and Throat Hospital), stands **Taiyuan Villa.** This elaborate structure, modeled on French designs of the era, was built in the 1920s by a French aristocrat, the Count de Marsoulies. It has since witnessed a veritable pageant of colorful historical events. To begin with, in a story that may be apocryphal but is too intriguing to resist narrating, the Count de Marsoulies—who happened to be a Shanghai lawyer—is said to have been poisoned by Du Yuesheng in the wake of a falling-out with the nefarious big-eared mobster. His wife, the countess, stayed on in the house until the outbreak of the Pacific War in 1941.

In 1945, Gen. George C. Marshall, the U.S. Army Chief of Staff, used the mansion as his headquarters in an unsuccessful bid to arrange an 11th-hour truce between the KMT and the CCP in the Chinese Civil War. After the latter's ultimate victory in 1949, the house was taken over by Mao Zedong's fourth wife, the redoubtable Jiang Qing (see sidebar p. 103).

Today the Taiyuan Villa is an upmarket guesthouse, still favored by Communist Party dignitaries.

Visitors who book in advance can stay in the suite once used as a Shanghai pied-à-terre by Madame Mao.

HUAIHAI ZHONGLU

North of Fuxing Park Huaihai Zhonglu is a bustling, tree-lined avenue. Bisecting the former French Concession, Huaihai Lu has emerged as the most fashionable

yang retained its richly deserved reputation for fake goods and knockoffs until 2006, when it was shuttered—permanently, perhaps—by municipal authorities eager to crack down on pirated goods and promote local understanding for the notions of copyright and respect for intellectual property rights. Many of the merchants who once traded here have

shopping street in modern Shanghai. On the south side of Huaihai Zhonglu, major commercial outlets include **Isetan** and the **New Hualian Commercial Building**—giant department stores and shopping malls selling everything from designer goods to children's toys. Until recently, here, too, you would have found the Xiangyang Shichang Fashion Market, a vibrant, noisy, raw shopping bazaar that specialized in clothing, electronic goods (especially CDs and DVDs), watches, shoes, and mobile phones. Xiang-

since shifted their business to busy Qipu Road Market in Zhabei (see p. 149).

Just across Xiangyang Park (Xiangyang Gongyuan) from Shaanxi Nanlu, on the west side of North Xiangyang Lu, a blue dome marks the site of the former **Russian Orthodox Mission Church** (Dongzhenjiao Shengmu Datang), built in 1934 and consecrated as the Cathedral of the Holy Mother of God. Though the church was forsaken for many years, its survival now seems certain—in a form that remains to be seen. You

An aura of aristocracy still seems to pervade Taiyuan Villa, once home to the Count de Marsoulies and now a guesthouse.

Cathay Theater
(Guotao Dianyingyuan)
- Map p. 107 E5
- 870 Huaihai Zhonglu
- 5404 0415

Shanghai Center for Jewish Studies
(Shanghai Youtai Yanjiu Zhongxin)
- Map p. 107 E5
- 7 Lane 622 Huaihai Zhonglu
- 5306 0606

Jinjiang Tower
(Xin Jinjiang Dajiudian)
- Map p. 107 E5
- 161 Changle Lu

Old Jinjiang Hotel
(Lao Jinjiang Fandian)
- Map p. 107 E5
- 59 Maoming Nanlu
- 6258 2582

Okura Garden Hotel
(Huayuan Fandian)
- Map p. 107 E5
- 58 Maoming Nanlu
- 6451 1111

Lyceum Theater
(Lanxin Daxiyuan)
- Map p. 107 E5
- 57 Maoming Nanlu
- 6256 4738
- Box office 9 a.m.–7 p.m.

can credit its rebirth to the dovetailing of two powerful forces: the fast-paced redevelopment of downtown Huaihai and the newfound appreciation of the people of Shanghai for their city's international past.

On the north side of Huaihai Zhonglu, as you make your way east, the giant **Parkson Department Store** and the **Cathay Theater** mark the junction with noisy, vibrant Shaanxi Nanlu.

One other site of interest on the north side of Huaihai Zhonglu merits a look-see not so much for its architectural merit as for its educational role. The **Shanghai Center for Jewish Studies,** intriguingly tucked away at the end of a short, dead-end alley, contains a library and information center. It also specializes in organizing tours of "Jewish Shanghai" (see pp. 146–47).

CHANGLE LU & BEYOND
A short walk along Changle Lu northwest of the Jewish Studies Center looms the 43-story-high **Jinjiang Tower,** offering wonderful views across the former French Concession from its observation room on the 42nd floor.

Continuing west and around the corner, brings you to No. 59 Maoming Nanlu, the **Old Jinjiang Hotel.** When this art deco complex was built in 1928 by famous Shanghai magnate Sir Victor Sassoon (1881–1961), it was styled the Cathay Mansions. Apart from its art deco facade, the hotel is best known as the place where Zhou Enlai and Richard Nixon signed the celebrated (and unexpected) 1972 Shanghai Agreement. The pact normalized Sino-American diplomatic relations for the first time since 1949—and, incidentally, hastened the end of the Vietnam War.

Directly opposite the Jinjiang Hotel, on the west side of Maoming,

is the **Okura Garden Hotel.** In previous incarnations this building was the prestigious Cercle Sportif Français, then a Shanghai retreat for Chairman Mao Zedong. Built in 1926 by French architect Paul Veysseyre—a contemporary of Ladislau Hudec's, and sometimes referred to as his counterpart—the hotel features the art deco style that was all the rage in colonial Shanghai, and especially in the French Concession. The Okura Garden Hotel has now been restored to its original splendor, replete with marble columns, bold stairways, and a grand ballroom. In its reclaimed

guise as a luxury hostelry, it targets Japanese businessmen in particular.

Just across Changle Lu from Jinjiang Hotel sits the venerable 1931 **Lyceum Theater** at 57 Maoming Nanlu. It, too, is in the art deco style. Renowned British ballerina Margot Fonteyn (1919–1991) danced here as a young girl (her father worked for the British Tobacco Company in Shanghai), but today's productions focus on traditional Chinese performing arts, pop concerts, and children's theater.

A quick jaunt west on Changle Lu and then north along Shaanxi Nanlu delivers you to yet another product of the extravagant French Concession architecture of the early 20th century. The **Moller House,** built by an eccentric Swedish shipping titan in the 1930s, is distinctly Gothic in style (the peaked towers are a dead giveaway). Having weathered the period of orthodox communist austerity before 1990—when it functioned for a time as the unlikely headquarters of the Shanghai Communist Youth League—the miniature château has since been redeveloped as an unusual boutique hotel, the Hengshan Moller Villa. ■

Moller House

(Male Bieshu)

🅰 Map p. 107 D5

✉ 30 Shaanxi Nanlu

☎ 6247 8881

Shanghainese flock to parks such as Fuxing on Sunday mornings to perfect various dance moves.

Walk around Xintiandi

The Xintiandi complex occupies just two blocks. It is bordered to the north by Taicang Lu (Taicang Road), to the south by Zizhong Lu (Zizhong Road), to the east by Huangpi Nanlu (Huangpi Road South), and to the west by Madang Lu (Madang Road). A walk around the district will not tax you physically, but it may open your eyes to the style and prosperity of New Shanghai at the dawn of the 21st century. Even the name of the complex is aspirational: Xintiandi means New Heaven and Earth.

Xintiandi is easy to reach. It's a 10-minute walk south from People's Square, or you can take the metro to the **Huangpi Road station ①**. From the station walk south on Huangpi to the Xintiandi complex, a creation of the New China, which opened in 2001.

Turn right on Taicang Lu and enter Xintiandi from the north; look for the Starbucks marking the narrow *longtang* alley leading south. Centered on a largely rebuilt area of *shikumen* housing (see sidebar p. 20; see pp. 100–101), here you'll find the **Xintiandi Visitors Information Center ②** where you can drop in for an overview of the complex and suggestions on where to eat. The place is distinguished by rows of trendy bars and restaurants (alfresco dining is very much in vogue here). Walk south past two narrow, covered side alleys; these lead to a

parallel longtang to the east, likewise lined with restaurants.

Located in Xintiandi North Block on the left, the **Shikumen Open House Museum ③** (Wulixiang Shikumen Minju Chenlieguan, *tel 3307 0337, 10 a.m.–10 p.m., $*) is a well-presented museum devoted to the architecture and lifestyle of the area before its recent gentrification. It depicts a century and a half of life in traditional shikumen housing through artifacts and photographs. This shikumen built in the 1920s houses seven exhibition rooms.

Continue your stroll south to Xingya Lu and turn east to the **Site of the 1st National Congress of the Chinese Communist Party ④** (see p. 109), a museum located in a typical shikumen house.

Across Xingya Lu, enter the South Block

via the single narrow longtang alley entrance. Here you'll encounter the **Central Academy of Fine Arts Gallery** ⑤, *(Unit 5, 2/F, 123 Xingye Lu, tel 6386 6161, 10 a.m.–10 p.m.).* Run by a graduate of the Beijing school of the same name, this gallery has revolving shows featuring several other graduates. Next door the tiny **Xintiandi Postal Museum** ⑥ showcases Chinese postal history.

Most of the South Block is given over to sheer indulgence. Here you will find everything from stylish restaurant dining to fast-food outlets imported from the West.

Exit the South Block via the narrow alley leading east to **Taipingqiao Park** ⑦ (Taipingqiao Gongyuan), which is located just across Huangpi Nanlu. This leisure area and 11-acre (4.5 ha) artificial lake (Shanghai's largest) is a place to relax—and perhaps to recover from any bouts of overindulgence at one of Xintiandi's numerous restaurants. The park features fountains and two islets, Magnolia

and Unison dotting the lake's surface.

If you'd like to witness a bit more of Shanghai's yuppie renovation, head back west down Xingya Lu and across busy Chongqing Nanlu to **Yandang Lu walking street** ⑧ on the east side of Fuxing Park. This "24-hour Pedestrian Leisure Street" also features restored traditional housing; it, too, is lined with bars and restaurants. ■

See area map p. 107
► Huangpi Road Metro station
↔ 1 mile (1.6 km)
🕐 1 hour
► Yandang Lu walking street

NOT TO BE MISSED
- Shikumen Open House Museum
- Museum of the First National Congress of the CCP
- Taipingqiao Park

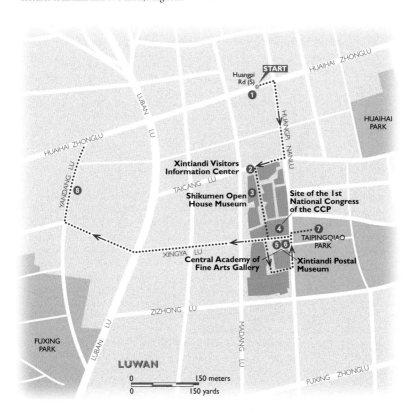

The Shanghai
Municipal Library
on Huaihai Lu
gives you time to
read and reflect.

Huaihai & Hengshan

HUAIHAI AND HENGSHAN ANCHOR AND STRETCH BEYOND
the western and southern limits of the former French Concession.
Home to the rich and influential in colonial times—when Huaihai Lu
went by the name Avenue Joffre—the western part of Huaihai remains
almost equally exclusive today.

**French
Consulate-
General**
(Faguo Lingshiju)
- Map p. 107 C4
- 1431 Huaihai
  Zhonglu

**Shanghai
Municipal
Library**
(Shanghai Tushuguan)
- Map p. 107 C4
- 1555 Huaihai
  Zhonglu
- 8:30 a.m.–
  8:30 p.m.

**Former
Residence of
Song Qingling**
(Soongqingling Gugju)
- Map p. 106 B4
- 1843 Huaihai
  Zhonglu
- 6474 7183
- 9 a.m.–4:30 p.m.
- $

West of the junction of Huaihai and
Wulumuqi Zhonglu, Shanghai's
consular district is distinguished by
the **French Consulate-General.**
This gracious French colonial-style
building is set back in spacious
gardens. Just across the road is
the **United States Consulate-
General** (1469 Huaihai Zhonglu),
a white neoclassic building that has
been rented out by a wealthy Shanghai industrialist since 1980. Another
major residence is the **Japanese
Consulate-General,** at 1517
Huaihai Zhonglu; the building dates
from 1900 and was once owned by a
powerful northern warlord. (The
consulates are closed to the public.)

A bit farther west stands another revered Shanghai institution, the
Shanghai Municipal Library.
Opened in 1996 and vaunted as
Asia's largest library, this prodi-
gious repository holds rare Chinese
books and manuscripts, as well
as photographs and documents

from the city's colonial period.

Still farther west, just as Huaihai
Zhonglu meets Wukang Lu (Wukang Road) and becomes Huaihai
Xilu (Huaihai Road West), you'll
find an eight-story redbrick apartment building, the **Normandie**
(Nuomandi Gongyu), that bears a
striking resemblance to New York's
Flatiron Building. Directly opposite
it is the **Former Residence of
Song Qingling.** Here Charlie
Song's second daughter, Song Qingling (see sidebar p. 109), spent her
childhood. It's a pleasant and spacious house, built by a Greek shipping magnate in the 1920s. Check
out the photos and other memorabilia on display of Song Qingling
and her husband (and revolutionary hero) Sun Yat-sen, whom Song
climbed out the window to marry.
The garage contains a pair of dated
communist limousines; far more
rewarding is the garden out back,
dominated by magnolia trees. ■

Xujiahui

ABOUT 550 YARDS (500 M) BEFORE THE START OF THE consular district on Huaihai Zhonglu, near Changshu Lu Metro Station, Baoqing Lu briefly heads due south, then does a dogleg southwest to become Hengshan Lu. This stretch of Baoqing Lu is the gateway to Xujiahui and southern Shanghai.

Xujiahui
▲ Map pp. 106–107
A3–C4

THE SONGS

The **Shanghai Conservatory of Music Middle School** (Shanghai Yinyue Xueyuan Zhongxueo) at 9 Dongping Lu has musical, historical, and culinary appeal. The vine-clad, redbrick building sits amid extensive gardens, with a lovely pond and a flock of attendant geese. Notes from flute, violin, piano, and cello waft through the air as students practice in the teak-floored conservatory.

Charlie Song bought the house for his daughter Meiling upon her 1927 marriage to Nationalist leader Chiang Kai-shek. The couple, who lived in Nanjing, used the house whenever they visited, so it is now (somewhat grudgingly) known as the **Former Residence of Chiang Kai-shek.** Meiling was

smitten with the house, which her husband dubbed *ai lu,* or love nest. After the Nationalist defeat in 1949, Meiling fled with her husband, where he died in 1975. She then moved to an apartment in Manhattan where, surrounded by black-clad bodyguards, she lived to the age of 106. Though the building has been restored twice, it retains the grand fireplaces, sweeping stairways, and wide windows that so beguiled Meiling.

Chiang Kai-shek's former residence is just one of nine villas in the old Song compound on Dongping Lu. Several have been converted into fine restaurants, forming a restaurant quarter of sorts. These include **Sasha's,** a French restaurant with a celebrated bar at 11 Dongping Lu; **Simply**

Visitors revel in the verdant respite of Xujiahui Park.

Shanghai Community Church
(Guoji Libai Tang)
- Map p. 107 C4
- 53 Hengshan Lu
- 6437 6576

La Villa Rouge
(Xiao Hong Lou)
- Map p. 107 B3
- 811 Hengshan Lu
- 6431 9811

Shanghai Library— Bibliotheca Zikawei
(Xujiahui Cangshulou)
- Map p. 106 B3
- 80 Caoxi Beilu
- 6487 4072
- 9 a.m.–5 p.m.

Wan Fung Art Gallery
- Map p. 106 B3
- 980 Caoxi Beilu
  (inside the Shanghai Library)
- 6487 4072, ext. 107
- 9:30 a.m.–7 p.m.

White Russians

Following the Bolshevik victory in the Russian Civil War (1918–1922), tens of thousands of defeated anti-communists, known as "White Russians" to distinguish them from the Bolshevik "Reds," fled their homeland many to the Far East. A large number of these refugees sought safety in Shanghai's Foreign Concessions, where they would be marginally protected by European and American administrative laws.

By 1932 about 25,000 White Russians lived in Shanghai. Some used the city as a stepping stone to the United States. Others managing to make a good living locally. The penurious majority, however, served as laborers, bodyguards, gangsters, entertainers, and prostitutes. Today's Huaihai Lu became the center of Russian life in Old Shanghai, with signs in Cyrillic and Russian restaurants and bars selling borscht, black bread, and vodka. Further shocks and uprootings occurred in 1941 and 1949, but today—with China open to free enterprise and the Soviet Union no longer extant—Shanghai's Russian population is staging a comeback. ∎

Thai at 5C; and the **Blarney Stone** at 5A, billed irrefutably as the city's "most authentic Irish pub." Nearby (but unrelated to the Songs) is **Yang's Kitchen,** which specializes in local cuisine.

A short distance south along Henghshan Lu stands the city's largest Christian place of worship, the 1925 English-style **Shanghai Community Church.** Built of red brick with an elaborate timber-work roof, it evokes a quiet parish church but in fact serves a multi-denominational community.

AROUND XUJIAUI PARK

Hengshan Lu continues southwest until it meets **Xujiahui Park** (Xujiahui Gongyuan, 6 a.m.–6 p.m.), a well-maintained expanse of lawns, flower gardens, and a lake. Mid-park, just east off Hengshan Lu, stands **La Villa Rouge,** a nicely restored redbrick villa dating from 1921. For years this was the EMI studio, recording home to stellar musicians and singers. Today it's an upscale French restaurant that hasn't forgotten its debt to the past. The owners have assembled a small museum of records and recording equipment from the colonial era.

Opposite Xujiahui Park, on the west side of Hengshan Lu, stands a gray monolith: the **Headquarters of the Shanghai Communist Party** (Zhonguo Gongchandang Shanghai Shiwei Yuanhui, *definitely not open to the public*). Its brooding presence lasts only as long as it takes to walk beyond the southwest corner of Xujiahui Park, where department stores and shopping malls cluster in a glittering celebration of consumerism, not communism. They include the **Hui Jin Department Store,** the huge **Pacific Department Store** (which has the widest selection), the **Grand Gateway, Metro City, Pacific Digital Plaza 2,** and **Orient Shopping Center.**

MISSIONARY LEGACIES

Long before the new capitalism there were old-school Jesuit missionaries, of whose work some fascinating memorials survive. Most significant of these is the **Shanghai Library Bibliotheca Zikawei** (Xujiahui Cangshulou) on Caoxi Beilu. This remarkable institution, opened by the Society of Jesuits in 1847, now houses more than half a million tomes in languages ranging from Latin and Greek to Chinese.

Shuttered for years in the wake of the 1949 revolution, the Bibliotheca Zikawei reopened in 2006 thanks to funding from the Ricci Institute for Chinese-Western Cultural History, a research arm of the University of San Francisco. The affiliation is apt: Matteo Ricci was an Italian Jesuit who worked in China from 1582 until his death in Beijing in 1610. The first Westerner allowed inside the Forbidden City, he was also the first to translate the Confucian Analects (selected writings) into a Western language. Indeed, Ricci created the Latinized name Confucius for the Chinese sage Kong Fuzi. He is thus the father of Western learning in China and Western knowledge of China.

The Bibliotheca Zikawei (the latter name is an obsolete 19th-century romanization of Xujiahui) is a beautiful library, so who can say why it is one of the most rarely visited sights in the city? It consists of two buildings, both meticulously restored. The main library occupies a two-story building. But start your visit in the four-story building next door, where traditional library tables and electric lighting deepen the 19th-century feel of the wood-paneled public reading room on the first floor. Free tours of the library are offered on Saturday from 2 to 4; the maximum group size is 10, and English-speaking guides are available. The ground floor of the main building is given over to the **Wan Fung Art Gallery.**

Another vivid evocation of Xujiahui's rich Jesuit past takes the form of St. Ignatius Cathedral, named for the Spanish founder of the Society of Jesus, St. Ignatius of Loyola (1491–1556). Today, the red-brick edifice in Franco-Gothic style is often called **Xujiahui Cathedral.** Beyond its twin gray spires you will find an imposing vaulted interior. Walk five minutes south to see a stone statue of Xu Guangqi (see sidebar below), in the distinctive cap of a mandarin, at his tomb in **Guangqi Park** (Guangqi Gongyuan, *Xiyang Lu*). ∎

Xujiahui

The name Xujiahui means Xu family village and derives from Xu Guangqi (1562–1633), a Ming dynasty mandarin who was Matteo Ricci's first convert to Christianity.

Yet Xu Guangqi was destined to distinguish himself as far more than a mere crossover statistic. He turned out to be a formidable scholar in his own right. After being named Ricci's personal secretary, Xu emerged as Ricci's ideal intellectual partner as well. Together the two men collaborated on translating Euclid's *Elements* from Latin into Chinese—a fair exchange, by international standards, for Xu's role in introducing the *Analects* of Confucius to the Western world. ∎

Toppled by Red Guards on the rampage in 1966, the spires rise again over Xujiahui Cathedral.

Xujiahui Cathedral
(Tianzhu Jiaotang)
✉ 158 Puxi Lu
☎ 6469 0930

The original power couple

The founding fathers of Chinese Communism—Chairman Mao Zedong (1893–1976) and Premier Zhou Enlai (1898–1976)—are both associated with Shanghai. In the minds of city dwellers, however, their respective legacies could not be more distinct.

Mao was born into a relatively prosperous-peasant family in Shaoshan Village, Hunan Province. He graduated from the First Provincial Normal School of Hunan in 1918 and headed for Beijing, where he got caught up in the revolutionary May 4th Movement of 1919. In 1921 Mao traveled to Shanghai to attend the first session of the Congress of the Communist Party (CCP) of China; within two years, he would sit on the CCP's Central Committee. He stayed in Shanghai for some

time but never made it a base of power. Instead Mao returned to Hunan, where he honed his concept of a peasant-based revolutionary war.

Zhou Enlai was born to a relatively poor mandarin family in Huaian, Jiangsu Province. Because his family prized education, he was sent to the prestigious Nankai School in Tianjin. He then attended university in Tokyo but abruptly returned to China to take part in the May 4th Movement. A year later found Zhou studying in Paris, where in 1922 he joined a

cell of the CCP. Zhou came back to China for a second time in 1924, this time to Shanghai, where he helped organize the city's 1926 general strike.

Politically savvy from an early age, Zhou Enlai neatly sidestepped the White Terror waged against the CCP and its allies by thugmeister Du Yuesheng's Green Gang on behalf of Chiang Kai-shek. Zhou next resurfaced in the Jiangxi Soviet area, where he forged what would become a lifetime alliance with Mao Zedong. Together Mao and Zhou survived the Long March, then organized and led the anti-Japanese resistance from the CCP base at Yan'an. They subsequently confronted—and conquered—Chiang Kai-shek and his Kuomintang forces in the Chinese Civil War.

During their years in power—notably the desperate years of the Great Leap Forward and the disastrous years of the Cultural Revolution—Zhou acted as a moderating influence on the impulsive Mao. Too bad his sway wasn't family-wide: Mao's irrational and vindictive fourth wife, Qiang Qing (see p. 103), made Shanghai her power base in the early 1970s, then led the notorious Gang of Four in causing more than half a million Chinese deaths and devastating the nation's economy. Both men died within a few months of each other in 1976—Zhou of cancer in January, Mao of Lou Gehrig's Disease in September.

That's about the extent of their shared legacy, for whereas Mao is remembered for his unpredictable irascibility, Zhou is revered for his suave urbanity. Indeed, though now officially deemed "70 percent good and 30 percent bad," Mao remains a difficult figure for many Chinese to evaluate. Respected for unifying the country and ousting its foreign invaders, Mao cannot escape the fact that his social policies yielded almost universally catastrophic results. Zhou, by contrast—though sometimes equally ruthless—remains genuinely loved and respected by most Chinese. At the foot of his statue near Fuxing Park, fresh flowers continue to materialize daily. ∎

Zhou Enlai (second from left) and Mao Zedong (center) sport nearly identical jackets—and gestures—in this 1950s photo.

Longhua & around

Longhua Temple
& Pagoda
(Longhua Si & Longhua Ta)

[M] Map p. 106 B1
[✉] 2853 Longhua Lu
[☎] 6457 6327
[🕐] 7 a.m.–5 p.m.
[$] $

Longhua
Cemetery
of Martyrs
(Longhua Lieshi Lingyuan)

[M] Map p. 106 B1
[☎] 6468 5995
[🕐] 9 a.m.–4 p.m.

SOUTH OF GUANGQI PARK, XUJIAHUI BLENDS GRADUALLY into Longhua District, home to yet more department stores and shopping malls but also to Shanghai Stadium and Longhua, Shanghai's largest temple. Easily accessed from Huaihai and Xujiahui by broad, north–south Caoxi Beilu (and Metro Line 3, which runs beside it), the area merits a visit for its appealing gardens and parks. The main draw remains glittering Longhua Temple and its incense-filled courtyards.

LONGHUA PARK

Longhua Lu lies south of Xujiahui and beyond the elevated Zhongshan Nanlu 2 (Inner Ring Road). **Longhua Temple**—the name means lustrous dragon—is Shanghai's largest Buddhist place of worship. The temple has five main halls, including the main Great Treasure Hall, flanked by a traditional bell tower and drum tower. Among the numerous fine Buddha images you can view here, those of the Laughing Buddha, the Maitreya Buddha, and the Sakyamuni Buddha are especially worth seeking out. Representations of gilded *arhat* saints (those who have attained enlightenment) fill the Thousand Luohan Hall.

Here you will also find a massive, 7-ton (6,350 kg) bell. Striking the latter, especially on Chinese New Year, is believed to dispel sins and promote good fortune. At all times of the year, worshippers throng the temple courtyards, and the air is redolent with the aroma (and thick smoke) of incense sticks lighted by the devout.

On the other (or east) side of Longhua Lu stands the 140-foot-high (44 m) yellow octagonal **Longhua Pagoda.** Shanghai's tallest pagoda is a significant place of pilgrimage for local Buddhists. Visitors are not allowed to climb the pagoda, which is said to date from 977 but has clearly been re-stored since then. In World War II the pagoda reportedly saw duty as

an anti-aircraft tower; in the Cultural Revolution a quarter-century later it suffered damage and desecration at the hands of iconoclastic Red Guards but has since been made whole. Now that 100 flowers of capitalism are blooming, Longhua Pagoda is girt round by stalls and small shops selling cold drinks, snacks, religious

paraphernalia, and souvenirs.

Nearby **Longhua Cemetery of Martyrs** is fraught with special significance for the communist authorities. It commemorates the victims of the 1927 White Terror, when Du Yuesheng's mobsters and Chiang Kai-shek's Kuomintang (KMT) colluded to murder hundreds of communists and striking workers—a massacre the young Zhou Enlai barely escaped. Other martyrs buried at the cemetery were victims of later KMT killings in and around Shanghai from 1927 until the Japanese invasion and occupation of 1937. Today the dead have found peace with honor here. The peach trees planted in the park blossom each spring, while outside a memorial hall an eternal flame burns to honor the fallen.

TO THE SOUTH

Farther southeast still, massive **Lupu Bridge** appears to vault the Huangpu River; it connects the southern part of Dapuqiao District with Zhoujiadu District on the Pudong side. Opened in 2003, this 1,804-foot-long (550 m) structure is the world's longest arched bridge. In order to allow freighters to pass under it, the span rises a dizzying 330 feet (100 m) above the surface of the river below. Bird's-eye views of the busy Huangpu River and both sides of Shanghai await those with the stamina to climb the 367 steps to the arch's apex. ■

Lupu Bridge
(Lupu Daqiao Qiao)

✉ 909 Luban Lu

🕐 10 a.m.–4 p.m.

💲 $$

Father and son savor a quiet stroll through Longhua Park.

More places to visit from Fuxing to Huaihai

PROPAGANDA POSTER ART CENTER

Though somewhat off the beaten track to the north and west of central Huaihai, the **Propaganda Poster Art Center** (Xuanchuanhua Nianhua Yishu Zhongxin) rewards politically or nostalgically minded visitors with its remarkable collection of socialist realist posters (see sidebar below) from China's recent revolutionary past. Maps of old Shanghai and other memorabilia are also on display. A separate section of the center sells reproduction posters and postcards lauding bumper harvests, eternal opposition to U.S. imperialism, boundless admiration of popular struggles in Africa and Latin America, and undying resistance to Soviet socialist imperialism. They make poignant souvenirs of a time that was actually more strident than our own.

🗺 Map p. 106 C5 ✉ 868 Huashan Lu
☎ 6211 1845 🚇 Changshu Lu 🕐 9:30 a.m.–4:30 p.m. 💲 $

SHANGHAI MUSEUM OF PUBLIC SECURITY

If you happen to be traveling with teenage boys, bring them here. Tucked away on Ruijin Nanlu in an otherwise uninteresting part of Dapuqiao east of Xujiahui, the **Shanghai Museum of Public Security** (Shanghai Gong An Bowuguan) constitutes that rarity: a subversive museum visit. Spread over four floors in an unprepossessing concrete building, the displays catalogue not just "public security" but multiple aspects of crime in Shanghai, both in the colonial period and since. Exhibits feature contemporaneous photographs and weapons, as well as such fascinating ephemera as mobster Huang Jingrong's cigarette-case gun, a brace of pistols once owned by Sun Yat-sen, racks of Al Capone–style tommy guns, weaponry used by the Green Gang in the vicious White Terror of 1927, opium-smoking pipes and equipment, and the business cards of high-class sing-song girls and prostitutes. As a souvenir you can purchase a rather sinister-looking high-caliber brass bullet; upon inspection, it turns out to be a cigarette lighter.

🗺 Map p. 106 C5 ✉ 518 Ruijin Nanlu
☎ 6472 0256 🚇 No metro—take a taxi or Bus Nos. 786, 932, 72 🕐 9 a.m.–4:30 p.m.
💲 $ ■

Socialist realism

After the Bolsheviks seized power in Russia in 1917, revolutionary art tended to be radical. It emphasized such idealized notions as the withering away of the state and the law. Following the death of Vladimir Lenin in 1924, however, his brutally pragmatic successor, Josef Stalin, decreed a more conservative approach. Art was to be traditional in form, aimed at the masses, laudatory of the party, and generally optimistic. As a result, by 1939 Soviet cultural life was cast in a constricting mold that ultimately dictated its own collapse.

In the dust-yellow hills of distant Yan'an, meanwhile, the Chinese communists were developing policies on literature and art designed to promote their cause in the bitter two-way struggle against the Japanese and the KMT. The resultant party line was spelled out in May 1942 with the publication of Mao Zedong's *Talks at the Yenan Forum on Art and Literature*. Mao's view: Revolutionary art was intended specifically for "the people"—that is, for workers, peasants, and soldiers. Above all else, literature and art should exalt "the Proletariat, the Communist Party, and Socialism." As a consequence, when the People's Republic of China was established in 1949, socialist realism (as this school of politicized esthetics has come to be known) cast an artistic straitjacket over a vast region stretching from the Adriatic to the South China Sea, constricting the cultural life of nearly half of humankind.

Since the easing of Party control over art in the 1990s, socialist realism is out of official vogue—but increasingly embraced by a populace in nostalgic search of the bad old days. ■

Pudong is Shanghai's new frontier. Rising on the east bank of the Huangpu River like a phoenix with wings of steel and scales of glass, this 21st-century megalopolis has been built from scratch since 1990. A shrine to international finance and commerce, it emblematizes everything to which the New China aspires.

Pudong

The Oriental Pearl TV Tower, icon of new Pudong

Pudong

PUDONG (EAST OF THE HUANGPU RIVER) IS A STARTLINGLY FUTURISTIC cityscape that leaves most visitors searching for superlatives. Before 1990, when Shanghai's modern development took off in the wake of China's economic reforms, little lay east of the Huangpu but rice paddies, market gardens, and rows of rundown warehouses. The years since then have witnessed a transformation of staggering proportions, as Pudong has blossomed into a thrumming urban landscape bristling with glittering skyscrapers reminiscent of Manhattan.

Pedestrians run the gauntlet of a crosswalk near Pudong Park.

Pudong is the new face of Shanghai. Already it has grown to be 1.5 times larger than the old city west of the Huangpu River. It's a modern monument to commerce and capitalism—impressive, yes, but at the same time rather soulless. So whereas it is reasonable to feel drawn to Pudong for its futuristic architecture and amazing views, don't waste your time searching for the Old World charm of The Bund or the former French Concession.

Pudong's most impressive skyscrapers cluster on the east bank of the Huangpu River, directly facing The Bund. This area, sometimes referred to as Shanghai's Wall Street, is easy to reach from The Bund via the Bund Sightseeing Tunnel (see p. 70) or by ferry; the latter offers fine views of both shores of the river. (Shanghai Subway Lines 2 and 4 also provide swift access.) Beyond the financial area, Century Avenue (Shiji Dadao) runs southeast to Century Park, the

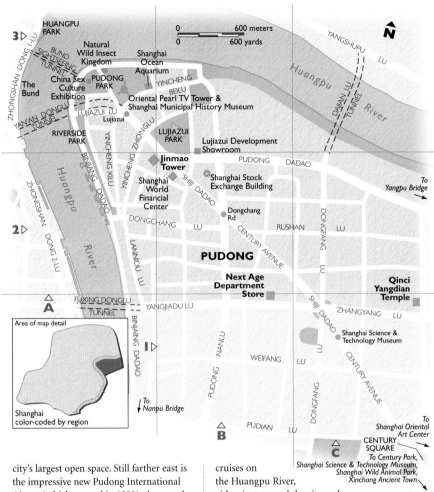

city's largest open space. Still farther east is the impressive new Pudong International Aiport (which opened in 1999), the mouth of the Yangtze River, and beyond it the East China Sea. The new airport was brought even closer with the 2003 opening of the Shanghai Maglev (magnetically levitated) Train, the fastest train in the world, which has come to symbolize the aspirations and achievements of Shanghai in general and Pudong in particular.

So what's there to see here beyond the mammoth architecture? Pudong offers a handful of intriguingly eclectic museums, as well as several out-of-town attractions, such as Shanghai Wild Animal Park and Xinchang Ancient Town. Best of all, perhaps, it is also the jumping-off point for

cruises on the Huangpu River, either just around the city and docks or farther downriver to the great Yangtze and Chongming Island.

One of the most rewarding excursions here is a simple stroll along the riverside. The avenue—Binjiang Dadao—runs south from the Bund Sightseeing Tunnel through Riverside Park to the ferry pier by Dong-chang Lu.

Otherwise, Pudong does not enjoy a reputation as a pedestrian-friendly place. Distances are considerable, attractions are spread out, and the boulevards, though wide, can get surprisingly winding. Fortu-nately, a phalanx of taxis are on hand to ferry visitors about. ■

Pudong's sky-scrapers dazzle the eye with height and light.

Pudong Park

Pudong Park
(Pudong Gongyuan)

🅰 Map p. 129 A3

🕐 6 a.m.–6 p.m.

💲 $

Oriental Pearl TV Tower
(Dongfang Mingzhu Guangbao Dianshi Ta)

✉ 2 Lane 504 Lujiazui Lu

☎ 5879 1888

🕐 8 a.m.–10 p.m.

💲 $$–$$$

Shanghai Municipal History Museum
(Shanghai Chengshi Lishi Fazhan Chenlieguan)

✉ Oriental Pearl TV Tower Basement

☎ 5879 1888

🕐 8 a.m.–9.30 p.m.

💲 $$

Pudong's sky-scrapers dazzle the eye with height and light.

THE SKYSCRAPERS ACROSS FROM THE BUND CLUSTER around Pudong Park, an attractive area of green lawns, weeping willow trees, and small waterways that is overshadowed—quite literally—by some of the tallest structures in all of China.

Rising above the southern part of Pudong Park, just a stone's throw from the eastern exit of the Bund Sightseeing Tunnel, is the iconic **Oriental Pearl TV Tower,** a 1,535-foot (468 m) tower that dominates the eastern shore of the Huangpu and sparks mixed emotions in those who see it. Alhough the majority of Shanghai residents seem justifiably proud of it—and the progress it represents—it is not the loveliest structure in Pudong. It is, however, true to its name, a TV tower. Nine TV channels and ten FM stations use the tower to broadcast their signals. However, tourists and locals come for the view—an undeniably impressive one from inside looking out. Or startling itself when illuminated at night.

Erected in 1995, the tower features 11 spheres of differing sizes joined by three columns. The design is said to be based on a Tang dynasty poem that describes the tinkling of pearls on a jade plate: The silver and dark-red spheres represent the pearls, while the Huangpu River symbolizes the jade plate. Still more fancifully, the architects liken the city's Yangpu and Nanpu Bridges to "Chinese dragons frolicking with the pearls of the Oriental Pearl TV Tower."

Dragon gambols or no, the tower is open to the public and has three observation levels. The highest, the Space Module, is at 1,148 feet (350 m); the Sightseeing Floor is at 863 feet (263 m); and Space City is at 295 feet (90 m). There's also a revolving restaurant at 876 feet (267 m). All offer views across the Huangpu to The Bund.

Beneath the tower is the excellent **Shanghai Municipal History Museum.** The well-designed exhibits shepherd the visitor through the history of Shanghai from the Opium War of 1842 to the present, showcasing all aspects of life from trade and transport to opium dens and crime. A number of exhibits take the form of audiovisual dioramas. Keep your eyes peeled for a stone that once marked the boundary of the International Settlement. You'll also want to be on the look-out for one of the bronze lions that once guarded the entrance to the Hong Kong and Shanghai Bank Building on The Bund.

On the east side of Pudong Park, the **Shanghai Ocean Aquarium** is a see-worthy sight. A joint venture between China and Singapore, it consists of a 509-foot-long (155 m) underwater tunnel that allows the visitor 270-degree views of sharks, turtles, and other marine creatures. An additional nine galleries furnish details and samples of 15,000 fish from all over the world, with a special emphasis on species indigenous to the nearby Yangtze River.

At the northwest corner of Pudong Park, the **Natural Wild Insect Kingdom** features snakes, lizards. and other reptiles, to say nothing of a host of bugs from around the world—everything from gorgeous butterflies and moths to distinctly less appealing creatures such as scorpions and centipedes. It's a good place to take children, and those under 2.6 feet tall (0.8 m) are admitted free of charge.

You may not necessarily want the youngsters along, however, when you visit the attraction next door. The **China Sex Culture Exhibition,** right next to the eastern exit of the Bund Sight-seeing Tunnel, is an unusual museum that catalogues and plumbs many aspects of Chinese eroticism and sexuality. These include the castration of eunuchs, the uniquely Chinese sexual custom of foot binding, sing-song girls, brothels, and prostitution. There's an educational side to the museum, too, with features on sexual health, female equality, and contraception.

It's an ocean up there: Inside the underwater tunnel at Shanghai Ocean Aquarium.

Sandwiched between Pudong Park and the Huangpu River, an attractive promenade known as **Binjiang Dadao** (Riverside Avenue) runs west and then south for 1.5 miles (2.5 km) from the northern end of Pudong Nanlu to Dongchang Lu. Hugging the river's east bank, this serene and carefully tended boulevard is one of the most evocative walks a visitor can take in Pudong. It offers fine views across the busy Huangpu River to The Bund, Waibaidu Bridge, and the impressive old Russian Consulate in Hongkou (see p. 142). ∎

Shanghai Ocean Aquarium
(Shanghai Haiyang Shuizuguan)
✉ 158 Yincheng Beilu
☎ 5877 9988
🕐 9 a.m.–6 p.m.
💲 $$$

Natural Wild Insect Kingdom
(Da Ziran Yesheng Kunchong Guan)
✉ 1 Fenghe Lu
☎ 5840 5921
🕐 9 a.m.–5 p.m.
💲 $$

Chinese Sex Culture Exhibition
(Zhonghua Xing Wenhua Hexing Jiankang Jiaoyuzhan)
✉ 2789 Binjiang Dadao
☎ 5888 6000
🕐 8 a.m.–10 p.m.
💲 $$$

Comfy chairs cushion a cruise down the Hangpu River to the sea.

Cruise the Huangpu River

A cruise on the Huangpu River transports the voyager back in time and unveils Shanghai's ultramodern future. Cruises ranging from the simple to the elaborate leave hourly from the Pearl Dock at 1 Shiji Dadao (Century Boulevard), right next to the Oriental Pearl TV Tower. They also leave from the Jinling Pier on the west side of the river, near the southern end of The Bund. It's a toss-up whether to take a river cruise by day or at night. The shorter cruises (about 30 minutes) are ideal for an evening excursion, when the lights of The Bund and the skyscrapers of Pudong Park stage a fantastic show, while the longer cruises (up to 3.5 hours) are best in broad daylight for viewing the docks.

The cruise described here departs from Pudong's Pearl Dock. It heads upstream (south) first, passing The Bund on the starboard (right) side and offering fine views of Pudong Park and the skyscrapers of Lujiazui on the port (left) side. The boat passes beneath the vast bulk of **Nanpu Bridge** (see p. 104) ❶, then turns in midstream and heads downriver. In the case of a short trip, your farthest destination will be the Yangpu Bridge. Longer cruises sail all the way to the Yangtze River, a 35-mile (60 km) round-trip that includes refreshments.

Heading downstream from The Bund, the river passes **Suzhou Creek** and the historic **Waibaidu Bridge** ❷ on the left bank, then sweeps past the old **Russian Consulate,** the docks of Tilanqiao, and the hulking **Yangpu Bridge** ❸. Spanning the inconceivable distance of 8,373 yards (7,658 m), this cable-stayed monster appears to vault the river, permitting easy clearance for the most massive commercial vessels. Opened in 1993, the Yangpu Bridge links Hongkou and north Shanghai to Pudong and the airport.

Dockyard cranes are active along both banks of the Huangpu River.

Farther downstream, the gritty personality of China's busiest port emerges. An estimated 2,000 oceangoing vessels and 18,000 river vessels dock here every year, and as you make your way downriver you're likely to spot every class from pleasure craft and ferry boats to container ships, oil tankers, and Chinese naval vessels *(which are off-limits to photography).*

Beyond the Yangpu Bridge, giant **Fuxing Island** ❹ heaves into view. Nestling the left bank of the river and the northern suburb of Yangpu, the island is being developed as a marina and a recreational area for yachting and pleasure cruising. Beyond Fuxing Island, on the left (west) bank of the Huangpu, one of Shanghai's largest wooded areas, **Gongqing Forest Park** ❺, hoves into view (see p. 154).

Historic **Wusongkou** awaits at the mouth of the Huangpu, where this so-called "yellow creek" empties into the mighty Yangtze River. It was here on June 16, 1842, that the British navy shelled the Qing batteries—the opening salvo of the First Opium War. The **Wusong-**

kou Lighthouse ⑥ on the left (north) bank marks the Wusong Bar, traditionally deemed the start of the Yangtze proper. Beyond, in the middle distance, lie Chongming and Changxing Islands, with their market gardens and fishing vessels.

As you cruise back upriver, focus on the Pudong bank (the east side of the river). Here a thicket of cranes signals the frenetic pace of the Shanghai docklands—and the still-busier pace of 21st-century Pudong as its skyline continues to rise and expand. ■

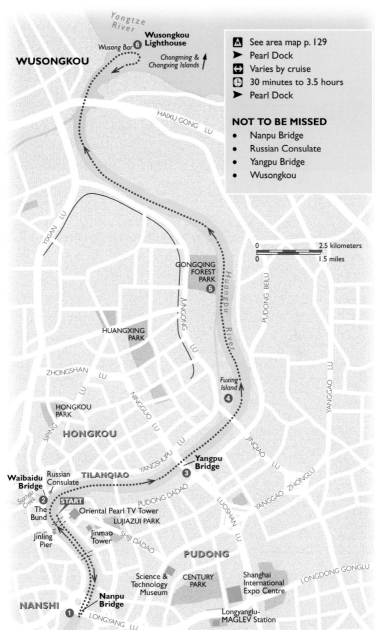

Lujiazui Park & around

HALF A MILE (700 M) SOUTHEAST OF PUDONG PARK IS another "green lung" for Pudong. This is Lujiazui Park, and as you might expect, it is a lunchtime magnet for the office workers pouring out of the skyscrapers looming nearby. Doubtless they are drawn to the park for its multiple bucolic blandishments: expanses of grass, borders of trees and plants, and a man-made lake with fountains and lots of fish.

East of the park you'll want to check out **Lujiazui Development Showroom,** sometimes called Lujiazui Development Museum. An anomaly by virtue of its traditional architecture, the 1917 courtyard mansion is a prized link to Pudong's past—and a stark reminder of the torrid pace of development in this sector.

Built for shipping magnate Chen Guichun, the showroom was one of the city's largest privately owned homes: Its floor space once covered 3,300 square yards (2,765 sq m). The Imperial Japanese Army commandeered the elegant structure during the Sino-Japanese War, and the house suffered further indignities during the Cultural Revolution—particularly damage to its elaborate interior woodwork.

Now faithfully restored, the showroom offers exhibits that chronicle the development of Pudong. You'll find looms and farming tools once used in the area, as well as some fine old rosewood furniture and other antiques.

Rising over the southern end of Lujiazui Park is the steel-and-concrete mass of the **Shanghai Stock Exchange Building** (visitors not allowed on trading floor). Mainland China's largest stock exchange—and a monument to industry looming over the communist state's largest city—the building is said to represent an antique Chinese coin: It is circular with a square hole in the center. ■

Jinmao Tower

SOUTH OF LUJIAZUI PARK, DOMINATING ITS ENVIRONS AND visible from just about anywhere in Shanghai, rises a glittering monolith of steel and glass: the Jinmao Tower. At a height of 1,379 feet (421 m), it's the tallest building in China (and third tallest in the world). Amid the frenzied construction zones of East Asia, however, don't expect those records to last long.

Jinmao Tower
(Jinmao Dasha)
Map p. 129
88 Shiji Dadao
5047 5101
8:30 a.m.–10 p.m.
$$

Jinmao was opened in 1998 and has 88 floors. High-speed elevators whisk visitors to the 88th-floor **Observation Deck** in less than a Shanghai minute, where (on a clear day) the views across Pudong and Puxi are worth the steep admission.

In a successful bid to blend modern and traditional Chinese architecture, the building rises through 16 distinct segments. Chicago architect Adrian Smith designed the structure to subtly evoke a pagoda. The first 50 floors are given over to office space; above rises the world's highest hotel, the **Grand Hyatt Shanghai** (Jinmao Kaiyue Dajiudian, *88 Shiji Dadao, 5049 1234*). A distinctive hotel by any standards (see Travelwise p. 245), the Hyatt also features a central atrium that soars 33 stories above the hotel lobby. (Vertigo, anyone?) From the Observation Deck on the 88th floor, those frantic ants below are actually hotel guests moving about the lobby.

Six years after the Jinmao Tower opened, it lost its claim of altitudinal superiority to the 1,671-foot-tall (509 m) 101 Tower in Taipei, Taiwan. Nor is the competition exclusively international: Right next door to the Jinmao Tower, a new behemoth is on the rise. When completed in 2008, the **Shanghai World Financial Center** (Shanghai Guoji Jinrong Zhongxin) will top out at 101 stories measuring 1,510 feet (472 m). Yes, the financial center will be second to Taipei 101—but only because of

the latter's 192-foot-high (60 m) spire. The center's original design featured a circular aperture atop the tower. This was hurriedly revised when numerous horrified Chinese—among them the mayor of Shanghai—pointed out that the finished structure would resemble a Japanese flag. A sky bridge has now been placed near the bottom of the aperture to sidestep this potentially inauspicious symbol. ∎

Your rise to the top will be swift: 45 seconds, to be precise, from basement to Observation Deck.

More places to visit in Pudong

CENTURY AVENUE

Sometimes rendered as Century Boulevard (Shiji Dadao), this huge 21st-century boulevard was designed to add grandeur to Pudong. Mission accomplished! French architect and urban planner Jean-Marie Charpentier envisioned a boulevard 3 miles (5 km) long and 320 feet (100 m) wide, with 25 acres (10 ha) of green belt running parallel to the road. Today Century Avenue leads southeast from Lujiazui financial district all the way to Century Park and constitutes one of the city's most attractive and pleasant drives.

 Map p. 129    Lujiazui, Dongchang Road, Dongfang Road, Yanggao Road South

CENTURY PARK

Century Park (Shiji Gongyuan) is the largest park in Pudong—indeed, in all Shanghai. Like Century Avenue, the park is a Charpentier original. Facilities include boating, cycling, and fishing. There are also picnic grounds and extensive amusement areas for children.

Map p. 129   1001 Jinxiu Lu   5833 5621   7 a.m.–6 p.m. $ Century Park (Shiji Gongyuan)

NEXT AGE DEPARTMENT STORE

Next Age (Xinshiji Shanghsha) is Pudong's largest department store and, perhaps, the largest in Asia—though superlatives are irrelevant given the region's breakneck pace of expansion. Biggest or not, Next Age is huge by any standards. Anchored by the Japanese supermarket Yaohan, the complex is 10 stories high and houses 150 separate shops and outlets, as well as a cineplex on the top floor.

Map p. 129   501 Zhangyang Lu   5830 1111   Dongchang Road

QINCI YANGDIAN TEMPLE

Tucked away at the junction of Yuanshen Lu and Shenjianong Lu about 1 mile (1.5 km) east of the Next Age Department Store, Pudong's Qinci Yangdian Temple (Qinci Yangdian Si) is the largest Taoist temple in Shanghai. Whereas it very likely dates from the Three Kingdoms Period (220–280), its present form is clearly a Qing dynasty restoration. In 1982 the Shanghai Taoist Association reopened the temple after years of neglect instigated by the Cultural Revolution. The temple is dedicated to such key Taoist figures as the Great Emperor of the Sacred Mountain of the East and the Primordial Lady of the Emerald Cloud.

Map p. 129   476 Yuanshen Lu   5882 8689   8 a.m.–4 p.m. $ Dongfang Road

SHANGHAI ORIENTAL ART CENTER

Designed by French architect Paul Andreu (the visionary behind Pudong International Airport), the Shanghai Oriental Art Center's (Shanghai Dongfang Yishu Zhongxin) stylish glass-and-steel concert hall opened in July 2005. Home to the Shanghai Symphony

Waibaidu Bridge provides a vantage point for viewing Pudong's skyscrapers.

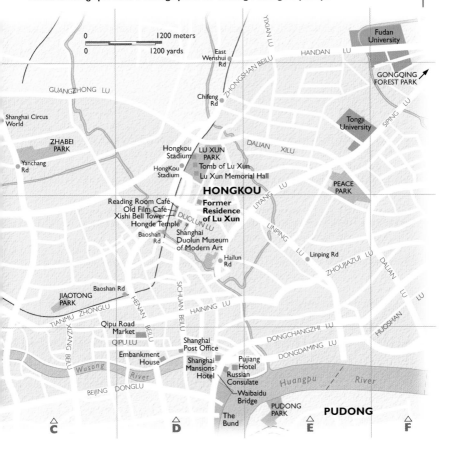

0   1200 meters

0   1200 yards

GUANGZHONG LU

YIXIAN LU

HANDAN LU

East Wenshui Rd

Chifeng Rd

ZHONGSHAN BEILU

Fudan University

GONGQING FOREST PARK

SIPING LU

Shanghai Circus World

ZHABEI PARK

Yanchang Rd

Hongkou Stadium

HongKou Stadium

LU XUN PARK

Tomb of Lu Xun

Lu Xun Memorial Hall

DALIAN XILU

Tongji University

PEACE PARK

HONGKOU

LIYANG LU

Reading Room Café

Old Film Café

Xishi Bell Tower

Hongde Temple

Former Residence of Lu Xun

DUOLUN LU

Baoshan Rd

Shanghai Duolun Museum of Modern Art

Hailun Rd

LINPING LU

Linping Rd

ZHOUJIAZUI LU

DALIAN LU

Baoshan Rd

JIAOTONG PARK

HENAN BEILU

SICHUAN BEILU

HAINING LU

TIANMU ZHONGLU

XIZANG BEILU

Qipu Road Market

QIPU LU

DONGCHANGZHI LU

DONGDAMING LU

HUOSHAN LU

Shanghai Post Office

Embankment House

Wusong River

Shanghai Mansions Hotel

Pujiang Hotel

Russian Consulate

Waibaidu Bridge

Huangpu River

PUDONG PARK

PUDONG

BEIJING DONGLU

The Bund

C   D   E   F

The 1924 Shanghai Post Office building contains a museum as well as a spectacular rooftop park.

Hongkou

The iron girders of Waibaidu Bridge are generally seen as the northern gateway to The Bund, but they are also the southern gateway to the historic Hongkou District. While distant from the city center, this area is experiencing something of a revival. The Duolun Road Cultural Street, a thriving arts scene, and nearby Fudan University give this area a less glitzy atmosphere than better known parts of Shanghai, but it is an interesting alternative to the tourist haunts downtown.

There are few actual sights here—the main draws, Duolun Road and the old Shanghai Ghetto, where thousands of Jewish refugees took refuge prior to World War II, are described in the following pages.

The area does boast some interesting architecture. Immediately beyond Waibaidu Bridge, for example, are two of colonial Shanghai's best-known landmarks. Dominating the north side of Suzhou Creek, **Shanghai Mansions Hotel** *(20 Suzhou Beilu, 6324 6260)* was built in 1935 as an immense 19-story apartment building called Broadway Mansions. During the 1930s and '40s, the upper floors functioned as the Shanghai Foreign Correspondents Club. The 18th-floor obser-

vation balcony still offers fabulous views south across The Bund and east toward Pudong.

Behind the Russian Consulate, the **Pujiang Hotel** (Pujiang Fandian, *15 Huangpu Lu, 6324 6388)* was once the Astor House. As Shanghai's premier hotel, it attracted such famous guests as Ulysses S. Grant, Albert Einstein, and Charlie Chaplin.

Other fine buildings in the area include the 1924 **Shanghai Post Office** (Shanghai Youzheng Ju, *250 Suzhou Beilu, 6306 0438)*, with its classical lines and clock tower, and **Embankment House** on Suzhou Beilu, built by Shanghai Jewish magnate Sir Victor Sassoon in 1932—the city's largest apartment building at the time. ■

Duolun Lu

Once the haunt of writer **Lu Xun** and other social activists, Duolun Lu is now best known for its teahouses, shops, and historic houses.

FARTHER NORTH OF WAIBAIDU BRIDGE ALONG SICHUAN Beilu, Duolun Lu is a lively center of creativity at the heart of Hongkou. Set in a restored area of *shikumen,* or stone gate housing, this area's official name is Duolun Lu Wenhua Jie (Duolun Road Cultural Celebrities Street) to honor and commemorate the Chinese literary circle that once lived here and remain associated with it.

Formerly grimy Duolun Lu has become a rather upscale walking street, home to art galleries, antiques shops, coffeehouses, and tea shops, as well as to statues of modern China's greatest literary figures: Lu Xun (1881–1936; see p. 145), Guo Moruo (1892–1978), Feng Xuefeng (1903–1976), Ye Shengtao (1894–1988), Shen Yimo (1883–1971), and others. There's also a statue of Uchiyama Kanzo (1885–1959), a native of Japan who ran a bookstore here and was a close friend of Lu Xun.

At the eastern end of the pedestrian zone, the **Shanghai Duolun Museum of Modern Art** is a seven-story collection of contemporary artworks, which also features artists in residence. Just off Duolun Lu, the **China Left Wing Writers Museum** (Zhongguo Zuolian Bowuguan, *2 Lane 201 Duolun Lu, 9:30 a.m.– 4:30 p.m., $*) marks the site of the original League of Left Wing Writers set up by Lu Xun and other intellectuals in 1930.

At 59 Duolun Lu, the distinctly Chinese upturned eaves of the **Hongde Temple** (Hongde Tang) seem to indicate a Buddhist or Taoist structure, but this is a Christian church built in 1928 (*Sunday services 7–8:30 a.m. & 9:30–11 a.m.*). It's the only one in the city built in the Chinese style. Also on Duolun Lu are small museums devoted to such curiosities as early 20th-century Shanghai (Nos. 179–181), Mao Zedong memorabilia (No. 183), Chinese porcelain (No. 185), and chopsticks (No. 191).

Café society is flourishing, and celebrated establishments are **The Old Film Café** at No. 123, next to the redbrick **Xishi Bell Tower,** and the **Reading Room Café** at No. 195. The area's atmosphere straddles the line between nostalgia for early 20th-century Hongkou and 21st-century passion for promoting and marketing that phenomenon. ∎

Duolun Lu
 Map p. 141 D2–D3

Shanghai Duolun Museum of Modern Art
(Shanghai Duolun Xiandai Meishuguan)
www.duolunart.com
✉ 27 Duolun Lu
☎ 6587 2503
🕐 9 a.m.–5:30 p.m. Tues.–Sun.
💲 $

Lu Xun's neighborhood

Writer Lu Xun's tomb occupies peaceful Lu Xun Park, where locals stroll and do tai chi.

ONCE A LOCALE FOR FOREIGNERS, DUOLUN LU AND CENtral Hongkou have become much associated with the writer Lu Xun. Widely acknowledged as the father of modern vernacular Chinese *(baihua)* literature, Lu Xun lived in this neighborhood between 1927 and 1936.

Writer with a cause

Born in 1881 at Shaoxing in Zhejiang Province, not far south of Shanghai, Lu Xun studied at Jiangnan Naval Academy before taking a Qing government scholarship to study medicine at Sendai University in Japan. Once there, he saw a lantern show of a Chinese man about to be decapitated by the Japanese for spying. Deeply shocked, he decided it was more important to cure his countrymen's spiritual woes than to minister to their physical welfare. An intellectual of pronounced left wing sympathies—though he never joined the communist party—Lu Xun devoted the rest of his life to writing more than 30 novels, essays, and short stories. He also translated literary works from Russian and English into Chinese, and edited literary magazines, notably *New Youth*. His first short story, "A Madman's Diary," was published in 1918. Inspired in part by Nikolai Gogol's story of the same name, it is considered the first published *baihua* story. His novella "The True Story of Ah Q" is also considered a masterpiece. In 1927 Lu Xun settled in Hongkou District, where he lived until his death from tuberculosis in 1936. A founding member of the China League of Left Wing Writers, he actively supported the revolutionary May 4th Movement. ■

Bronze bust of Lu Xun

Former Residence of Lu Xun
(Lu Xun Guju)
🅰 Map p. 141 D2
✉ 9 Lane 132, Shanying Lu
☎ 5666 2608
🕘 9 a.m.–4 p.m.
💲 $

Hongkou Stadium
(Hongkou Tiyuguan)
✉ 444 Dongjiangwan Lu
🄰 HongKou Station

A short distance north of Duolun Lu is the **Former Residence of Lu Xun.** Born Zhou Shuren, he lived in this unpretentious three-story, redbrick-and-tile-house for six years. The residence acts as a museum, displaying his furniture and belongings. (The writer's library of 16,000 books is not here, however, but is instead preserved at the Lu Xun Museum in Beijing.)

Located a few minutes' walk north of the residence is **Lu Xun Park** (Lu Xun Gongyuan, *6 a.m.–6 p.m.*). This pleasant open space centers on a small lake, where local residents come to exercise. It is also home to a bronze seated statue of Lu Xun and the **Tomb of Lu Xun** (Lu Xun Ling), as well as the **Lu Xun Memorial Hall** (Lu Xun Jininguan, *9 a.m.–5 p.m., $*). The inscription on the tomb was Mao Zedong's tribute, while the trees on either side of it were planted by the Premier of the People's Republic of China Zhou Enlai and by Lu Xun's widow, Xu Guangping. The memorial hall displays an extensive collection of Lu Xun memorabilia, including his horn-rimmed spectacles, pens, and hand-written essays.

On the northwest side of Lu Xun Park is the huge **Hongkou Stadium** (Hongkou Tiyuguan), a popular soccer venue with a capacity for 35,000 people. ■

Jewish Shanghai walk

In the late 19th and early 20th centuries, Shanghai emerged as the center of Jewish settlement in the Far East. An initial wave of largely Sephardic Jewish emigrants from Baghdad via Bombay had arrived by the 1870s, including wealthy businessmen from the Sassoon and Hardoon families, who would become some of the city's most celebrated magnates. A second wave of largely Ashkenazi Jewish emigrants arrived under very different circumstances in the 1920s and '30s, following the Bolshevik Revolution in Russia and the subsequent rise of Nazism in Germany.

A residential street in Hongkou's former Jewish Quarter

By the late 1930s, Hongkou had become Shanghai's major area of Jewish settlement, with an estimated 20,000 Jewish residents, many of them stateless refugees. During the Japanese occupation of the city during World War II, they were ghettoized in the few blocks surrounding the old Hongkou synagogue. Most left after the war's end, and the community declined to just a few dozen people after the 1949 communist takeover. Although Shanghai's Jewish population is a far cry from what it once was, it's still possible to walk around Hongkou and get some idea of the area's Jewish history.

Head east from **Waibaidu Bridge** ❶ along Dongdaming Lu for about 1.2 miles (2 km) and turn northeast onto Huoshan Lu. Halfway along this street is the Broadway Disco—once the **Broadway Theatre** ❷

(65 Huoshan Lu), which housed the Jewish-owned Vienna Café. This was the only area of Hongkou to have lights at night during the '30s.

Continue east along Huoshan Lu, passing a series of small town houses with gardens in front that were once owned by Jewish families. Enter tiny **Huoshan Park** (6 a.m. –6 p.m.) to view the stone plaque in Chinese, Hebrew, and English that commemorates the area's former role as a "haven for stateless refugees"— until 1939 Shanghai had no visa requirements. This monument was erected for the visit of then–Israeli Prime Minister Yitzhak Rabin in 1993.

Turn north along Zhoushan Lu, another street lined with small town houses—this area was once known as "Little Vienna" for its shops and cafés. Famous former residents include former U.S. treasury secretary Michael Blumenthal, movie mogul Michael Medavoy and *Far Eastern Economic Review* founder Eric Halpern; many others have penned memoirs.

At tiny Changyang Lu, turn west and continue to the recently refurbished **Ohel Moishe Synagogue** ③ (Moxi Huidang, *62 Changyang Lu, tel 6541 5008, 9 a.m.–4:30 p.m. weekdays, $),* the area's centerpiece, now called the **Jewish Refugee Memorial Hall of Shanghai** *(62 Changyang Lu).* The synagogue was built in 1927 to serve the mainly Russian Ashkenazi Jewish community of Hongkou and was administered by Meir Ashkenazi, the chief rabbi of Shanghai from 1926 to 1949. No longer a place of worship, it serves as a center for remembering Shanghai's Jewish past and addressing the questions of tourists who stop by. On various floors you'll find historic photographs of Shanghai Jewish life and of recent visits by Jewish luminaries (Yitzhak Rabin's likeness takes pride of place), as well as furniture and everyday items of Jewish life from the pre-1949 period.

Books on sale at the Memorial Hall

include studies of Jewish Shanghai (in Chinese and English), along with a study of the much earlier Sung dynasty Jewish settlement at Kaifeng in Henan Province (in English only).

For further information on the Jewish settlement in Hongkou, as well as the former Jewish presence elsewhere in Shanghai (notably in the French Concession), contact the **Shanghai Center for Jewish Studies** (Shanghai Youtai Yanjiu Zhongxin, *7 Lane 622, Huaihai Zhonglu, tel 5306 0606;* see p. 115). ∎

- See area map pp. 140–141
- ► Waibaidu Bridge
- ↔ 3 miles (4.8 km)
- ⏱ 1.5 hours
- ► Ohel Moishe Synagogue

NOT TO BE MISSED
- Huoshan Park
- Broadway Theatre
- Jewish Refugee Memorial Hall of Shanghai

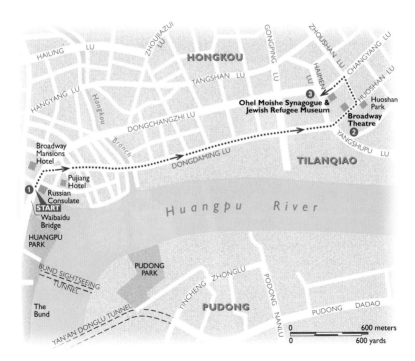

Zhabei

Zhabei, the district lying immediately to the west of Hongkou, has shared many of the latter's hardships and suffered even more than its neighbor at the hands of the Imperial Japanese Army. In 1932 and again in 1937, much of the district was completely leveled by artillery fire and aerial bombing, so relatively few historic buildings survive. Today broad swaths of Zhabei are given over to residential housing. Although the area is quieter than Hongkou, there are still places of interest to visit here, as well as in neighboring Jingan, just on the other side of Suzhou Creek.

Southern Zhabei extends west along Suzhou Creek beyond Shanghai Railway Station. A gritty industrial area of factories and warehouses, it also houses the extensive Qipu Road Market and Jiaotong Park. In an attempt to transform the area and promote investment, Zhabei District authorities are now developing the Suzhou Creek Modern Services Zone, including Meitai Ancient City and Sihang Warehouse, site of a famous battle with the Japanese army in 1937 (see p. 152).

Just to the west of Suzhou Creek—in fact in Jingan District but easily accessible from Zhabei via Tianmu Lu West—is the Jade Buddha Temple, one of the most interesting and important Buddhist temples in Shanghai. Jingan is also home to trendy Moganshan Lu, a burgeoning arts district filled with art galleries and artists' lofts and studios.

Northern Zhabei is home to Zhabei Park and the tomb of Song Jiaoren, revolutionary nationalist and first president of the Kuomindang (KMT). Beyond lie a number of open-air attractions, including Daning Green Land Park, where the annual Zhabei Tourism Festival is held, and Shanghai Circus World, home to the Shanghai Acrobatic Troupe. ∎

Travelers and commuters crowd busy Shanghai Railway Station in Zhabei.

Suzhou Creek area

A well-stocked fruit market near Suzhou Creek tempts shoppers with color.

SUZHOU CREEK (ALSO KNOWN AS THE WUSONG RIVER) is a narrow waterway just 78 miles (125 km) long, which rises in Lake Tai to the west of Shanghai. Its small size belies its historic importance as an artery for all manner of waterborne trade in and out of Shanghai and as a frontier between the British and American Settlements in the 19th century. Lined with industrial and agricultural warehouses, by the early 20th century, Suzhou Creek—locally known as the "stinking river"—was the city's most polluted stretch of water.

The waterway forms the southern boundary of Zhabei District. It is being gradually cleaned up as part of the Suzhou Creek Rehabilitation Project, which was launched in 1998 with a budget of 11.35 billion yuan (1.37 billion dollars). The warehouses, a protected heritage zone, are being restored and designed to attract shopping plazas, restaurants, and bars, and to encourage the city's flourishing art scene. The project, due to be completed in 2010, also includes new parks and 250 acres (100 ha) of greenbelt.

North of Suzhou Creek, about 700 yards (650 m) along Henan Beilu, is **Qipu Road Market** (Qipu Lu Shihchang, *Henan Beilu at Qipu Lu, dawn to dusk)*, a huge market mainly selling shoes and clothing. With an emerging reputation for fake goods and knockoffs, it has inherited the mantle of Xiangyang Market, which closed in 2006.

Farther west looms the giant **Shanghai Railway Station** (Shanghai Huochezhan, *385 Meiyuan Lu, tel 6317 9090)*, the main terminus on the Shanghai–Beijing line, offering rail links across the country. This area is fairly rough, housing new migrants from the countryside. ∎

Suzhou Creek
🅐 Map pp. 140–141
B2–D1

Chinese temples

Three recognized and interlinked faiths belong to traditional China—the *san jiao* or three teachings of Confucianism, Taoism, and Buddhism. Of these, the first two are purely indigenous while Buddhism traveled to China from India at least two millennia ago via the Silk Road. Although most Chinese temples are readily identifiable as being predominantly Confucian, Taoist, or Buddhist, the syncretic nature of san jiao means that symbols and deities from all three interrelated faiths often appear in a single temple.

Confucian temples, or *wenmiao,* are essentially dedicated to tradition, education, and filial piety. They commonly house stone stela mounted on the backs of stone tortoises recording the names of literary graduates, honoring the tradition of learning, which "hangs like perfume through the ages." Most contain a statue of the great sage Kong Fuzi (Confucius, 561–479 B.C.) as well as images of his disciples, especially the Confucian philosopher Meng Zi (Mencius, 372–289 B.C.). There are relatively few Confucius temples, the most important being in the master's hometown of Qufu, in Beijing, and in Hanoi in Vietnam. In Shanghai visit the Wen Miao in southwest Nanshi (see p. 99).

Taoist temples, or *guan,* are dedicated to the teachings of Laozi (6th century B.C.), founder of the faith and author of the *Tao De Jing (The Book of the Way and its Virtue).* Besides images of Laozi, Taoist *guan* generally contain images of the Eight Immortals, the Jade Emperor, and often the goddess charged with protecting seafarers, Tianhou (aka Mazu). Taoism teaches practicing harmony with *tao,* The Way, and is often described as naturist. Taoist monks, or *taoshi,* wind their long hair up in knots and wear jackets and trousers. The Qinci Yangdian Temple, Shanghai's largest, dates back to the first millenium.

Buddhist temples, or *simiao* (those dedicated to Zen Buddhism are called *chansi),* are distinguished by images of Milefo (the

laughing, jovial Buddha) and by images of Sakyamuni, also called Gautama (the historic Buddha), Maitreya (the Buddha of the future), and Amitabha (the infinite Buddha). Also enduringly popular is the goddess of mercy, Guanyin, who was somehow transformed into a female deity in her passage across the Himalaya, from her Indian male form Avalokitisevara. Buddhist temples are guarded by four heavenly kings, filled with incense smoke, and inhabited by shaven-headed, robe-

Affluent Shanghainese stroll on West Nanjing Road.

Changfeng Park neighborhood.

Hongqiao and Gubei are known for the Shanghai Zoo, the Shanghai Children's Museum, and the neighboring Song Qingling Mausoleum in addition to its expatriate residents, shops, and bird market.

The district of Jiading includes Nanxiang, known for its Garden of Ancient Splendor and *xiao long bao* dumplings (see p. 165). Jiading is a canal town with a Confucian temple and museum.

To the southwest of Shanghai, Sheshan's highlights include its observatory, the Basilica of Notre Dame, the Xiudaozhe Pagoda, and the tilting pagoda at Huzhu Ta. Neighboring Songjiang features the Square Pagoda and the Garden of the Poet Bai Juyi. The Chinese-style Songjiang Mosque, built in the mid-14th century, is one of the oldest mosques in China. ■

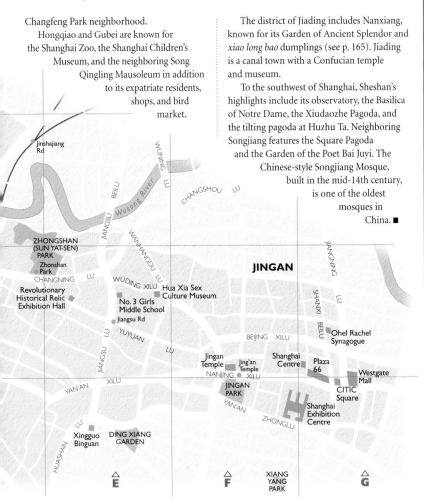

Jingan

**Chinese yachts
are part of the
boat fair at
the Russian-
built Shanghai
Exhibition Centre.**

JINGAN WAS ALWAYS A WEALTHY AREA, HOME TO SOME OF Shanghai's richest taipans (foreign businessmen). It was also a favored shopping district for their wives. Even today, Jingan is the place to go for fine silks and couturier clothing.

On the north side of Nanjing Xilu, **Westgate Mall, CITIC Square, Plaza 66,** and **Shanghai Centre** attest to the area's continuing affluence. Just to the north, along Shanxi Beilu beyond CITIC Square, the former **Ohel Rachel Synagogue** survives. Built by

banker Jacob Sassoon in 1920, this synagogue has been refurbished. Though it remains consecrated, it now serves primarily as a museum *(open to the public only by special arrangement with the Shanghai Center for Jewish Studies; see p. 115).*

South of Nanjing Xilu, almost directly opposite the Shanghai Centre, the **Shanghai Exhibition Centre** (Shanghai Zhanlan Zhongxin, *1000 Yan'an Lu*) on the former estate of Silas Hardoon—once the city's richest man—is a remarkable example of high Social-ist Realist kitsch from the heady days of Sino–Soviet solidarity in the early 1950s. Designed by a Soviet architect, the Christmas cake-like structure combines a five-pointed communist star atop classical pillars and floral wreaths with elements of Eastern Orthodox church architecture, including a gilded steeple.

Near the western end of Nanjing Xilu, **Jingan Temple** is said to have been built in A.D. 247, but it has been repeatedly restored and rebuilt over the centuries, most recently in 2005. Dedicated to Sakyamuni Buddha, it now seems equally dedicated to commerce, with a shopping mall located within the temple precincts. In the 1930s Jingan Si was the richest Buddhist temple in Shanghai and the preserve of an extraordinary abbot, Khi Vehdu, who was almost 6 feet, 6 inches (2 m) tall. Protected by White Russian bodyguards, he reportedly maintained seven concubines, each with her own house and car! ■

Bubbling Well Road

Bubbling Well Road was once the name of Jingan's Nanjing Xilu. A carbonated spring that stood at the intersection of Nanjing Xilu and Wanhang Lu was paved over long ago, but a re-creation of the spring is in Jingan Park *(Jingan Gongyuan, 6 a.m.–8 p.m.)*, the former Bubbling Well Cemetery. In dry weather, calligraphers practice writing Chinese ideographs on the stone flags using giant *maobi* brushes and water—a transient art form. ■

Changning

LIKE JINGAN, CHANGNING HAS LONG BEEN ONE OF Shanghai's wealthier districts. Several historical and cultural sights make it worth a visit.

The great British *hong* (trading company) Butterfield and Swire chose to build Hazlewood, its extensive Shanghai headquarters, in Changning. It replicates an English country estate, complete with playing fields and tennis courts. After the company left Shanghai following the communist seizure of power in 1949, Hazlewood became Mao's favored residence. It now serves as the **Xingguo Binguan,** or Prosperous Kingdom Guesthouse *(78 Xingguo Lu, 6212 9998).*

North of the guesthouse, at the intersection of Jiangsu Lu and Wuding Lu, is the **No. 3 Girls Middle School** (Di San Nu Zhong, *Lane 155 Jiangsu Lu).* The prestigious institution was founded as the McTyeire School for Girls in 1890. The Song sisters—Ailing, Qingling, and Meiling (see p. 109)—all studied here, which helps to explain the school's cachet.

About 600 yards (550 m) east down Wuding Lu from the school is the **Hua Xia Sex Culture Museum.** This unusual museum details five millennia of Chinese sexual and erotic behavior through more than a thousand exhibits about fertility, sex toys, foot binding, chastity belts, classical pornography, and so on.

Back in central Changning, the **Revolutionary Historical Relic Exhibition Hall** displays books, maps, pamphlets, posters, and other revolutionary literature in a building once devoted to producing the underground Marxist publication *Bolshevik.*

A taxi is the best way to reach **Changfeng Park** *(6 a.m.–6 p.m.)* on Zhongshan Lu. At Gate 4 of the park, **Changfeng Ocean World** is the city's finest aquarium, if not in China. Its vast tanks house a variety of marine life, including whales, penguins, and sharks.

On the north side of Changfeng Park at the **Jingdezhen Ceramics Art Center** (Jingdezhen Ciqi Yishu Zhongxin, *1253 Daduhe Lu, 9:30 a.m.–4 p.m.),* thousands of ceramic pieces from Jingdezhen and Yixing (see p. 94) are displayed. Watch potters work and purchase contemporary ceramics. ∎

Children play at the popular adventure playground in Zhongshan Park.

Changning
- Map pp. 156–157

Hua Xia Sex Culture Museum
(Hua Xia Xing Wenhua Bowuguan)
- Map p. 157 E2
- 1133 Wuding Lu
- 6230 1243
- 10 a.m.–6 p.m.
- $

Revolutionary Historical Relic Exhibition Hall
(Changning Qu Geming Wenwu Chenlie Guan)
- 1376 Yuyuan Lu
- 6251 1415
- Mon.–Sat. 1 p.m.– 4 p.m.

Changfeng Ocean World
(Changfeng Haiyang Shijie)
- Map p. 156 D3
- 451 Daduhe Lu
- 5281 8888
- 8:30 a.m.–5 p.m.
- $$$

Western architecture in Shanghai

It's difficult to generalize about Western architecture in Shanghai because it's as varied as the institutions and individuals who settled in the city and erected buildings. Some settlers were motivated by religion, resulting in fine churches, like St. Ignatius Cathedral in Xujiahui, the blue-domed former Russian Orthodox Mission Church near Fuxing Park, and the Basilica of Notre Dame at Sheshan. Others were driven by commerce, erecting great temples to wealth, notably along The Bund. Many buildings were designed by the British architectural firm Palmer & Turner, which remains active in Shanghai. Its land-

mark structures include the Bank of China, the Yokohama Specie Bank, the Customs House, and the Hong Kong and Shanghai Bank. When the latter opened in 1923, the six-floor, neo-classic building was the largest bank in East Asia and, astonishingly, the second largest in the world after the Bank of Scotland in the U.K.

As foreign-concession Shanghai grew wealthier, grand hotels were built to house the travelers and tourists who flocked to the city for its sophistication and style, as well as for its dubious but compelling reputation. Palmer & Turner also played a role in the travel industry,

4

Nanxiang

TEN MILES (17 KM) NORTHWEST OF SHANGHAI—LOCATED
in Jiading District on the road to Jiading and therefore easily visited on
the way there or back—lies the small town of Nanxiang. Its fame rests
partially on the 16th-century Garden of Ancient Splendor and partially on the ancient Yunxiang Temple.

A formal, Suzhou-style garden
designed by local bamboo sculptor
Zhun Shansong, the lovely **Garden
of Ancient Splendor** served as
the private garden for a Ming dynasty official. Chinese pavilions,
pebble paths, peaceful ponds, and
exotic birds are part of its allure.
Highlights include a Song dynasty
pagoda and a Tang dynasty (618–
907) stela.

Yunxiang Temple is said to be
the only surviving Tang dynasty
temple in the Shanghai area and to
date, in its original form, from A.D.
505. That date, however, is pre-
Tang, so the claim must be taken
with a grain of salt. The temple was
originally called White Crane
Nanxiang Temple to honor the pair
of auspicious birds that reportedly
inspired its construction. It was
renamed Yunxiang Si during the
reign of the Qing Emperor Kangxi
(1654–1722). Today, it's an active
Buddhist temple, with shaven-
headed monks in yellow robes
wandering the corridors. ■

Dumpling heaven

Nanxiang may be best
known as the original
home of the enduringly popular
Shanghai culinary delicacy *xiao
long bao,* or "little basket bun."
Traditionally steamed in small
bamboo baskets, these bite-size
treats can be filled with broth
and ground pork or vegetables.
Be careful biting into them, as
the hot broth can scald your
mouth. Although popular
across China, experts agree
that the Shanghai version of
xiao long bao was originally
prepared and sold at a restaurant next to Nanxiang's historic
Guyi Gongyuan, from where its
fame spread into the big city.
Today, they are sold throughout
Nanxiang (and indeed all points
beyond) and make a delicious
and satisfying lunch, especially
in cold weather. ■

Even adults
enjoy the parks
of Nanxiang.

Nanxiang
🅰 Inset map p. 156

**Garden of
Ancient
Splendor**
(Guyi Gongyuan)
✉ 218 Huyi Lu
🕐 8 a.m.–4:30 p.m.
💲 $

Yunxiang Temple
(Yunxiang Si)
✉ 8 Huyi Lu
🕐 7 a.m.–5:30 p.m.
💲 $

Sheshan

Sheshan

🅜 Inset map p. 156

THE TOWN OF SHESHAN, ABOUT 19 MILES (30 KM) WEST OF Shanghai and almost due south of Jiading, is home to Sheshan Mountain, where the Jesuits established an observatory dating in 1898. You'll also find several other religious institutions that bear a closer look.

The handsome redbrick and stone basilica of Sheshan Cathedral

Start with the refurbished **Sheshan Observatory** (Sheshan Tianwentai, *9 a.m.–4:30 p.m., $*), which houses a small museum dedicated to the history of Chinese astronomy.

The Jesuits are also responsible

for erecting the impressive church next door that started life as the Cathedral of the Holy Mother in 1866. In 1935 it was replaced by the redbrick-and-stone Basilica of Notre Dame, one of the area's finest churches, more commonly called **Sheshan Cathedral** (Sheshan Shengmu Dadian, *Mount Sheshan, $*). Red Guard iconoclasts damaged the church during the Cultural Revolution, but it has been restored. Look for the letters "M" for Mary (the Mother of God) and "S" for *Societas Jesu* (the Society of Jesus) inscribed into the old church gate.

To the east of the church stands a 65-foot-high (20 m), seven-story tower, the **Xiudaozhe Pagoda** (Xiudaozhe Ta, *7:30 a.m.–6 p.m., $*), said to have been constructed between 976 and 984 during the Song dynasty.

About 5 miles (8 km) distant from Sheshan is the "pagoda for guarding pearls," **Huzhu Pagoda** (Huzhu Ta, *Tianma Mountain, 7:30 a.m.–6 p.m., $*), a 62-foot-high (19 m) pagoda chiefly remarkable for its tilt—locals have dubbed it the "leaning tower of China." Though it's much smaller and less impressive than the Leaning Tower of Pisa, the pagoda does tilt at a slightly greater angle and therefore is no place for vertigo sufferers. It is claimed that the octagonal stone Huzhu Ta was originally built in 1079 but that its trademark slant did not develop until 1788, when villagers pulled out some supporting stones at the base while looking for buried treasure. ∎

Songjiang

JUST SOUTH OF SHESHAN, ON THE HUHANG EXPRESSWAY between Shanghai and Hangzhou, the small town of Songjiang is the capital of Songjiang County and another ideal place for a day trip out of Shanghai.

Songjiang
 Inset map p. 156

The town's most celebrated monument is the **Square Pagoda**, a 160-foot-high (48.5 m), nine-story tower that was erected during the Song dynasty (A.D. 960–1279), probably about 1070, as part of Songjiang's Xingshengjiao Si—a long gone temple. The screen in front of the pagoda portrays a *tan*, or legendary monster with a deer's antlers, lion's tail, and bull's hooves—associated with greed in Buddhism. According to legend, the tan drowned while attempting to drink all the water in the sea. The pagoda is set in a lovely restored garden; concessions around the park include silent-running electric boats and children's scooters.

Other Songjiang attractions include the **Garden of the Poet Bai Juyi** (Zubaichi, *Zhongshan Lu, 7 a.m.–6 p.m., $*), a traditional Suzhou-style garden built by Gu Dashen—a Qing dynasty official and admirer of the celebrated Tang dynasty poet Bai Juyi (772–846). Songjiang's historic past is reflected in the **Xilin Pagoda** (Xilin Ta, *Zhongshan Zhonglu & Xilin Beilu, 8 a.m.– 5:30 p.m., $*), a 152-foot-high (46.5 m) pagoda within a recently renovated Buddhist temple. The pagoda, said to date from 1440, can be climbed (for a small fee) and offers fine views across Songjiang. Much older—in fact, supposedly the oldest Buddhist structure in the Shanghai area—is the **Toroni Sutra Stela** (Tang Jing Zhang, *Zhongshan Xiaoxue, Zhongshan Zhonglu*). This 30-foot-high (9 m) structure made of 21 separate stone blocks stands on the grounds of

Zhongshan Primary School *(open during school hours)*.

Perhaps Songjiang's best attraction is the remarkable **Zhenjiao Mosque** (Zhenjiao Qingzhensi, *Zhongshan Zhonglu*), the oldest Islamic structure in the area. It dates from the Yuan dynasty, perhaps having been completed in 1367, and was most recently restored in 1985. Once called "White Crane in the Clouds Mosque," it now bears the more Islamic designation Zhenjiao, or true religion, though

The carefully tended Garden of the Poet Bai Juyi evokes the beauty of Suzhou-style gardens.

Square Pagoda
(Fang Ta Yuan)
✉ Zhongshan Lu
🕐 8:30 a.m.–4:30 p.m.
💲 $

The elegant up-turned eaves of Songjiang's Square Pagoda rise above Square Pagoda Park.

most locals simply call it Songjiang Mosque. Among the oldest mosques in China, this architectural gem spans both Islamic and Chinese traditions, though it has little in common with the typical Islamic architecutre of Nanshi's mosques (see p. 102). Like Beijing's Niujie Mosque, it recalls a Chinese temple with upturned eaves, hidden courtyards, and massive wooden roof joists, as well as a *mihrab* (niche) indicating the direction of Mecca, a *mimbar* pulpit, the small Bangke Minaret, and Quranic suras written in the unique Sino–Arabic *sini* script of China's Hui Muslim community, around 300 of whom live in Songjiang.

Set in low-lying, rice-farming country transected by waterways, Songjiang is a pleasant escape from the big city—but perhaps not for long. Atkins, an international landscape and urban design company, has been awarded a contract to build **Songjiang Garden City,** a model community with its own central business district and housing for 500,000. A a water-filled quarry is being developed as a five-star resort with an aquatic theme, including rooms and restaurants below water level. ■

Thames Town

The newly built Thames Town, a pricey Songjiang County suburb designed by the British architectural firm Atkins, is an uncanny clone of a small English town. Cobbled streets, Georgian terraces, village greens, Victorian brick warehouses, a turreted castle, pubs, even a fish-and-chips shop make you think you're on a totally different continent. One of nine foreign-style towns that have been sanctioned by the Shanghai Municipality, Thames Town is expected to house ten thousand people. It's an interesting sign of the times that the Shanghainese, while ultramodern and contemporary, also seem to hunger for a lost past. ■

South of Shanghai, along Hangzhou Bay, lie such exotic destinations as culturally rich Hangzhou, historic Shaoxing, and Buddhist Putuoshan. Inland, the mountain resort of Moganshan sits amid giant bamboo forests.

Excursions south of Shanghai

Elaborately decorated silk scarves on sale on Xinhua Road, Hangzhou

Excursions south of Shanghai

THERE ARE SOME WONDERFUL EXCURSIONS SOUTH OF SHANGHAI, ALL IN easy striking distance of the city and all increasingly easy to reach as the network of expressways, bridges, and high-speed trains continues to expand. The historic city of Hangzhou—a major destination in its own right—is the gateway to historic Shaoxing, the Buddhist pilgrimage island of Putuoshan, and peaceful Moganshan. Along the way, breathtaking countryside makes you feel as if you've traveled far away from the urban bustle.

At a time when Shanghai was a sleepy fishing village attached to Songjiang County, Hangzhou was the capital of China. During the Southern Song dynasty (1127–1279), when it was called Lin'an, Hangzhou served as the seat of government and an important center of Chinese civilization. This imperial tradition means that Hangzhou retains many ancient pagodas, temples, and other historic sites, as well as the world-famous Xi Hu, or West Lake, which the Chinese consider an archetypal lake. Hangzhou, which is now the capital of Zhejiang Province, is the 11th largest city in China.

To the northwest of Hangzhou, Moganshan is an isolated area of hills and mountains celebrated for its bamboo groves, cool climate, fresh air, and natural beauty. It has long been a favored weekend retreat of

wealthier Shanghainese—not to mention Western missionaries, local warlords, gangsters, and Kuomintang generals.

South of Hangzhou, Shaoxing is a small city on the south bank of the Qiantang River. Famous for its rice wine, it is also renowned as the birthplace and childhood home of the noted Chinese literary figure Lu Xun (see p. 145). The tomb of Emperor Da Yu, the founder and first ruler of the Xia dynasty (ca 2070–1600 B.C.), is still honored to the south of the city. Beyond Shaoxing, the port of Ningbo is the headquarters of the People's Liberation Army's Navy's East Sea Fleet, which is responsible for monitoring the Taiwan Straits. Primarily a military town, Ningbo is a vital communications center for travel south and east of Shanghai, home of the region's only major domestic airport, and

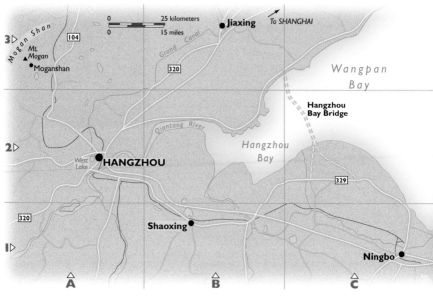

Pilgrims congregate at the main altar shrine in Puji Temple, Putuoshan.

the southern terminus of the amazing Hangzhou Bay Bridge, due to open in 2008.

Putuoshan was affected particularly badly during the Cultural Revolution, when zealous Red Guards desecrated temples and smashed Buddha images. The resident population of Buddhist monks dwindled to fewer than 30, from a pre-revolutionary high of about 2,000. Buddhism has made a comeback in China since the mid-1980s, and Putuoshan has reemerged as a popular pilgrimage center for Buddhists and other vacationers, who visit the island for its temples, beaches, caves, and tranquil hills. ■

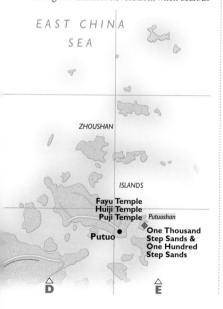

Economic powerhouse

China's awe-inspiring growth rate during the last two decades, 9.5 percent per annum, owes much to the area around Shanghai, encompassing the Yangtze River Delta. The delta covers a relatively small area of 38,650 square miles (100,100 sq km), yet it is home to 10.4 percent of the country's population. In 2002 it accounted for 22.1 percent of China's gross domestic product, 24.5 percent of its revenues, and a staggering 28.5 percent of the country's import and export volume. ■

Hangzhou

Hangzhou is often described as an excursion from Shanghai, and that is precisely how many people will visit the city. It's not a small place, however, having a population of about 6.5 million people and a considerable history of its own, as well as extensive parkland to the south and west of the city center.

The Venetian merchant Marco Polo visited Hangzhou in the late 13th century and described the city as "beyond dispute the finest and noblest in the world." He added, "The number and wealth of the merchants, and the amount of goods that pass through their hands, is so enormous that no man could form a just estimate thereof." In imperial times, much of the city's wealth was due to its position at the southern end of the Grand Canal, which runs for 1,115 miles (1,794 km)

to connect with the capital, Beijing, in the north. The city has suffered disasters, too, most notably being razed during the Taiping Rebellion in 1861 (see pp. 224–225). Cultural treasures also suffered gravely during the Cultural Revolution, and many of those that survive have been carefully restored over the past two decades.

The city is again wealthy, with an economy based on silk and textile production, electronics and other light industries, and green tea.

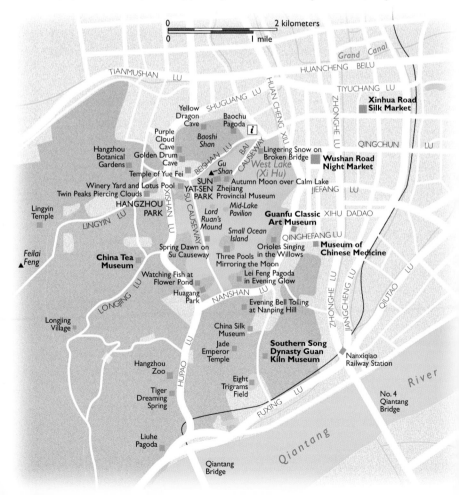

Wooded paths, bamboo groves, and small pagodas bedeck tranquil Tiger Dreaming Spring, a popular place to stroll.

Tourism is increasing every year, as Chinese travelers and overseas visitors flock to see Hangzhou's ancient temples and pagodas, along with Xi Hu, the lovely, willow-lined West Lake. Young lovers and newlyweds enjoy being photographed by the lake and drinking the famous Longjing tea in the teahouses lining its shores.

As a city, Hangzhou lacks great distinction, but just about every amenity found in Shanghai is available here, including fine restaurants and upscale hotels. Since Hangzhou is just about China's favorite tourist destination, though, they are not particularly cheap, and it's advisable to make reservations well in advance. ∎

Xi Hu (West Lake)

THERE ARE MANY BODIES OF WATER KNOWN AS WEST LAKE in China, but Hangzhou's Xi Hu is certainly the most celebrated. Traditionally, ten famous scenic spots around West Lake should be visited, each distinguished by a four-character epithet engraved on a stone stela in the hand of the Qing Emperor Qianlong (1711–1799).

Even if you don't try to track down each of these stelae, West Lake is lovely enough, and large enough, to merit the better part of a day's exploration. You can walk around the 2.6-square-mile (6.8 sq km) lake, wander across it via two ancient causeways, and also explore the waters by boat. At various points around the lakeshore, boat rentals are available.

At the lake's northeastern shore,

Peaceful scenes such as a pagoda in the mist explain West Lake's fame.

Bai Causeway (Bai Di) is named for the Tang dynasty poet Bai Juyi (see p. 167). The Broken Bridge (Duan Qiao) named in the Ten Scenes is at the eastern end of the causeway, but you will have to visit during a cold January or February to see it dusted with snow. The causeway leads to **Sun Yat-sen Park** (Zhongshan Gongyuan) on **Gu Shan**, West Lake's largest island. Visitors flock here to enjoy fine teahouses and also Louwailou Fandian, West Lake's famed restaurant, dating from 1848—local specialties include Hangzhou beggar's chicken, West Lake vinegar fish, and Dragon Well shrimp. Also on the island, **Zhejiang Provincial Museum** houses an estimated 100,000 items, but it is most famous for its unique collection of celadon; on the museum grounds stands the **Flourishing Literature Pavilion** (Wen Lan), a former imperial library dating from 1782. A stroll up **Gu Shan**, the Solitary Hill that gives the island its name, leads to the **Huayanjing Pagoda** (Huayanjing Ta). Dating from 1924, this eleven-story structure offers fine views across West Lake.

THREE ISLANDS

South of Gu Shan, accessible only by boat, are three smaller man-made islands. The **Mid-Lake Pavilion** (Huxinting) and **Lord Ruan's Mound** (Ruangongdun) are both wooded and tiny. Farther to the south lies the much larger **Small Oceans Island** (Xiaoying

Zhou, *8 a.m.–6 p.m.),* created from West Lake silt in 1607. The island is studded with pavilions and pagodas and has four small ponds within the island itself as well. Stand at the southern shore to see another of the Ten Scenes of West Lake: Three Pools Mirroring the Moon (Santan Yinyue)—three small pagoda-like towers set in the midst of the waters.

SU CAUSEWAY & MORE

Running approximately north–south and paralleling the western shore of West Lake, Su Causeway (Su Di) is named for the Song dynasty poet Su Dongpo (1036–1101). Lined with willow, peach, and plum trees, the causeway is a wonderful place to stroll or ride a bike. The causeway runs north from Nanshan Lu past Xiaoying Island to a point near the Temple of Yue Fei.

From the Nanshu Lu end of the causeway, it's a five-minute walk west to **Huagang Park** (Huagang Guangyu, *9 a.m.–4:30 p.m.),* where you can indulge in a third of West Lake's Ten Scenes: Watching Fish at Flower Pond. Huagang Guangyu, which literally translates as flower harbor view fish, is a former Song dynasty garden that is now home to red carp.

Turn east instead of west at the southern exit from Su Causeway and, in the lee of Xizhao Hill, rises one of West Lake's greatest attractions, the **Lei Feng Pagoda** (Lei Feng Ta, *8 a.m.–6 p.m., $*). Lei Feng, or thunder peak, is a fourth traditional West Lake sight: Lei Feng Pagoda in Evening Glow. However, the original five-story, brick-and-wood pagoda collapsed in 1924. A new Lei Feng Pagoda was recently built in the traditional style, but with a sturdy, state-of-the-art steel-and-glass structure. It offers fantastic views across West Lake and Hangzhou City. The brick base of the original pagoda has been carefully preserved in the new pagoda's futuristic basement. ■

The Ten Scenes of West Lake

- Spring Dawn on Su Causeway
- Orioles Singing in the Willows
- Watching Fish at Flower Pond
- Winery Yard and Lotus Pool
- Evening Bell Tolling at Nanping Hill
- Autumn Moon over Calm Lake
- Lei Feng Pagoda in Evening Glow
- Three Pools Mirroring the Moon
- Lingering Snow on Broken Bridge
- Twin Peaks Piercing Clouds ■

Visitors relax by West Lake near sunset. Locals go to the lake to read, play chess, gossip, or just look at the water.

West Lake
Map p. 170 A2

Zhejiang Provincial Museum
(Zhejiang Bowuguan)
No. 25 Gushan Lu
8797 1177
8:45 a.m.–4:30 p.m.
$

Baoshi Shan

**Yue Fei
Memorial Area**
Map p. 172

**Temple of Yue
Fei**
(Yue Wang Miao)
✉ 1 Hougushan Lu
☎ 8799 6663
🕐 7:30 a.m.–5:30
p.m.
💲 $

ALONG THE NORTH SHORE OF XI HU, OR WEST LAKE,
overlooking Beishan Lu, is Baoshi Shan, or Precious Stone Hill. This
rocky outcrop sandwiched between Hanzhou and the lake has a
number of important historic sites, the most important of which
are the Temple of Yue Fui and the Tomb of Yue Fei (Yue Fei Mu).
The view across West Lake from the top of Baoshi Shan is compelling,
especially in the early morning, when the rising sun illuminates the
islands, causeways, temples, and pagodas below.

Military patriot

Yue Fei (1103–1142) was a
Song dynasty military commander who fought bravely for
Emperor Gaozong (1127–1162)
against the Jurchen Manchu, who
had occupied the Song capital
of Kaifeng and captured Qinzong
(1126–27), then the Song emper-
or. As Yue Fei was about to take
back Kaifeng, the Song premier
Qin Hui advised Gaozong to
recall him, as a Jurchen defeat
might lead to Emperor Qinzong's
release. Since Gaozong valued
his throne more than the lost
Chinese territories, he and Qin
Hui had Yue Fei arrested. The
commander was executed in
1142. One year after Emperor
Gaozong died in 1162, Yue Fei
was officially exonerated and
reinterred with full honors
beside West Lake. ■

mountains—a message that echoes
powerfully to the present day. Eight
murals relate key episodes from
Yue Fei's life, and a walkway leads
through a formal Song-style garden
to the tombs of Yue Fei and his son.

Inside a low, caged enclosure, four
iron statues—representing Qin Hui,
his wife Lady Wang, and two other

Yue Fei is revered as a patriot
nationally and as a local hero in
Hangzhou. At the **Temple of
Yue Fei,** his memorial hall is
generally filled with fresh flowers
and coils of smoking incense. A
statue of the military hero in
green-and-yellow robes, clutching
the hilt of his sword, dominates
the main hall. The Chinese characters above the statue read *huan wo
he shan*—return my rivers and

Fans, tea, and revolutionary memorialia abound at Hangzhou's Wushan Road Night Market.

More places to visit in Hangzhou

CHINA TEA MUSEUM

The China Tea Museum (Zhongguo Chaye Bowuguan) is located beyond West Lake at Shuangfeng Village. Opened in 1991, it is surrounded by tea plantations (see sidebar p. 182). Six exhibition halls are dedicated to all aspects of tea culture, from cultivation to serving to drinking. On display are different varieties of tea, teapots and cups, ceremonial instruments for serving tea, and exhibits showing how different nationalities prepare and serve tea. Naturally enough, Hangzhou's famous Xi Hu Longjing Cha—West Lake Dragon Well Tea—is much in evidence and can be enjoyed in the teahouse at the museum or bought as prepared leaf.

✉ Shuangfeng Village, Longjing Lu ☎ 8796 4222 🕒 8:30 a.m.–4:30 p.m.

GUANFU CLASSIC ART MUSEUM

The Guanfu Classic Art Museum (Guanfu Gudian Yishu Bowuguan) to the east of West Lake is devoted to the history of Chinese furniture and features a wide range of beds, tables, chairs, wardrobes, portable vanities, and floor coverings.

✉ 131 Hefangjie Lu ☎ 8781 8181 🕒 8:30 a.m.–5 p.m. 💲 $

MUSEUM OF CHINESE MEDICINE

Just to the southeast of the Classic Art Museum, the Museum of Chinese Medicine (Huqingyutang Zhongyao Bowuguan) is one of China's two most celebrated traditional medicine stores (the other being Tongrentang in Beijing). Established in 1878 by the wealthy businessman and pharmacologist Hu Xueyan, it is located in the historic pedestrian area around Qinghefang Lu. Like the street itself, the museum has been recently and lovingly restored. Listed since 1988 as a national monument, it's set in a traditional courtyard house dating from the late Qing dynasty. The traditional dispensary is supported by carved wooden pillars and illuminated by red Chinese lanterns. Rows of wooden drawers contain a huge assortment of leaves, dried funguses, barks, roots, dried flowers, seeds, and dried or powdered animal parts. The various notices and explanations are given in Chinese and English throughout.

✉ 95 Dajing Xiang ☎ 8702 7507 🕒 8:30 a.m.–5 p.m. 💲 $

QINGHEFANG OLD STREET

On the east side of West Lake, in the heart of downtown Hangzhou, Qinghefang Lu—

sometimes styled Qinghefang Laojie, or Old Street, and sometimes Qinghefang Lishijie, or Historical Street—has been part of the commercial district of Hangzhou since Tang dynasty times (6th century). Its present

Longjing tea

Hangzhou's Longjing tea is one of the best known and most highly esteemed teas in China. The tea is grown in the Longjing Hills southwest of West Lake, on terraced plantations surrounding the ancient stone well that gives the area its name—*Longjing*, or Dragon Well. Tea has been produced here for more than a thousand years. The earliest reference to tea production in Longjing is in the Tang dynasty *Chajing*, which Chinese experts claim is the first book ever written about tea. Longjing first gained notice during the Southern Song dynasty (1127–1279) and became world-famous by Qing times (1644–1911). Longjing tea leaves, which are flat, smooth, and green, must be picked during a very short season that traditionally runs from April 5 to April 21 each year. Specialists and connoisseurs believe the best Longjing tea is yellowish-green in color when brewed, while medium-grade tea is green without any yellow tones, and the lowest grade tea is dark green. They recommend pouring water heated to 185°F (85°C)—well below boiling point—onto a pinch of tea in a porcelain or glass cup. Enthusiasts say that the aftertaste of the top-grade Longjing tea is a little sweeter than that of other green teas. ■

incarnation dates from the 18th and 19th centuries, during the Qing dynasty. The pedestrian-only shopping area was completely restored and refurbished in 2001, and many of the buildings are in fact re-creations of Ming and Qing dynasty styles.

SOUTHERN SONG DYNASTY GUAN KILN MUSEUM

Away from the town center, between Jade Emperor Mountain and the Qiantang River, the Southern Song Dynasty Guan Kiln Museum (Nan Song Guanyao Bowuguan) is built on the site of a Southern Song dynasty ceramics works. Under the Southern Song, Hangzhou was a center of porcelain production, particularly serving the imperial court. Its most celebrated product was Guan ware; the museum brochure states: "With its dignified and graceful shape, sparkling jade-like color, thin body and heavy glaze, Guan ware was recognized as the best among the five wares produced by the Southern Song." Visitors can see part of the preserved kiln, a traditional workshop, and ancient Guan ware.

✉ 42 Shijiashan Nanfu Lu ☎ 8608 2071 🕐 8:30 a.m.–4:30 p.m. Tues.–Sun.

WUSHAN ROAD NIGHT MARKET

The bustling night market called Wushan Lu Yeshi is located near West Lake's eastern shore in the commercial center of Hangzhou. It's a great place to shop for revolutionary memorabilia, souvenirs, ceramics, clothing, Longjing tea, fans, lanterns—but no longer quite as many pirated CDs or other goods, as the authorities are cracking down on this illicit business. Although much of the night market activity recently has moved to neighboring Jiefang Lu, Wushan Lu is a better choice for visitors seeking snacks.

✉ Wushan Lu

XINHUA ROAD SILK MARKET

Northeast of West Lake, Xinhua Road Silk Market (Sichou Shichang) is the best place in Hangzhou to shop for silk. Tailors will whip up a traditional *qipao* (Chinese dress) or a shirt, blouse, or jacket to your specifications in a short time and at a very reasonable price.

✉ Xinhua Lu ■

Moganshan

LOCATED NEAR THE SUMMIT OF 6,560-FOOT (2,000 M) Mount Mogan, 125 miles (200 km) southwest of Shanghai, the mountain resort of Moganshan flourished in the early 20th century. After suffering from neglect during the first four decades of communist rule, the compact hilltop, with all major sights within walking distance, is enjoying a renaissance.

Moganshan
Map p. 170 A3

Because of its close proximity to Hangzhou, Suzhou, and Shanghai, Moganshan, with its cool climate and quiet valleys, is an appealing weekend getaway for city dwellers. Visitors follow in the footsteps of early missionaries, foreign businessmen, and wealthy or powerful Chinese, including Green Gang leader "Big Ears Du" (see pp. 78–79) and Chiang Kai-shek and his wife, Song Meiling (see p. 108). The carefully restored **Moganshan Lodge** (Songliang Shanzhuang, *Yin Shan Jie, tel 0572 8033011, www/moganshanlodge.com*) uses a glowing description taken from the *North China Daily News* in 1936 to promote the location: "The skies of Italy, the verdure of Japan, the grandeur of the Rockies."

VISITING

Part of the pleasure of visiting Moganshan is the journey up the hills to reach the small isolated settlement. Some still approach the old-fashioned way—by sedan chair.

You'll find most of the places to stay and eat along **Yinshan Jie,** the main street (if you can call it that). From here, you can explore the whole town in an hour or two. The draw, however, is the slow pace, the panoramic views at every turn, the fresh mountain air. You must stroll through the ubiquitous bamboo groves—one of the resort's three wonders, along with springs and clouds. A small **Bamboo Museum** honors this plant—long the area's main crop—with exhibits

showing many varieties of bamboo and demonstrating their myriad uses. Bamboo is a remarkably versatile plant, still used, for example, on massive construction sites as natural scaffolding.

Beyond the museum at 126 Yinshan Jie stands a rather nondescript gray stone house, where Chairman Mao once stayed. In

Early 20th century artwork on display in Moganshan

Bamboo Museum
(Zhuzi Bowuguan)
Yinshan Jie
9:30 a.m.–3:30 p.m.
$

The pine-crested summits of Moganshan offer welcome relief from the heat of the nearby plains.

1953 he visited Moganshan to recover from an illness and left a note in the Moganshan Clinic guest book: "It takes patience to recuperate from an illness, and furthermore it requires the spirit to struggle."

Other historical houses on Yingshan Jie include **No. 546** and **No. 547,** both of which belonged to the notorious gangster Du Yuesheng; the latter is now an upscale guesthouse. Beyond Yinshan, on the far side of the mountain, is the former retreat of Chiang Kai-shek and Song Meiling, who honeymooned here in 1927 at a house called White Cloud Castle, now part of the Baiyun Hotel (see p. 253).

The Moganshan skyline is dominated by the former **Protestant Church** and the former **Assembly Hall,** whose crenellated tower recalls a medieval keep. Still active, in contrast to the church and hall, is the tiny **Huang Si,** or Yellow Temple.

Moganshan's natural attractions include **Jian Chi,** the Sword Pond, set in a lovely gully, and the adjacent **Sword Pond Falls.** According to legend, swordsmith Gan Jiang forged two magical swords that made their bearers undefeated in battle at this spot during the Spring and Autumn Period (722–481 B.C.). Gan Jiang's wife was called Mo Ye; Mount Mogan's name is said to be derived from hers.

Carefully maintained stone paths, many of them laid more than a century ago, wind around and across Moganshan, leading to such scenic spots as **Guai Shi Jiao,** or Strange Stone Corner. Below the famous overlook, the **Qing-caotang Tea Plantation** *(open by special arrangement with the estate manager, Mr. Pan)* offers tours. ∎

Shaoxing

A DELIGHTFUL WATER TOWN, SHAOXING SHOWCASES attractive canals, bridges, footpaths, and houses. It is built on the site of the capital of the Spring and Autumn Period Kingdom of Yue; the tomb of the contemporaneous ruler, Yu the Great, lies just beyond city limits. Shaoxing is also celebrated as the birthplace of writer Lu Xun (see p. 145) and for Shaoxing wine, which has been made here for 15 centuries. It's the perfect stopover, especially if you are en route between Hangzhou and Putuoshan on the main road or rail line.

The childhood **Home of Lu Xun** and the **Lu Xun Memorial Hall** (Lu Xun Jinianguan) both stand near the center of the old part of town, an area of narrow canals and arched bridges. Also worth visiting is the **Ancestral Home of Zhou Enlai.** Although Zhou never actually lived here (see pp. 122–123), Shaoxing is proud of the family association with Communist China's first premier and enduringly popular politician.

The legendary **Yu the Great** (Da Yu), considered the founding father of China's complex, immense water control system, is commemorated at an unlikely tomb 2.5 miles (4 km) southeast of town. Yu was the mythical founder and first ruler of the Xia dynasty (2070–1600 B.C.). The putative tomb is marked by a statue of Da Yu, surrounded by pavilions, memorial halls, and gardens.

Also of interest in Shaoxing are the hexagonal **Dashan Pagoda** (Dashan Ta) on Guanming Lu, and the **Yingtian Pagoda** (Yingtian Ta) in the southern part of town. Both have been restored frequently. Finally, the **Orchid Pavilion** (Lanting) is famous for its association with the fourth-century calligrapher Wang Xizhi. His most famous work, the *Lanting Xu,* or *Preface to the Orchid Pavilion,* was penned to commemorate a literary feast held at the pavilion in A.D. 353. It is one of the favorite destinations of local Chinese. ∎

Revolutionary heroine

Qiu Jin (1875–1907) was a Shaoxing native who sought the overthrow of the ruling Qing dynasty. Unhappily married, she advocated freedom of choice for women in marriage. Crippled with bound feet from childhood, she was virulently opposed to foot binding. Her left wing, nationalist views were strengthened during her studies in Japan. On returning to China, she joined an anti-Qing Triad society, and in 1905, she joined the revolutionary Tongmenghui led by Sun Yat-sen.

In 1907, after a failed rebellion called the Xu Gao Rising, Qiu Jin was captured by Qing forces and tortured. Instead of writing her accomplices' names on the paper proffered for her confession, Qiu Jin wrote: "The autumn winds and autumn rains agonize over the killing of the people." She then calmly walked to her public execution. Qiu Jin lies in a tomb by West Lake, and a museum at her former home in Shaoxing celebrates her achievements. ∎

Shaoxing
- Map p. 170 B1

Visitor information
- CITS, 341 Fushan Xilu
- ☎ 0575 515 5669

Home of Lu Xun
(Lu Xun Guju)
- 208 Lu Xun Zhonglu
- $

Ancestral Home of Zhou Enlai
(Zhou Enlai Zuju)
- 369 Laodong Lu
- $

Home of Qiu Jin
(Qiu Jin Guju)
- Hegang Tang

Putuoshan

Putuoshan

⚠ Map p. 171 E1

Visitor information

✉ CITS, 117 Meicen Lu

☎ 0580 609 1414

Note: Hangzhou Bay Bridge is scheduled to open in 2008, providing the first direct road link between Shanghai and Ningbo and promising much easier and faster access to Putuoshan. At 22.5 miles (36 km) long, it will also be the longest transoceanic bridge in the world, and the second longest bridge in the world (after Lake Pontchartrain Causeway in Louisiana).

FOR CENTURIES, BUDDHISTS HAVE BEEN MAKING PILGRIM-ages to Putuoshan—Mount Putuo—a sacred Buddhist mountain located on an island in the Zhoushan Archipelago of the same name. Like other such sites, its structures were badly damaged during the Cultural Revolution, but many have been carefully restored since. Among Putuoshan's many draws are Buddhist temples and unforgettable scenery.

GETTING THERE

For now, ferry is the only way to reach Putuoshan. It's a 15-minute boat ride from Zhoushan, and an hour ride from the Ningbo Ferry Wharf. You'll find an information booth at Putuoshan's wharf; from here, it's a short walk to the temple area. Sights are close enough to one another to explore on foot; otherwise, minibuses connect the attractions as well.

THE TEMPLES

Though the numerous temples on Putuoshan are all under the auspices of the Chinese Buddhist Association, the most important three are Puji, Fayu, and Huiji.

Puji Temple (Puji Si, *6 a.m.–9 p.m., $*) was established in 1080, but it has been rebuilt several times and the present buildings date from the late Qing era. It's a lovely complex of pavilions, pagodas, and lotus ponds shaded by large rain trees. The main hall houses a golden seated Buddha flanked by Taoist immortals, and a second hall houses the fat, laughing Buddha that brings prosperity. Standing near the back of the temple, and especially venerated, is a golden statue of Guanyin. Puji, which is near the geographical center of the island, is surrounded by shops, restaurants, and teahouses.

Fayu Temple (Fayu Si, *6:30 a.m.–6 p.m., $*) stands to the north of Puji on the densely wooded slopes of Foding Mountain (Foding

Shan). Dating from the Ming dynasty (1368–1644), the large temple extends through six levels back up the mountain. The most important building is the Dayuan Hall (Dayuan Tang), which once stood in Nanjing but was moved to Putuoshan on the orders of the Qing Emperor Kangxi (1654–1722). It houses another famous

Guanyin image that serves as the center of the goddess of mercy birthday celebrations held here on the 29th day of the second lunar month, which generally falls in March or April. Nine exquisitely carved, intertwining wooden dragons decorate the hall's dome.

Huiji Temple (Huiji Si, *6:30 a.m.–7 p.m., $*) lies still farther to the north, near the summit of Foding Shan. Dating from the Ming era, the temple feels pleasantly venerable and offers panoramic views across the island. In times past, getting to the temple required quite a climb, but a cable car now whisks visitors to the summit. The pious may still prefer to walk the beautiful wooded path up the mountain, however,

prostrating themselves every three steps. The walk takes about an hour (without prostrations).

MORE SIGHTS TO SEE

Far from Huiji, at the southern tip of the island, the **South Seas Guanyin** (Nanhai Guanyin) is a 108-foot-tall (33 m) gilded statue of the goddess of mercy. Her right hand is raised in blessing and her left hand holds what is probably intended to be a *darmachakra*, or Buddhist wheel of law, but which looks very much like a ship's helm—no doubt a visual reassurance to local seafarers. The image-packed hall in which the statue stands is decorated with wooden murals depicting the Guanyin rescuing shipwrecked seafarers.

Among Putuoshan's many Buddhist pilgrimage sights is Huiji Temple, on the top of Mount Putuo.

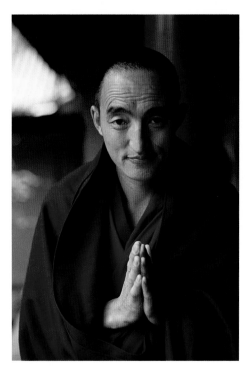

A reverent Buddhist monk in residence at Huiji Temple, Putuoshan

Enter to see the island's largest Reclining Buddha and a wealth of other Buddha images, as well as gray-clad Chinese nuns with shaved heads. Near Puji, the three-story **Duobao Pagoda** (Duobao Ta, or Many Treasures Pagoda), built in 1334, dates from the Yuan dynasty.

BEACHES & BEYOND

Although Putuoshan is a small island, just 3.5 miles (5.5 km) long and 2 miles (3 km) wide, it has two attractive beaches: **One Thousand Step Sands** (Qianbusha) and **One Hundred Step Sands** (Baibusha).

South of Baibusha, on a small promontory, the **Hall of the Unwilling to Depart Guanyin** (Bukenqu Guanyinyuan) marks the spot where, according to legend, the Japanese monk Hui'e was shipwrecked. Nearby is the **Sound of Tides Cave** (Chaoyindong), where the waves thunder into the hollowed-out cliff. Visions of the Guanyin have appeared at this spot to the pious over the centuries.

Other caves to explore include **Buddhist Tidings Cave** (Fanyindong), with a small Guanyin temple, and **Morning Sun Cave** (Zhaoyangdong), located between the two stretches of beach. ∎

She is clearly the patron saint of the island, though there seems to have been some crossover locally with the Taoist immortal Matsu, the goddess of the sea, who also protects fishermen.

Other points of religious interest are **Dasheng Nunnery** (Dasheng An, *8 a.m.– 5:30 p.m.*).

The legend of Putuoshan

In Mahayana Buddhism, Putuoshan is considered the *bohimanda,* or place of enlightenment, of the Bodhisattva Avalokitesvara, better known in the Far East through the female manifestation Guanyin—the beloved goddess of mercy. The mountain's name, Putuoshan, is a Sinified version of Potalaka, the mountain home of Avalokitesvara in the Avatamsaka Sutra.

According to legend, the Bodhisattva Guanyin was enshrined on Putuoshan in A.D. 916 when a Japanese monk called Hui'e, carrying an image of Guanyin, was shipwrecked on the island. The goddess appeared to him in a vision and promised to ensure his safe return home if he installed her image on the island. The monk did so, and Putuoshan became a famous place of pilgrimage. ∎

West of Shanghai lie Lake Tai, its water towns, and the ancient city of Suzhou. Bustling Nanjing, a burgeoning modern city, merits at least a weekend for all its historic charms.

Excursions west & north of Shanghai

Detail of Ming dynasty domestic scene in Chen Residence, Zhouzhuang

Sun Yat-sen's Mausoleum in Nanjing honors the founder of modern China.

Excursions west & north of Shanghai

THE REGION WEST AND NORTHWEST OF SHANGHAI AROUND TAI HU (LAKE Tai, or Grand Lake) includes some of China's loveliest countryside. Here you'll discover the region's traditional water towns. The classical gardens and fine silks of the medieval city of Suzhou have been celebrated for centuries. Nanjing, China's capital under both the Ming and the Nationalists, is replete with memories both glorious and terrible. And through the whole area snake two of the world's most historic waterways, the mighty Yangtze River and the 1,500-year-old Grand Canal.

Long lauded for its beauty, Lake Tai, located in the southern Yangzte River Delta, is the third largest freshwater lake in China (its surface area measures 870 square miles/2,250 sq km). Dotted with 48 islets, it's plentiful with fish, including the "Lake Tai three whites": white shrimp, whitebait, and whitefish, typically prepared aboard popular boat cruises.

The fertile flatlands around Lake Tai are famed for a number of canalside or riverside communities that date back to imperial times, commonly referred to as water towns. These peaceful, scenic villages, with picturesque bridges arching across willow-lined canals, make wonderful day trips from

Shanghai, though it is also possible to stay overnight in some of them—a good idea, since that's when the crowds have left and the tranquil spirit of the towns emerge.

Near Lake Tai's shores, Suzhou—together with Hangzhou (see pp. 172–173)—has long retained a special place in Chinese affections. An old saying attests: "In heaven there is paradise, on earth there are Suzhou and Hangzhou." While Suzhou's outskirts are heavily industrialized, the core of the ancient city, surrounded by moats, retains the most exquisite collection of classical gardens in China, as well as numerous ancient temples and pagodas. The city is also legendary for the beauty of its women, and another hoary Chinese adage advises: "Marry in Suzhou, live in Hangzhou, eat in Guangzhou." (Today, however, the restaurants of Suzhou also offer some exceptionally fine dining.)

Some distance north and west of Suzhou, but readily accessible by fast train or the new Shanghai-Nanjing Expressway, the Ming capital of Nanjing is too far from Shanghai for a day trip. The city does make a fine weekend excursion, though, and it is worthy of at least a week's visit. Packed with historic sites, from the world's longest city wall to the Ming Tombs, it is also home to the magnificent Mausoleum of Sun Yat-sen, the founder of modern China. More recent historic sites include a sobering memorial to the Nanjing Massacre of 1937–38, better known internationally as the Rape of Nanjing, and the Yangtze Great Bridge, redolent of the socialist achievements of China's Maoist heyday. ■

Suzhou's Master of the Nets Garden was established in 1770 by a retired court official who wanted to be a fisherman.

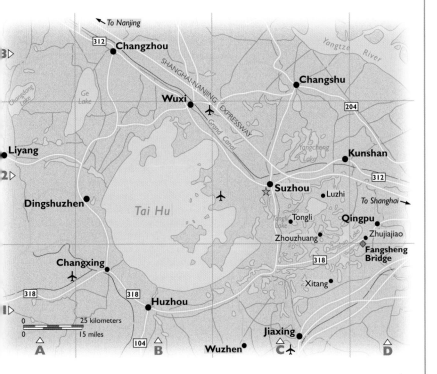

A line of moored boats waits for passengers along one of Wuzhen's waterways.

Water towns

West of Shanghai, an arc of small towns and villages known in Chinese as *shui xiang,* or water towns, extends from Wuzhen in the south to Changzhou on the Grand Canal in the north. Acclaimed for their arched bridges, ancient buildings, and serene waterways, these are living towns, where daily life goes on: Coppersmiths and silk spinners work at their age-old crafts, people carry water, tend gardens, and congregate at the squares to chat.

The water towns make an easy day trip from Shanghai (Suzhou makes a good alternative base). The easiest and cheapest way is to take a tour (inquire at your hotel). Alternatively, you can take a bus or taxi from Shanghai (or Hangzhou or Suzhou). Few people choose to visit more than two or three water towns total, sticking to one a day.

Keep in mind that the towns can be crowded during the day, and for this reason an overnight is preferable. In the evenings and early mornings, after the visitors have left, the waterways become calm, mirroring the ancient houses in a scene straight out of old China. With the place to yourself, rent a boat and explore the narrow back canals and surrounding countryside—you will be awestruck by the classic beauty.

One of the most famous, and most popular, is vehicle-free, compact Zhouzhuang in Jiangsu Province, 60 miles (96 km) west of

Shanghai. Given its popularity (it's been called a Chinese Disneyland), it's an excellent candidate for an overnight stay.

Some of the less-visited water towns (though they can still get crowded) include the traditional towns of Wuzhen, 65 miles (100 km) from Shanghai, and Xitang, 55 miles (90 km) southwest of Shanghai; both are in Zhejiang Province. In Jiangsu Province, there are ancient Tongli, 50 miles (80 km) west of Shanghai, and literary Luzhi, 47 miles (75 km) northwest of Shanghai.

Also in Jiangsu Province are tourist favorite Zhujiajiao, which is less than an hour from Shanghai's Hongqiao Airport, and the more distant, less-visited Changzhou. The latter is a much larger town with additional attractions, including the world's tallest pagoda.

In the following pages, you'll find more detailed descriptions of the main water towns. ■

Wuzhen

SANDWICHED BETWEEN SHANGHAI AND HUZHOU, WUZHEN is one of the region's most authentic water towns. Ancient timber buildings, dating from Qing times (1644–1911) and even earlier, edge cobbled lanes along picturesque waterways.

The long, narrow town edges the canal for 1.25 miles (2 km), passing through six different areas: Traditional Workshop District, the Traditional Housing District, the Traditional Culture District, the Traditional Food and Drink District, the Traditional Shopping District (where the locals will be particularly happy to see you), and the Traditional Life and Customs District. The best plan of attack is to make an east–west circuit beginning at Feng Yuang.

Walk west along Dong Dajie on the canal's north side. **Feng Yuang Qiao** (Feng Yuang Bridge, aka the Bridge in Bridge) is a recently restored double bridge, one of which, **Tongji Qiao,** crosses the water from east to west, while the

other, **Renji Qiao,** runs from north to south.

A short distance west, in the Traditional Workshop District, artisans practice traditional handicrafts in a row of shops: painting silk, hand-sewing cloth shoes, weaving rattan baskets, making indigo-dyed printed calico cloth, spinning fiber into yarn, and carving wood. Many of these workshops will allow you to try your hand at the craft of your choice.

The workshop district's narrow, cobblestone street continues between rows of predominantly brown, two-story buildings housing restaurants, pubs, pawnshops, homes, and souvenir shops. At the **Rice Wine Distillery** on the street's north side, you can sample

Wuzhen

◭ Map p. 191 C1

Visitor information

www.wuzhen.com.cn/oldweb/wuzhen.eng

✉ Tongxiang Wuzhen Tourism, 18 Shifo Nanlu Wuzhen Tongxiang

$ $$, single entry ticket for all attractions

Wuzhen's residents convene along a canal around midday to chat, smoke, and play mah-jongg.

and purchase this traditional local product, called *sanbai*, or three-times white. Just to the north, the small **Cotton Mill** manufactures the indigo-dyed cloth that is then fashioned into curtains, tablecloths, wall hangings, and clothing.

FARTHER WEST

Farther along, the narrow, arched bridges become more frequent. Just before the intersection with Heng Jie (Heng Street), a gabled building houses a collection of locally produced wooden carvings called the **Exhibition of Wooden Sculpture.** Beyond Ren Shou Qiao and again on the north side of the street is the **Yu Liu Liang Coin Exhibition,** which features an extensive collection of ancient Chinese coinage.

Right next door stands the **Former Residence of Mao Dun** (Mao Dun Guju), a traditional building dating from the late Qing era that was the family home of Shen Dehong (1896–1981), a Chinese

Detail of a carving at the Exhibition of Wooden Sculpture. The Chinese characters on the gable read, "The Whole Family Blessed."

revolutionary writer who used the pen name Mao Dun (which means contradiction). A founding member of the Chinese Communist Party and a member of Lu Xun's League of Left Wing Writers (see p. 143), he had a long career as a distinguished journalist and published more than a hundred short stories and novels, including *Ziye*, or *Midnight*. The house has three exhibition rooms featuring Wuzhen, the hometown of Mao Dun; the way of Mao Dun; and the renovation of the former

residence of Mao Dun. There is also a small **Mao Dun Museum** (Mao Dun Bowuguan) in the former Li Zhi Academy of Classical Learning, where the writer studied as a child.

Just beyond Mao Dun's former home on Chang Xin Jie is the **Han Lin Residence,** another traditional house that is open to the public. A left turn here leads to **Ying Jia Qiao** and the **Fang Lu Pavilion,** Wuzhen's most famous teahouse. It is named for Lu Yu, patron saint of tea during the Tang dynasty (618–907). According to legend, Lu Tong, the teahouse's owner, was taught the art of tea making by Lu Yu, author of *Chajing (The Classic of Tea)*. Lu Tong's resulting expertise led to the success of his teahouse and that success continues to this day. Certainly it's a fine place to sit and watch the succession of small boats moving along the river and the stream of pedestrians crossing the Ying Jia Qiao.

South of the bridge lies Chang-feng Jie, another busy traditional thoroughfare that is home to the **Hui Yuan Pawnshop and Pawn Museum.** In the past, the pawnshop was an essential feature of everyday life, providing government-regulated credit to borrowers at a fixed, relatively low rate for up to three years. The scales, abacus, and other tools of the pawnbroker's trade are preserved and displayed here.

MORE SIGHTS TO SEE
Among Wuzhen's additional attractions are the seven-story **White Lotus Tower,** the **Footbinding Museum,** the **Hundred Beds Museum,** and the **Temple of General Wu,** commemorating a Tang dynasty general believed to be the town's namesake. ∎

Former Residence of Mao Dun
- ✉ 13 Yuanensi
- ☎ 6225 2042
- 💲 $

Xitang

Xitang

🅰 Map p. 191 C1

Visitor information

www.xitang.com.cn/eyou.asp

✉ Xitang Town Tourism, JiJia Xiang Youdian Lu

💲 $$, single entry ticket for all attractions

A VISITING UNESCO WORLD HERITAGE OFFICIAL ONCE commented, "Xitang is like the melodious and limpid music of a flute; people need to appreciate it with their hearts." Until 2005, this lovely village near the eastern shore of Lake Tai was, perhaps, the quietest and most laid-back of the water towns. But all that changed after it appeared in *Mission Impossible III* (supposedly depicting old Shanghai); after the movie's release in China, domestic tourism increased dramatically.

Xitang dates back to the Warring States Period in the fourth and third centuries B.C., when it was strategically situated on the borders of Wu and Yue States, earning it the name "Corner of Yue, Base of Wu." It developed into a prosperous town during the Ming and Qing dynasties and now consists largely of restored Qing dynasty housing. Ancient names for the town translate as "nine dragon old pearl" and "wind from eight sides."

Xitang is the quintessential water town. It lies on flat land latticed by nine small rivers that divide the town into eight sections connected by 104 bridges, most of them arched and all of them dating from Ming and especially Qing dynasty times.

As in the other water towns, the inhabitants of Xitang go about their business—now overwhelmingly tourism-related—along narrow lanes with flagstones polished by centuries of footsteps. The local authorities claim that there are 122 lanes and roads in the township, with the narrowest being a mere 30 inches (80 cm) wide. Due to Xitang's unusually rainy climate, many of these lanes are traditional covered walkways strung with the ubiquitous red lanterns. Each family was responsible for roofing over the part of the lane immediately contiguous to their property. These roofs were joined together to make covered corridors. The mainly two-story houses along the lanes are painted gray or white and roofed in black tiles with characteristic curved gables.

VISITING XITANG

Certainly the best way to see Xitang is to wander the narrow covered lanes, crossing from one section of town to another by one of the lovely arched bridges. From the apex of any of these, you can watch small boats carry vegetables or visitors on the tranquil waters. More red lanterns are hung over the rivers from the eaves of the houses; these look particularly lovely at night when they are illuminated across the whole town.

Be sure to seek out the longest **covered corridor,** running 1,421 yards (1,300m) along the riverside. Tile-roofed and decorated in places with elegant carvings, it provides a gorgeous, sheltered promenade with uninterrupted views of water-town life. High-backed benches at strategic points allow you to sit and reflect.

The Song dynasty's (960–1279) **Wangxian Qiao** is Xitang's oldest and most notable bridge. According to legend, a Taoist sage used to stand on the bridge watching for immortal spirits *(wang xian* means looking for spirits).

Also keep an eye out for **Xiyuan Garden,** traditionally

laid out to integrate the flowers and willow trees with the water and bridges; the unusual **Pearl Button Museum,** where you can watch pearl buttons being handcrafted; the nearby **Fan Museum,** where handheld painted fans are produced, displayed, and sold; and the **Xue Residence,** a carefully restored traditional house that belonged to a wealthy merchant during the Qing dynasty.

Xitang's eateries serve local specialties, including pork steamed with rice flour and lotus leaves, glutinous rice dumplings, and freshwater crabs from Lake Tai, all best enjoyed with Jiashan yellow rice wine. ∎

Xitang harbors 104 bridges arched across scenic waterways.

Zhouzhuang

Zhouzhuang
⬛ Map p. 191 C2
Visitor information
www.zhouzhuang.com
☎ 86215 5721 7303
💲 $$$, single entry ticket for all attractions

OF ALL THE WATER TOWNS, BEAUTIFUL ZHOUZHUANG, located near Lake Tai's eastern shore, is the most developed and best known. It's also the busiest, so avoid visiting on weekends and holidays, when the ancient narrow streets are jam-packed. Surrounded by lakes on four sides and laced with canals and waterways, it's no wonder Zhouzhuang calls itself the Venice of China—some of the boatmen even sing as they carry you on gondola-reminiscent rides.

Many of Zhouzhuang's charming restaurants evoke the past with traditional music and decor.

from the water. Or wander the narrow traditional stone-block paved lanes. As you roam, you might encounter some of the hundred historically preserved houses or 30 gate towers with carved brick ornamentation. Red lanterns illuminate the canals in the evening, providing a soft, romantic glow.

Zhouzhuang is generally entered from the north on foot—a short stroll from the bus station and parking lot past many small shops selling souvenirs and snacks. Watch for the delicious roasted pig's feet called *wansanti,* which are a local specialty.

In the northwestern part of town awaits **Quanfo Temple** (Quanfo Si), the town patron's Buddhist temple. Its pagoda, Quanfo Ta, boasts extravagantly upturned eaves, somewhat reminiscent of *chofa* in Thai temple architecture. Beyond, you'll pass **Zhouzhuang Museum** (Zhouzhuang Bowuguan) and cross a narrow humpbacked bridge to the town's second temple, **Chengxu Daoyuan,** which—as the name suggests—is dedicated to Taoism; it dates from the Song dynasty.

A short distance to the east, spanning the river and canals at the center of town, are the famous **Shuang Qiao,** or Twin Bridges. Dating from the reign of Ming dynasty emperor Wanli, this composite structure has become

Like Xitang, Zhouzhuang dates back to the Warring States Period (4th and 3rd centuries B.C.) and perhaps even earlier. During the Northern Song dynasty, in 1086, a devout Buddhist named Zhou Digong donated the settlement, originally called Zhenfengli, to the estate of Quanfo Temple, which still survives. The name was changed in his honor to Zhouzhuang or Zhou Village. Little remains from that ancient time; the majority of buildings you see today date from the Ming and Qing eras.

VISITING ZHOUZHUANG

The town's main axis is a small river running north–south, while the canals extend east–west on either side. You can hire a boat (*$$*) to see the back alleyways and bridges

iconic for Zhouzhuang. Shide Qiao arches across the Nabei River from east to west and has a rounded arch, while Yongan Qiao crosses Yinzi Creek and has a square arch. Together the two bridges look like an antique key, hence their nickname, Key Bridge. In 1984 the American oil millionaire Armand Hammer bought a painting of the bridge by famous artist Chen Yifei, which he subsequently presented to China's then paramount leader Deng Xiaoping (1904–1997). The same painting was chosen for a United Nations postage stamp in 1985; Zhouzhuang's fame was made, and the town has never looked back.

BRIDGES & MORE
Of a dozen other venerable stone bridges in town, the most notable are the single-arch **Fuan Qiao** (late Yuan dynasty, 1365), at the eastern end of Zhongshi Jie, and **Zhenfeng Qiao** (Ming dynasty) on Xiwan Jie. Both lie in the western part of Zhouzhuang.

In the far south of town, **Nanhu Gardens** (Nanhu Yuan) consist of a series of lovely pagodas sitting on tiny islets directly contiguous with **South Lake** (Nanhu). East of town, across the Nabei River, are the **Shan Residence** (Qing dynasty, 1742), a wealthy merchant's house with seven courtyards and more than a hundred rooms divided into three sections that are connected with aisles and arcades, and the **Zhen Residence** (Ming dynasty, 1449), which has six courtyards and more than 70 rooms. Both residences are well worth visiting for the extensive antique collections on display, in addition to their beautiful gardens and pagodas.

Historic attractions aside, Zhouzhuang is filled with cafés, restaurants, and pubs. Along the narrow streets, numerous galleries purvey contemporary Chinese art and copies of traditional paintings. ■

Colorful Buddha figures in Zhouzhang's Quanfo Temple

Tongli

Ancient whitewashed buildings and flagstone streets edge Tongli's main canal, giving credance to the town's naming by the *China Daily* in 2006 as one of the "Top Ten Charming Chinese Towns."

ONE OF THE LARGER WATER TOWNS, TONGLI SITS ON A complex of canals and rivers on the western shore of Tongli Hu (Tongli Lake). The lovely town is neither as famous as Zhouzhuang nor as crowded with visitors, though its pace has picked up since the mid-1980s, when Chinese filmmakers discovered the city. More than a hundred films and television shows have been made here since, including a tremendously popular version of the Qing dynasty classic *Hong Lou Meng, The Dream of the Red Chamber.*

In typical water-town fashion, Tongli is built on flat land, surrounded by five lakes and divided into seven separate districts—effectively small islands—by 15 rivers and canals that flow through the area. These waterways are crossed by at least 49 ancient bridges, most of them arched.

While both Zhouzhuang and Wuzhen are famed for their double bridges, Tongli seeks to outshine them with a triple bridge. In the center of town, **Taiping Qiao** (Great Peace Bridge), **Jili Qiao** (Lucky Bridge), and **Chanqing Qiao** (Long Celebration Bridge), stand in such close proximity that they form an almost continuous

Most face onto narrow lanes or directly onto the canals, which are reached by a short flight of steps from each house, permitting residents access to small rowboats. Most houses are whitewashed, with elegantly carved windows, upturned eaves, and black tiled roofs. Some have fine gardens concealed behind walls.

The most celebrated of these, and the old town's main attraction, is **Tuisi Yuan** (Retreat and Meditation Garden, aka Garden Close to the Water), constructed in 1886 by an official named Ren Lansheng. It's a fairly substantial garden, covering 1.65 acres (6,600 sq m), with residential buildings in the west and a lush area of trees, ponds, pavilions, and terraces in the east. Red carp swim through waters crisscrossed by winding causeways.

Among the finest residences in town are **Gengle Hall** (Gengle Tang), built by the Ming dynasty aristocrat Zhu Xiang and featuring more than 40 rooms around three large courtyards; **Chongben Hall** (Chongben Tang), built by Qian Youq in 1912 and sprawling around four courtyards filled with stone sculptures and finely carved wooden panels; and **Jiayin Hall** (Jiayin Tang) dating from 1922 and once the property of the scholar Liu Yazi.

Tongli's most unexpected attraction must be the **Museum of Chinese Sex Culture in Ancient Times** (Zhongguo Gudai Xing Wenhua Bowuguan, *Wujiang Jie, 6332 2973, 8 a.m.– 5:30 p.m., $*). Professor Liu Dalin has amassed almost 4,000 artifacts relating to the history of erotica and sexual relations in China. These include sex toys, instructive figurines once given to brides, chastity belts, and furniture designed to enhance sexual intercourse. ■

Tongli

🅰 Map p. 191 C2

Visitor information

☎ Tongli Tourist Information Center, 0512 6349 3027

💲 $$$, single entry ticket for all attractions

link around and across three ancient waterways. Known together as **San Qiao,** the triple bridges have long been revered by Tongli's citizens, who walk across them for good fortune on auspicious occasions, such as weddings and birthdays.

Other significant bridges include **Siben Qiao,** or Reflecting Origin Bridge, the town's oldest, dating from the Song dynasty (960–1279), and **Dubu Qiao,** or Single Step Bridge, the town's smallest—just 5 feet (1.5 m) long and about 3 feet (0.9 m) wide.

ANCIENT ARCHITECTURE

Tongli is also a town of ancient Chinese architecture—an estimated 40 percent of the buildings date back to the Ming and Qing periods.

Grand Canal

China's Grand Canal (Da Yunhe) is the oldest and longest man-made waterway in the world. Dating from the fifth century B.C., the canal links Beijing with the East China Sea at Hangzhou, winding a north–south path through the provinces of Hebei, Shandong, Jiangsu, and Zhejiang. It also crosses six major rivers: the Hai, Wei, Huang, Huai, Yangtze, and finally, the Qiantang (see p. 180).

The founding of the Grand Canal is generally attributed to Fu Chai, Duke of Wu—present-day Suzhou—who ordered the construction of a canal to transport soldiers in an attack on the neighboring state of Qi in 486 B.C., during the Warring States Period. This initial canal was extended and improved under the Sui dynasty (A.D. 581–618), attaining approximately its current form around 610. After Beijing became the capital of the Yuan dynasty in 1279, a

westward extension to Luoyang was abandoned. In the late 1200s, a new section was cut through hilly terrain in Shandong, considerably shortening the route between Hangzhou and Beijing. This addition effectively established the canal as it is today, with an overall length of 1,115 miles (1,794 km).

In 1855 the Huang He, or Yellow River, suffered particularly severe flooding and changed course. The Shandong section of the Grand Canal was severed and fell into a decline exacerbated by improvements in oceanic shipping routes and the subsequent

introduction of railways. Reconstruction did not take place in any meaningful way until after the establishment of the communist People's Republic in 1949. Even today, only the section between Hangzhou and Jining in Shandong Province is navigable.

The main purpose of the Grand Canal in imperial times was to transport grain from southern and central China to Beijing. At its peak, records show that as many as 8,000 river boats transported between 250,000 and 360,000 tons (226.8–326.6 kt) of grain annually to the capital. The canal was also used to transport other commodities, including luxury goods for use by the imperial court. Not surprisingly, the towns along its banks prospered.

The Grand Canal also served as an important cultural link between northern and southern China, helping to unify the state and to establish a sense of common cultural identity. Qing emperors, notably Kangxi (1661–1722) and Qianlong (1735–1796), used its waters to make inspection tours of the south. It was also traveled by early European visitors, including Marco Polo (13th century) and Matteo Ricci (16th century; see p. 121). Some skeptics have raised doubts that Polo ever visited China, but his accounts of Hangzhou (see p. 172) as well as of Suzhou (see p. 208) seem very authentic to most readers, as does his description of the Grand Canal's arched bridges, prosperous trade, and great warehouses.

Today the navigable sections of the Grand Canal handle cargo that neither Marco Polo nor the Emperors Kangxi and Qianlong could possibly have imagined. Vast quantities of heavy goods—sand, gravel, coal, bricks, fuel oil—traverse its waters. The Jianbi locks at the junction with the Yangtze handle 75 million tons (68,040 kt) of cargo each year, and the Li Section in Jiangsu Province is projected to reach a staggering 100 million tons (90,720 kt) of cargo handled per year in the near future. The Grand Canal's founder, Fu Chai, would doubtless have been amazed and, one hopes, more than a little proud. ■

The busy, diverse traffic on the Grand Canal reflects China's rapid industrialization and growing need for transportation.

Narrow waterways and traditional arched bridges add to Luzhi's appeal.

Luzhi

ONE OF THE LESSER KNOWN WATER TOWNS, AND ONE OF the smallest, picturesque Luzhi, east of Suzhou, is at least 1,400 years old. Despite its tiny size (about one square mile), the town has a distinguished literary tradition, having once been home to the 9th-century Tang dynasty poets Lu Guimeng and Pi Rixiu, the Ming dynasty poet Gao Qi (1336–1374), and the novelist and educator Ye Shengtao (1894–1988).

Luzhi
Map p. 191 C2
Visitor information
$$, single entry ticket for all attractions

Literature aside, Luzhi is noted for its beautiful tranquil canals, as well as the distinctive traditional costume worn by its women—embroidered cloth shoes, black cotton trousers, a pale blue cotton blouse, and a black turban elaborately decorated with red pom-poms and flowers.

Luzhi's attractions include 41 ancient humpbacked bridges dating from the Song, Yuan, Ming, and Qing dynasties. Proud locals, who claim that each bridge has a different design, call their town "a museum of ancient Chinese bridges." The best known bridge is the **Zhengyang Qiao,** dating from the reign of the Ming dynasty Emperor Wanli (1572–1620). The

largest stone arched bridge in town, it is said to receive the first rays of the morning sun. The **Dongmei Qiao** is celebrated both for its unusual structure—said to be a complete circle, with half above the water and half below—and for the Buddhist designs carved on it. The best way to see the bridges, with their detailed carvings of flowers, bats, frogs, dragonflies, and lotus roots, is by boat.

Established in A.D. 503, **Baosheng Temple** (Baosheng Si) is Luzhi's most important historic site. During the Song dynasty, it is said to have had 5,000 halls and 1,000 monks. Inside its venerable cloisters are nine clay *luohan* (arhat) figures—considered

Among Suzhou's famous gardens, Blue Wave Pavilion is the oldest, dating back to the Northern Song dynasty (906–1127).

HISTORY

Ancient Suzhou's history begins at least as early as 514 B.C., when, during the Spring and Autumn Period (722–481), King Helu of Wu established it as his capital, Great City of Helu. It was renamed Suzhou in A.D. 589, under the Sui dynasty, and became wealthy after the Grand Canal's completion around 610. The city continued to prosper under the Tang and Song. The famous Confucius Temple was founded in 1035.

In 1367 the royal city at the center of the walled city was destroyed during the establishment of the Ming dynasty. Despite this setback, Suzhou reached the height of its prosperity under the Ming and Qing dynasties, a period when most of the famous gardens were built, generally by imperial officials. In 1860, Suzhou was sacked by the Taiping rebels (see pp. 224–225). In 1863, however, it was recaptured for the Qing by the Ever Victorious Army of British general Charles "Chinese" Gordon. When the city was captured by the Japanese in 1937, many of the classical gardens were damaged or destroyed. After the communist victory in 1949, the old city walls, which followed the moat's path, were torn down. Grubby industrial suburbs were built around the city. Suzhou's difficulties did not end until reformist Deng Xiaoping took power in 1981.

Today, Suzhou is one of the richest cities in China, with satellite cities like Kunshan,

are described, including its gorgeous gardens, a pleasant bike ride, museums, pagodas, and more.

One intriguing sight is the **Confucius Temple** (Wen Miao, *Renmin Lu, 8:30–11 a.m., 12:30–4:30 p.m.*), one of the city's oldest temples. Founded in 1035 by the mandarin and poet Fan Zhongyan (989–1052), this temple was long the venue for imperial examinations. It is filled with stelae recording the names of past doctoral graduates. Though still revered by some, nowadays it is fairly quiet.

Confucianism, which some view as

Ceramic and copperware artifacts can be found at the **Confucius Temple Antique Market.**

Taicang, and Zhangjiagang producing vast quantities of such high-tech goods as computers and digital cameras, whose value far exceeds the income produced by tourism and silk.

VISITING SUZHOU'S SIGHTS

Throughout Suzhou's long and varied history, the core of the ancient walled city survived remarkably well. Despite the loss of the former royal city and, more recently, the ancient city walls, much remains for the visitor to see. Most sites of interest lie within the moats in the protected historic heart of town, ringed by canals and waterways crisscrossed by about 200 arched stone bridges.

In the following pages, Suzhou's best sights

symbolic of a class-stratified society, does not yet seem to have made the same comeback in the affections of the Chinese people as have Buddhism and Taoism. More visitors are attracted by the **Confucius Temple Antique Market** on the temple's grounds than by their adherence to the teachings of "Master Kong." A fine stone statue of the master stands in the courtyard, surrounded by centuries-old trees. Behind him, the rust-red temple rises, supporting a magnificent two-level, raised-eaves tiled roof. The temple houses Confucius-related artifacts and musical instruments, including a large, well-preserved set of bells, which temple attendants play several times a day. ∎

Legacy of the Great Master

Kong Fuzi (ca 551–479 B.C.) was a Chinese philosopher whose teachings have deeply influenced—and continue to influence—Chinese, Japanese, Korean, and Vietnamese societies. "Master Kong," whose name was Latinized as Confucius by the Jesuit missionary Matteo Ricci (see p. 121), was born in the city of Qufu in Shandong Province, which is still the site of China's most famous *wen miao*, or Confucius temple.

Master Kong came of age during an era of great political and social unrest associated with the Spring and Autumn Period (722–481 B.C.), when China disintegrated into as many as 170 small states and statelets competing for power. As a young man, he despaired of the self-seeking, immoral actions of the rulers and people. He sought to develop a rational philosophy that would encourage them to live orderly, peaceful lives. Central to his teachings was respect for the past and for authority, including both rulers and families. He stressed the importance of education and moral propriety. The system he established became the basis for state authority until the 20th century, not just in China, but also in Japan, Korea, and Vietnam. With Buddhism and Taoism, Confucianism became one of the *san jiao*, or three teachings, that defined Chinese society, as well as the central pillar by which the Chinese state was governed.

Today, the Chinese authorities are ambivalent about Confucianism, which offers an unwelcome alternative vision of state authority to communism, yet provides a welcome set of moral standards in a society increasingly troubled by social disorder, greed, and crime. Confucianism has started to make a comeback in neighboring Vietnam, where Ho Chi Minh was a discreet but active lifelong admirer of the Great Master. Quite possibly the same may occur in China. ■

A statue of "Master Kong," China's sage philosopher, presides over the outer courtyard of the Confucius Temple in Suzhou.

**Master of the
Nets Garden**
(Wangshi Yuan)
🅰 Map p. 215
✉ Shiquan Jie
🕐 7:30 a.m.–5:30 p.m.
🅂 $

The beauty of
the **Blue Wave
Pavilion** is its
harmonic
intermingling
of man-made
buildings with
the natural
environment.

Suzhou's gardens

IF SUZHOU IS FAMOUS FOR ONE THING ABOVE ALL ELSE, IT
is the classical Chinese gardens that still distinguish the city, though
they are much fewer in number than during their heyday under the
Qing dynasty. Most were established by affluent yet pious Confucian
mandarins who sought to create oases of tranquility. Intended for
inward reflection, they are based on the principles of *shan-shui*, or
mountains and waters, which also dovetails with Taoist concepts of
natural harmony. As places designed for quiet meditation, they
should not be rushed through.

Small and lovely, the enduringly
popular **Master of the Nets
Garden** had its beginning in the
12th century. Just over an acre (0.4
ha) and the smallest of Suzhou's
residential gardens, the design and
use of space presents an illusion of
tranquility and harmony. A visit in

the evening might present a chance to hear traditional Suzhou music or see local dancers perfom.

Walking clockwise discover the **Blue Wave Pavilion,** which dates from 1696, one of Suzhou's larger and more informal gardens. Set beside a canal, it is home to several rare varieties of bamboo. Once the home of the classical scholar Su Zimei, it extends over 2.5 acres (1 ha) but appears larger due to the illusion of distant hills created by the garden's designer. Follow narrow paths that rise and fall in a suggestion of rocky hills.

The enchanting **Garden of**

Harmony was once the property of Wu Kuan, a Ming dynasty chancellor, though its present form dates from the late 19th century. At just over one acre in size, it is known for its tranquility and for its elaborate rock gardens.

At the beginning of the 16th century, another Ming dynasty mandarin, Wang Xianchen, laid out the **Humble Administrator's Garden.** One of the largest and most luxuriant of Suzhou's classical gardens, it extends over 11.5 acres (5 ha) of streams, ponds, and pagodas and offers some of the best quiet walks in town. It is known for its bamboo-covered islands, which are connected by traditional bridges and causeways. The adjacent bonsai garden and small gardening museum are also interesting to visit (included in admission).

To the south, the **Lion Grove** is named for its largest rock, said to be lion-shaped. The stones are originally from the Lake Tai area and are famous throughout China, luring many visitors.

The **Couples Garden,** located in the eastern part of the old city near the old city wall and surrounded by water on three sides, was designed by a former governor of Anhui Province during the Qing dynasty. A little away from the city center, it's often quieter than most other gardens. A stroll through rock gardens and traditional circular gateways leads to the elegant Moon-Viewing Pavilion.

Somewhat removed from the other gardens to the west, the **Garden for Lingering In** promises an increasingly unattainable dream. It's still worth visiting, though, for the traditional landscapes and pagodas, impressive bonsai collection, and the **Crown of Clouds Peak,** an 18.5-foot-high (6 m) limestone rock shaped like a miniature mountain. ■

Blue Wave Pavilion
(Canglang Ting)
✉ Canglangting Jie
🕐 7:30 a.m.–5:30 p.m.
💲 $

Garden of Harmony
(Yi Yuan)
✉ Remin Lu
🕐 7:30 a.m.–5:30 p.m.
💲 $

Humble Administrator's Garden
(Zhuozheng Yuan)
✉ Dongbei Jie
🕐 7:30 a.m.–5:30 p.m.
💲 $$

Lion Grove
(Shizilin)
✉ Yuanyin Lu
🕐 7:30 a.m.–5:30 p.m.
💲 $

Couples Garden
(Ou Yuan)
✉ Cang Jie
🕐 7:30 a.m.–5:30 p.m.
💲 $

Garden for Lingering In
(Liu Yuan)
✉ Liu Yuan Lu
🕐 7:30 a.m.–5:30 p.m.
💲 $$

Around Suzhou by bike

The old city of Suzhou remains a good place for a bicycle ride, something that is becoming increasingly rare in traffic-congested modern China. This ride takes you from the Pan Men Scenic Area (see p. 219) in the southwest of the city, past various gardens, temples, pagodas, and canals, to Changmen Gate in the northwest. If you have the nerve and stamina to proceed beyond the old city, you can continue on to West Garden Temple to view the giant statue of Guanyin. Bikes are available for rent from various hotels, guesthouses, and shops in the area.

Start in the southwest of the city by high-arched **Wumen Qiao,** one of the loveliest bridges in Suzhou. Next cycle east past **Pan Men Scenic Area,** where it's hard to miss towering **Ruiguang Pagoda** ❶. Turn east along Xinshi Lu and then north along Renmin Lu as far as the 11th-century **Confucius**

North Temple Pagoda is the tallest historic pagoda in all South China, 250 feet (76 m).

Temple (see p. 211) and antiques market.

From here, turn right, continuing east along Canglangting Jie past the **Blue Wave Pavilion** ❷ (see p. 213), one of Suzhou's most celebrated classical gardens. After a short distance, turn left (north) along Quque Qiao Lu, then continue east along Shiquan Jie as far as the **Master of the Nets Garden** (see p. 212). Backtrack about 150 yards (138 m) to Fenghuang Jie and continue north, passing the 10th-century **Twin Pagodas** ❸ (see p. 217) on your right; Taiping rebels burned down the temple that they once adorned (see pp. 224–225).

Ride slightly to the west on Ganjiang Dong-lu, then cross the small canal and take the first right turn onto Lindun Lu. Continuing north, you pass the **Suzhou Bazaar** on your left and approach a pedestrian street called **Quanqian Jie,** where you will have to park your bike. Proceed on foot to the third-century A.D. **Xuanmiao Temple** ❹ (see p. 219). Quanqian Jie is a good place to stop for a break; numerous small restaurants and cafés provide a selection of cold drinks and local delicacies. After retrieving your bike, proceed north as far as Baita Donglu, where you turn right and head east to the next intersection on the left, Yuanyin

---

- 🗺 See area map p. 191
- ▶ Wumen Qiao
- ↔ 4.5 miles
- 🕐 Half a day
- ▶ West Garden Temple

NOT TO BE MISSED
- Blue Wave Pavilion
- Twin Pagodas
- Xuanmiao Temple
- North Temple Pagoda

Lu. Turn up the small street and continue north until you reach **Lion Grove,** one of the city's famous gardens (see p. 213).

Beyond Lion Grove, bike north once more to the intersection with Dongbei Jie, directly opposite the **Humble Administrator's Garden ⑤** (see p. 213), then turn west toward the vertigo-inducing **North Temple Pagoda** (see p. 217) on your right. Secure the bike and climb to the top for fine views across the old city and beyond. Next make a left turn south to join Baita Xilu, and continue west all the way to **Changmen Gate ⑥.** From here, it's a straight shot across busy Changxu Lu to the intersection with Fengqiao Lu. *(Be careful, as traffic in this area is usually heavy.)* At this point, a smaller road, Liu Yuan Lu, branches slightly to the northwest, leading past the **Garden for Lingering In** (see p. 213) to **West Garden Temple ⑦** (see p. 219). If you feel like extending your ride beyond this point, Huqiu Lu leads north from West Garden Temple to **Tiger Hill** (see p. 219). ∎

A worshipper lights a giant stick of incense at Suzhou's venerated Confucius Temple.

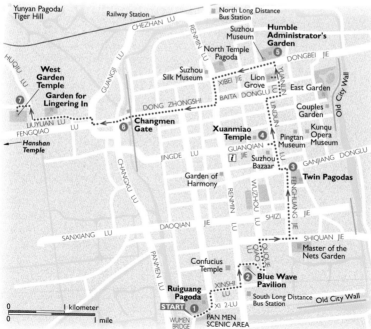

Suzhou's museums

Kunqu Opera Museum
(Kunchu Bowuguan)
✉ Zhongzhangjia Xiang
🕐 8:30 a.m.–4:30 p.m.

Pingtan Museum
(Pingtan Bowuguan)
✉ Zhongzhangjia Xiang
🕐 8:30 a.m.–4:30 p.m.

Suzhou Museum
(Suzhou Bowuguan)
✉ Dongbei Lu
🕐 8:30 a.m.–4 p.m.
💲 $

Suzhou Silk Museum
(Suzhou Sichou Bowuguan)
✉ Renmin Lu
🕐 9 a.m.–5:30 p.m.
💲 $

SUZHOU HAS A NUMBER OF EXCELLENT MUSEUMS FOCUSing on local arts and traditions. They all are well worth visiting, though the Silk Museum takes pride of place.

KUNQU OPERA MUSEUM

One of the oldest forms of Chinese opera, *Kunqu* dates back at least 600 years, reaching its zenith of popularity in the 16th to 18th centuries. It is particularly associated with Suzhou, as well as nearby Nanjing and Hangzhou. Housed in elegantly carved buildings dating from the Ming dynasty, the museum features objects related to the opera's history; performances are given daily.

PINGTAN MUSEUM

Across from the Kunqu Opera Museum, this associated institution relates the history of *pingtan*, a locally celebrated musical genre that mixes singing with spoken dialogue in the local Wu dialect. There are performances daily from 1:30 to 3:30 p.m.

SUZHOU MUSEUM

Set in a historic building that was once the residence of senior Taiping leader Li Xiucheng (1823–1864), this provincial museum offers exhibits related to Suzhou's history. These include Song, Yuan, Ming, and Qing dynasty artifacts, a collection of fine porcelain, funerary relics, calligraphy, paintings, and old maps.

SUZHOU SILK MUSEUM

This informative and well-displayed museum covers just about everything there is to know about Suzhou's most famous product, silk. Combining ancient and modern architecture, the museum is predominantly decorated in white, representing silk's purity. Its several exhibit halls include Introductory Hall, Ancient Hall (which looks at the history of the Silk Road in China), Silkworm Rearing Hall, Silk Weaving Hall, and Modern Hall. Several shops built in Ming and Qing style represent silk stores past and present, purveying different kinds of silk. ∎

Suzhou silk

An antique Chinese name for Suzhou is Capital of Silk. It has long been the most famous center of silk production in China. Since at least as early as Tang dynasty times, the city has been renowned for its high-grade silk, woven locally from silkworms that are raised on Jiangsu mulberry leaves. In times past, much of Suzhou's silk was destined for the imperial court. In the 13th century, Marco Polo commented on the great quantities of silk produced in Suzhou, as well as on the "gold brocade and other stuffs" made here. Suzhou is also famous for its handmade silk embroidery work, known as Su embroidery, one of four traditional styles of embroidery in China. (The other three are Xiang, Yue, and Shu.) Today, numerous modern factories continue the tradition of silk production, and shops selling silk fabric and garments are everywhere. A particularly good place to go shopping for silk is Shiquan Jie (Shiquan Street) in the southeast of the old city, near the Master of the Nets Garden. ∎

Suzhou's pagodas

SEVERAL OF SUZHOU'S PAGODAS ARE CONSIDERED AMONG the finest in China. Some, like Ruiguang Pagoda, have been beautifully restored. Others, like North Temple Pagoda, await restoration and remain a little intimidating to climb for those who suffer from vertigo. All are historically fascinating.

As its name suggests, **North Temple Pagoda** (Bei Si Ta, *Xibei Jie, $*) is located in the northern part of the old city. Originally dating from the third century A.D., it was rebuilt in 1582, attaining a height of 11 stories. Following a fire, the brick-and-wood structure was rebuilt and is still a dizzying nine stories—250 feet (76 m) high—today, thereby maintaining its status as the tallest historic pagoda south of the Yangtze River.

Dating from the Northern Song dynasty, the **Twin Pagodas** (Shuang Ta, $) are tucked away in Dingshuishi Alley off Fenghuang Jie in the eastern part of the old city. Tall, narrow, and elegant, they stand 22 yards (20 m) apart, and are identical, seven-story octagonal brick structures with doors on four sides (but alternating from floor to floor). Named Clarity Dispensing Pagoda and Beneficence Pagoda, they have long been icons of Suzhou.

In the southwest part of the old city, in what is now Pan Men Scenic Area, 1,000-year-old **Ruiguang Pagoda** (Ruiguang Ta, $), the Pagoda of Auspicious Light, is said to be the oldest pagoda in Jiangsu. Standing 142 feet (43 m) high, the recently restored octagonal brick structure is embellished with finely carved wooden eaves, banisters, and balconies. In 1978 a number of historic relics were found concealed in a recess on the third floor of the pagoda, including two gilded

bronze *chedi* and nine images of the Buddha and of the goddess of mercy, Guanyin (Avalokitesvara). These relics are now on display at Suzhou Museum (see p. 216).

To the west of town, on top of Tiger Hill (Huqiu Shan), **Yunyan Pagoda** (Yunyan Ta, *Huqiu Lu, $$*) is chiefly celebrated for its disconcerting incline—indeed, publicists have dubbed it China's Leaning Tower of Pisa. The blue-brick

The thousand-year-old Yunyan Pagoda rises above Tiger Hill in the west of the city.

Traditional dancers perform regularly in the gardens around Suzhou's temples.

octagonal structure was erected during the Five Dynasties Period (A.D. 907–960) on ground that was partly rock and partly softer soil. Over time, the tower began to tilt. Though it has been restored and repaired many times since, the tilt has not been fixed. Today it stands 154 feet (47 m) tall, and the difference in angle between the top and bottom of the tower is 7.6 feet (2.32 m). In 1957 the pagoda was stabilized by pumping concrete into the foundations. During the process, a stone container holding Buddhist scriptures was uncovered; it dated the tower's original construction to A.D. 961. Public access to the tower is not permitted for safety reasons. ■

Covered with dense woods, Purple-Gold Mountain was named for the purple clouds that seem to hover overhead.

Sacred Way
(Shandao)
✉ Shixiang Lu
🕐 8 a.m.–6:30 p.m.

Ming Tombs
(Ming Xiaoliang)
🕐 7:30 a.m.–4:30 p.m.
💲 $$

Zijinshan Observatory
(Zijin Shan Tianwentai)
🕐 8 a.m.–4:30 p.m.
💲 $

Linggu Temple
(Linggu Si)
🕐 7:30 a.m.–5:30 p.m.
💲 $$$

and an indication of the respect in which Sun is still held.

To the west of the mausoleum along Shixiang Lu, the 1,970-yard (1,800 m) **Sacred Way**—lined with 12 pairs of Ming dynasty stone animals, including camels, lions, and elephants—leads to the **Ming Tombs.** This is the last resting place of the Hongwu Emperor Zhu Yuanzhang, founder of the Ming dynasty, who ordered the construction of the tomb in 1381, the 14th year of his reign. The mausoleum was completed in 1405, seven years after his death, having taken 100,000 laborers 24 years to complete. Beyond this tomb, a path leads through the pine forest to the reputed **Mausoleum of Sun Quan,** Monarch of Wu during the Three Kingdoms Period (220–265). In 2003, together with the other Ming Tombs just north of Beijing, the complex was registered by UNESCO as a World Heritage site. The mausoleum is marked by the **Ling Ta Altar Tower** that stands in front of it.

West of the Ming Tombs, along Taiping Men Lu and up a steep path to the north, stands **Zijinshan Observatory.** Although dating from 1929, the observatory also

houses displays of Ming and Qing dynasty astronomical instruments, as well as a small museum documenting the development of astronomy in China.

On the eastern flank of Zijin Shan, at the northern end of Linggu Si Lu, stands the park's third most important major site, **Linggu Temple.** Originally dating from A.D. 515, it has experienced the vicissitudes common to many temples in China, having been destroyed and restored several times. Its present form dates from the reign of the Qing Emperor Tongzhi (1861–1875) and comprises several restored Ming era temple buildings, including the 1831 **Beamless Hall,** or Wuliang Tang, which is 72 feet (22 m) high and 177 feet (54 m) wide. Originally used to house Buddha images and scriptures, in 1928, it was turned into a memorial hall for the estimated 30,000 Nationalist soldiers who died in the Kuomintang Northern Expedition (1926–27) against fractious warlords. Beyond the temple, nine-story **Linggu Pagoda** (Linggu Ta), which was erected in 1929 and rises to a height of 198 feet (60.5 m), also honors the Northern Expedition martyrs. ■

More places to visit in Nanjing

BELL TOWER

Nanjing's Bell Tower (Zhong Lou) supports a huge bell cast in 1388 that once rang to warn of danger. According to legend, on the orders of the Hongwu Emperor (1368–1398), the great bell was cast of an amalgam of iron, silver, gold, and the blood of virgins. The Bell Tower has been lovingly restored and doubles as a popular teahouse.

Map p. 221 ✉ Beijing Donglu 🕐 8:30 a.m.–5:30 p.m.

DRUM TOWER

A short distance west of the Bell Tower, the city's Drum Tower (Gu Lou) dates from 1382 and stands in the center of a downtown traffic circle. It houses a single drum and, like the Bell Tower, has been carefully restored. It also features a pleasant teahouse that stays open late in the evening.

Map p. 221 ✉ Zhongyang Lu 🕐 8 a.m.–11:30 p.m.

FUZI TEMPLE

In the southern part of the city, on Gongyuan Jie, Fuzi Miao is an ancient Confucius temple dating back more than 1,500 years. Once the center for imperial examinations in Nanjing, it has been restored and now stands as an unlikely adjunct to a bustling pedestrian zone packed with souvenir shops, restaurants, teahouses, and bars. Across from Fuzi Miao is the **Imperial Examinations History Museum** (Jiangnan Gongyuan Lishi Chenlieguan, *8 a.m.–6 p.m., $*), which details the immense amount of work faced by

Yangtze Great Bridge

Crossing the Yangtze River just north of Nanjing is the Yangtze Great Bridge (Nanjing Yangzi Da Qiao), a visually impressive, if architecturally dated, tribute to Maoist autarchy and the "great days" of socialist construction. Completed in 1968 in the face of Sino-Soviet rivalry and Moscow's withdrawal of funding and experts, the bridge is only the second to cross the Yangtze. It was hailed by Mao as a symbol of China's ability to "go it alone."

Massive, double-decker construction provides for road traffic above and trains passing below. Upon its completion, the 22,212-foot-long (6,772 m) span provided the first direct rail link between Beijing, Nanjing, and Shanghai. It's worth visiting for the sheer scale of the structure itself, for the fine—if dizzying—views it offers of the Yangtze River and its shipping far below, and for the massively muscled Socialist Realist statues standing at either side of the bridge. Politically correct at the time of construction, the statues feature workers, soldiers, and peasants clutching weapons, tools, and little red books of the collected quotations of Mao Zedong (*Mao Zedong quanji*). ■

Prayer flags flutter over Jiming Si, or the Temple of the Cock's Crow, in Nanjing.

scholars attempting to enter the mandarin civil service in imperial times.

Map p. 221 ✉ Gongyuan Jie ⏱ 8 a.m.– 9 p.m. $ $

JIMING TEMPLE

South of Xuanwu Lake Park, near Beijing Donglu, is Jiming Si, or the Temple of the Cock's Crow. Dating in its original form from A.D. 527, it has been rebuilt or restored many times since, most recently following a serious fire in 1973. One of the city's most venerated Buddhist temples, it is usually filled with worshippers. Nearby, the recently constructed **Yaoshi Pagoda** (Yaoshi Ta) offers panoramic views of the city and of the Yangtze River.

Map p. 221 ✉ Xuanwu Hu Gongyuan ⏱ 8 a.m.–5 p.m. $ $

JINGHAI TEMPLE

At the foot of Lion Hill (Shi Shan) rises Jinghai Temple (Jinghai Si), built on the orders of the Ming Emperor Yongle (1402–1424) to honor admiral Zheng He. The admiral was a Muslim eunuch from Yunnan Province who directed Yongle's great Treasure Fleets across the Indian Ocean to East Africa and Mecca. The temple also houses the small **Nanjing Treaty Museum** (Nanjing Tiaoyue Shiliao Chenlieguan), which details the unequal treaty forced upon China by the British at the end of the First Opium War (1839–1842).

Map p. 221 ✉ Shi Shan ⏱ 8 a.m.– 4:30 p.m. $ $

MEMORIAL HALL OF THE NANJING MASSACRE

Not for the faint-hearted, but essential to understanding China's recent history and contemporary Chinese attitudes toward Imperial Japan, the Memorial Hall of the Nanjing Massacre (Nanjing Datusha Jinianguan) makes compelling, if disturbing, viewing. Between mid-December 1937 and early February 1938, the Imperial Japanese Army systematically raped and killed between 150,000 and 300,000 Chinese soldiers and civilians, a crime that Japanese history books continue to downplay. The Nanjing memorial hall is designed to confirm that the massacre did indeed happen, a contention supported by masses of contemporary witness accounts, photographs, and, not least, the public viewing hall erected over skeletons of massacre victims in a mass grave.

Map p. 221 ✉ 418 Shuiximen Dajie ⏱ 8 a.m.–5:30 p.m. $ $

TAIPING HEAVENLY KINGDOM HISTORICAL MUSEUM

The Taiping Heavenly Kingdom Historical Museum (Taiping Tianguo Lishi Bowuguan) is located near the South Gate and the Confucius Temple. This institution houses displays of maps, weapons, and other materials from the time of the Taiping Rebellion, including coins minted by Hong Xiuquan and his personal seals as "Heavenly King."

Map p. 221 ✉ 128 Zhanyuan Lu ⏱ 8 a.m.–6 p.m. $ $ ■

Travelwise

Jingan transportation
center

PLANNING YOUR TRIP

TRAVELWISE INFORMATION

PLANNING YOUR TRIP

WHEN TO GO

Given the choice, a trip to Shanghai should be timed to achieve both temperate weather and avoidance of crowds.

Winters can be cold and wet, and summers hot and humid. Crowded periods are Chinese New Year (known as Spring Festival in China), Labor Day, and National Day, commemorating the founding of the People's Republic in 1949. Chinese New Year is based on a lunar calendar, thus the date is not fixed, although it usually falls in February. In 2008, the auspicious day falls on February 7; in 2009, January 25; and in 2010, February 14. Labor Day is fixed on May 1 and National Day on October 1. All of these major holidays are in fact week-long events. Nearly all employees and students are given time off and travel stipends, resulting in a massive wave of domestic travel throughout the country. Hotel prices soar, and planes, trains, and buses are booked solid. Many small restaurants and tourist attractions, such as museums, will close for the week beginning with the official holiday.

An ideal time to visit Shanghai would thus be in the spring between Chinese New Year and Labor Day or in the fall after National Day. All this said, if you find yourself safely ensconced in your hotel during any of the three holiday rushes, observing the locals discover their own country can be a real pleasure. In a country where travel beyond one's hometown was, until fairly recently, either forbidden or an unaffordable luxury, the excitement is palpable.

CLIMATE

Members of the older generations regale grandchildren with stories of Shanghai blanketed in snow, but increased urbanization and vehicular traffic have caused the temperatures to climb, so it's more likely to be rain that falls in Shanghai during the winter months. Summers are hot and humid; though air-conditioning is the rule, early mornings and evenings are still agreeable for a stroll.

Shanghai is located at 31 degrees northern latitude. Temperature and humidity ranges are not unlike the coastal regions of the southeastern United States, though it's more likely to rain in Shanghai during the summer months.

Temperature ranges are:
January 34–46°F (1–8°C)
April 50–66°F (10–19°C)
July 73–90°F (23–32°C)
October 57–73°F (14–23°C)

Rainfall is highest during the summer months, but it is sporadic and often brings a cooling relief from the heat.

WHAT TO BRING

Shanghai is China's capital of chic, and while foreigners are not expected to follow the locals' obsession with the latest fashions, one is certainly going to feel more comfortable dressing smartly, especially in upmarket venues.

Since the weather varies dramatically by season, prepare accordingly. Winter in Shanghai is not as bitterly cold as in other parts of China, so you can leave your heavy woolen overcoat at home, but layering with silk long underwear can be a good idea. The heat and humidity of summer call for loose-fitting, breathable cottons. The Chinese rarely wear shorts, but they are acceptable attire for foreigners, except in temples. A jacket with a waterproof shell and removable fleece liner will cover all outdoor weather eventualities.

Most of the world's high-tech outdoor wear, such as down and fleece jackets, is made in China, but it's best to buy at home; these aren't cheaper in China, unless you find the right stall (see Shopping, pp. 255–258), selling bargain overruns or irregular items in your size.

A folding travel raincoat or an umbrella is almost always likely to come in handy here. A pair of comfortable, water-resistant walking shoes is vital. In all seasons except winter, a sun hat, sunglasses, and a sun-block cream are useful.

Any prescription or specifically required over-the-counter medicines should be carried with you, as not all foreign medicines are easy to find. The multinational cosmetic and toiletry manufacturers have discovered the Chinese market and Western branded soaps, toothpastes, and the like abound.

Book lovers should bring a selection of reading material, since most of the English books for sale in China are geared to Chinese who are studying English language and culture. Weekly newsmagazines such as *Time, Newsweek,* and *The Economist* are available, as are the daily *International Herald Tribune* and *Asian Wall Street Journal,* except editions that carry articles critical of the Chinese government.

A Chinese phrase book is worthwhile and often essential. The Chinese love swapping business or name cards, so if you have some, bring them along. The ritual exchange requires presenting and accepting the cards using the thumbs and forefingers of both hands.

INSURANCE

Check with your health insurance company regarding the extent of coverage offered while traveling abroad. Most plans exclude care outside the country of the policy's issuance, but extended coverage is available.

Medical care in Shanghai itself is quite good, but if you are traveling to more remote areas plans are available offering immediate medical evacuation. Likewise for property insurance; many plans do not cover losses while traveling abroad, but special temporary policies are available. Expensive jewelry and the like is probably best left at home while traveling, but if you choose to bring it along, talk to your insurance agent at home before departure.

ENTRY FORMALITIES

VISAS
All foreign passport holders require a visa in advance of travel to China—there is no visa-on-arrival provision except in extraordinary cases.

Nonetheless, acquiring the standard one-month tourist visa is not difficult. You should apply to the Chinese embassy or consulate closest to your home. Your passport must be valid for six months from your proposed date of entry and contain two blank visa pages. Visas for longer periods, business visas, or multiple-entry visas are also available, with a commensurate increase in the fee.

The standard one-month tourist visa can be extended for an additional month at the offices of the Public Security Bureau throughout the country. The PSB office (gonganju) in Shanghai is located at 1500 Minsheng Lu, tel 6834 6205 or 2895 1900.

If you happen to be entering via the Hong Kong Special Administrative Region for which no visa is required except for those holding Middle Eastern or African passports, you can get most any length and type of visa using a local travel agent.

Some embassies and consulates accept applications by mail, while others require that you either submit the application in person or use a visa service—contact the embassy or consulate from the list below for specific details.

Selected Chinese embassies and consulates are listed below;

for a complete list check the Chinese Ministry of Foreign Affairs website: www.fmprc.gov.cn/eng.

United States
2201 Wisconsin Ave.
Room 110
Washington, DC 20007
Tel 202/338-6688
Fax 202/588-9760
www.china-embassy.org

443 Shatto Pl.
Los Angeles, CA 90020
Tel 213/807-8088
Fax 213/807-8091

100 West Erie St.
Chicago, IL 60610
Tel 312/803-0095
Fax 312/803-0110

Canada
515 Patrick St.
Ottawa, ON K1N 5H3
Tel 613/789-3434
Fax 613/789-1911
www.chinaembassy.
canada.org

United Kingdom
31 Portland Pl.
London W1N 3AG
Tel 020/7631-1430
Fax 020/7588-2500
www.chinese-embassy
.org.uk

Denison House
71 Denison Rd.
Rusholme
Manchester M14 5RX
Tel 161/224-7443
Fax 161/257-2672

Australia
15 Coronation Dr.
Yarralumla, ACT 2600
Canberra
Tel 02/6273-4783
Fax 02/6273-5189
www.chinaembassy.org.au

39 Dunblane St.
Camperdown
NSW 2050
Tel 02/8595-8002
Fax 02/8595-8001

New Zealand
2–6 Glenmore St.
Wellington
Tel 04/472-1382
Fax 04/499-0419
www.chinaembassy.org.nz

CUSTOMS
Foreign visitors are allowed to bring all personal effects, such as cameras, video recorders, laptop computers, GPS systems, etc., into China without problem. The duty-free allowance permits three bottles of alcoholic beverages and two cartons of cigarettes. Foreign currency exceeding the equivalent of $5,000 is supposed to be declared, but in fact foreigners are only sporadically issued with customs declaration forms at large entry points such as Shanghai.

Avoid carrying any books on sensitive political subjects, such as Tibet. Pornography and religious materials in Chinese are also unwelcome. During periods of concern about contagious diseases, such as SARS or avian flu, arriving passengers may have their temperatures taken using touch sensors.

Upon departure, note that Chinese law stipulates antiques dating from 1795 to 1949 be accompanied by an official certificate stating their provenance, and that antiques dating prior to 1795 may not be legally exported.

DRUGS & NARCOTICS
No illegal drugs, including marijuana, may be carried into or consumed in China. While foreigners will not usually be subjected to the penalties meted out to Chinese citizens for such infractions, discovery of even small quantities of illegal drugs will doubtlessly lead to an unpleasant encounter with the judicial system, followed by deportation.

If you take medicine that has an abuse potential, such as painkillers, diet pills, or sleeping pills, be sure to keep them in the container bearing a prescription label, and if possible carry a letter from your doctor noting that they are prescribed for you.

HOW TO GET TO SHANGHAI

BY AIRPLANE

All international flights arrive at the futuristic and efficient Pudong International Airport (PVG) 30 miles (45 km) from the city center.

Three Chinese carriers arrive directly in Shanghai from abroad: **Air China** (www.airchi na.com.cn), **China Eastern Airlines** (www.flychinaeastern .com or www.ce-air.com), and **China Southern Airlines** (www.cs-air.com). China Eastern is probably your best choice, since it is based in Shanghai and has the most nonstop flights from abroad, including Los Angeles and New York.

From North America, airlines serving Shanghai include:

United Airlines
800/864-8331
www.united.com
Northwest Airlines
800/225-2525
www.nwa.com
American Airlines
800/433-7300
www.aa.com
Air Canada
888/247-2262
www.aircanada.com

From Australia, **Quantas** (www.quantas.com) flies non-stop from Sydney.

From Great Britain, both **British Airways** (www.british airways.com) and **Virgin Atlantic** (www.virgin-atlantic.com) fly to Shanghai.

Note that all of these airlines practice "code sharing," meaning that even if you buy a ticket from your carrier of choice, you may well fly on a different airline entirely. This should not be worrisome, however, since the old days of aging Russian aircraft once used by Chinese airlines are long gone. If anything, the Chinese carriers

offer a better standard of service and often at a lesser price.

From Southeast Asia, there are regular nonstop flights to Shanghai, and Hong Kong's **Dragonair** (www.dragonair .com) has several flights daily to Shanghai.

If you're a determined cost-cutter, cross from Hong Kong to Shenzhen by train or high-speed ferry and pick up a domestic flight there. This, however, is likely to take you to Hongqiao Airport (SHA), which is used for domestic flights. While closer to the city, it offers a less foreigner-friendly experience than Pudong.

Once you've cleared immigration and customs, you'll need to make your way into the city. Top hotels offer private cars for a fee, but no airport shuttle buses. The easiest way to make the transfer is by taxi. Official taxis are found outside the airport and charge between 160 and 200 yuan ($20–$25) for the trip to downtown Shanghai. The trip will take at least one hour depending on traffic conditions. For hotels in Pudong, the time is much less, but not the fare. Avoid anyone approaching you in the arrivals hall offering taxi services—these are unlicensed drivers who will grossly over-charge you. If you arrive on a domestic flight at Hongqiao Airport, taxis should cost no more than 80 yuan ($10) and take about half an hour to reach downtown.

Official airport buses serve all parts of Shanghai and can get you into town for about 30 yuan ($4) depending on your destination. There are many different routes, so get information from the airport bus service counter in the arrivals hall.

A final alternative is the high-speed magnetic levitation (Mag-lev) Train, which leaves from Pudong every hour and travels at speeds of up to 260 mph (430 kph). While indeed a technical marvel, it is impractical for most travelers since it only reaches the eastern terminus of the Shanghai subway, where you

will need to transfer. It's best to save this adventure for another time and take the round trip, appreciating China's technical prowess once you've gotten rid of your luggage and jet lag.

BY TRAIN

If you're coming directly to Shanghai from Hong Kong, you might consider the train. It leaves every other day from the Hung Hom KCR station in Kowloon, and the trip takes 27 hours. Prices are according to class and range from HK $550 ($80) for a hard sleeper to HK $1,200 ($170) per person for a deluxe two-berth cabin. Tickets can be purchased at Hung Hom KCR station or through travel agents.

GETTING AROUND

TRAVELING IN SHANGHAI

Finding your way around urban China can be difficult, especially if you don't speak or read the language. In large cities like Shanghai, many of the major roads will have their names given in Romanized Chinese, or pinyin script, as well as Chinese characters.

A useful starting point for the beginner is learning the four cardinal points in pinyin, as well as the ideograms, if possible. North is *bei*, east is *dong*, south is *nan*, and west is *xi*. To this should be added the word *zhong* for center or central.

Nearly all Chinese cities have long avenues or freeways, as well as shorter streets and lanes. Other useful related terms are *lu* or road, *jie* or street, and *xiang* or lane. By convention these are often sub-divided according to the cardinal directions. Thus, Shanghai's famous Nanjing Road is divided into Nanjing Xilu, or Nanjing Road West, and Nanjing Donglu, or Nanjing Road East.

Other variants are, for example, Henan Beilu, or Henan Road North, Henan Zhonglu, or Henan Road Central, and Henan Nanlu, or Henan Road South.

Unfortunately, the Shanghainese can be as inconsistent as anybody else, so sometimes—as in Dong Daminglu, or Daming Road East, the word for east—dong—precedes the road name. Still, learn these cardinal directions and getting about Shanghai, or any major Chinese city, will be considerably simplified.

Also, there is no numbering convention in Shanghai. The odd and even numbered buildings intermingle.

BY AUTOMOBILE

Only foreigners who hold a residence permit are allowed to apply for a Chinese driver's license, which is required to own or rent a car. This is a blessing in disguise, since traffic in the city is chaotic and road signs are not always in English. The real danger begins once you leave urban areas where those unused to the unwritten rules of the road here would be in for a hair-raising experience, or far worse. If you wish to travel by private car, it should be with a driver. This can be arranged through your hotel; otherwise, rental cars with drivers are available from Hertz (tel 6211 6381) or Avis (tel 6241 0215). Both of these companies have offices at Pudong International Airport and in the city.

BY BICYCLE

The days when all of China commuted by bicycle are well and truly gone in Shanghai. While millions still pedal through town, and there are dedicated bicycle lanes in some areas, the pollution and danger of collision with cars makes it less fun than this mode of transportation once was.

If you're an experienced cyclist, give it a try. Rentals are hard to come by and either worn out or pricey—it's best to spend 300 yuan ($38) for a

brand-new basic model, which you can buy at any department store. Be sure to get a lock and park in the guarded bicycle parking lots the locals use.

BY BUS

The bus system is inexpensive but crowded and a place to be vigilant of pickpockets, especially if you're carrying a handbag or backpack.

The system is also a bit hard for non-Chinese speakers to navigate, unless you know the desired line and stop. If you want to see as you go, take a taxi or walk.

Something Special: One bus line in Shanghai is worth the ride: the double decker buses imported from Hong Kong (Route 911), which ply Huaihai Lu through the old French Concession. Recently arrived, they have an open upper deck and music to accompany the scenery. Board at the old city gate, just north of the Yu Gar.

BY SUBWAY

Shanghai's ever growing underground and light-rail mass transit system is probably the most efficient way to get from point to point within the city, since it is not affected by the notorious traffic congestion above ground. The trains, however, do get rather crowded during both the morning and evening rush hours, and, needless to say, offer little in the way of scenery. Still, the Metro is Shanghai's best way of getting around. Known as the MRT, or ditie in Chinese, there are comprehensive route maps in each station and car. Announcements are made in English, and the stored-value fare cards (Shanghai Public Transportation Card, or jiaotong-ka) can even be used in taxis. Currently four of the planned seven lines are in operation, with others due to open soon, as follows:

Metro Line 1: Runs north and south, passing through the Shanghai train station, the old

French Concession, and People's Square

Metro Line 2: Runs east and west, from Zhongshan Park to the terminus of the Maglev high-speed train to Pudong International Airport. Passing through the main shopping street of Nanjing Donglu, and crosses Line 1 at People's Square

Metro Line 3: Mainly above ground and reaches the train station and Shanghai stadium

Metro Line 4: Essentially a ring around the city, useful for travel from Pudong to the train station

Metro Line 5: South extension from Dongchuan Lu to Jinshan Chemistry Industrial Zone; first phase, which extends to Fengxian, started construction in mid-2006

Metro Line 6: Scheduled to open in late 2007. Planned route runs in Pudong from Jiyang Lu to Gangcheng Lu

Metro Line 7: Will run from Chentai Lu to Longyang Lu and cross the Expo 2010 zone; Projected opening in 2009

Metro Line 8: The first phase (Shiguang Lu to Xizang Nanlu) and second phase (Xizang Nanlu to Chengshan Lu) are both due to open fall 2007

Metro Line 9: Will run from Songjiang New City to Chongming Island. The first phase, from Songjiang New City to Yishan Lu, is scheduled to open fall 2007, with the line reaching completion by 2009

Metro Line 10: Will run from Hongqiao to New Jiangwan City (first phase) and is due to open in 2009

BY TAXI

Taxis in Shanghai are plentiful and comfortable, using mainly locally built Volkswagen Santana and Passat models. During rush hour and in the rain, taxis are not as easy to find. The fare is 11 yuan ($1.35) for the first 3 kilometers (1.75 mi) and 2.10 yuan ($0.26) for each additional kilometer. Fares increase after 11 p.m.

Several taxi companies compete for your service, the largest and most reliable of which is the Da Zhong taxi fleet, characterized by its turquoise-colored vehicles. While most taxi drivers are honest (and a fair portion of them are women), the usual caveats in dealing with such situations apply: The meter lever should be upright and lighted in red when you board and lowered when you start off. If not, say "Qing da biao," or point at the meter. When boarding, it's a good idea to have your destination written in Chinese characters on a slip of paper. Also carry the card of your hotel for the return trip. When disembarking, ask for a receipt (fapiao), which is automatically printed by the meter, since it notes the taxi's number and the company's telephone number should you forget something in the cab.

Tipping is not expected, and you can pay with the same Shanghai Public Transportation Card, or jiaotongka, used in the subway. If you don't have a card, be sure you have something smaller than a 100 yuan note.

Decline any offers from a person on the street for a taxi and use only those parked in a taxi rank or cruising for fares. If you are going around in circles, or if the driver stops to ask directions more than once, the driver is probably lost. (This is not a regular occurrence, but if it happens, just pay the metered fare and find a different taxi. You're technically not responsible to pay, but you have better ways to spend your time than arguing over a few dollars with a taxi driver who speaks no English.)

TRAVELING OUTSIDE SHANGHAI

Hangzhou
Buses leave from all three of Shanghai's bus stations about every half hour. The 105-mile (170 km) trip takes two to three hours, depending on traffic. There are also buses directly to Hangzhou from both Pudong and Hongqiao Airports in Shanghai. Five express trains make the trip in two hours, departing five times daily from Shanghai's Meilong train station in the south of the city.

Nanjing
Buses to Nanjing depart from the Hengfeng bus station every half hour; the trip takes four hours. It's better to take one of the double-decker trains, which leave from the main station in Shanghai and, even with some stops, only take three hours.

Suzhou
Buses leave for Suzhou primarily from Shanghai's Hengfeng bus station, and less frequently from the Xiajiahui Long Distance bus station. The 60-mile (100 km) trip takes two hours. Double-decker express trains (no smoking allowed, refreshments served) leave Shanghai's main train station every hour and cover the trip in 45 minutes. Train tickets should be booked in advance. Buses also go directly from Pudong and Hongqiao Airports in Shanghai.

It is also possible to travel between Suzhou and Hangzhou by boat on the Grand Canal, but service runs overnight; if you choose this route, you'll miss most of the scenery.

GUIDED BUS TOURS
The **Shanghai Bus Sightseeing Tour Center** (Shanghai Stadium, 666 Qianyaogiao, Gate 12, Staircase 5, tel 6426 6666) offers many tour options, both within Shanghai and beyond to such neighboring areas as Hangzhou and Suzhou. Some are day tours, others include an overnight stay.

For a comprehensive day tour of Shanghai, including the former French Concession, The Bund, Jade Buddha Temple, Yu Gardens, and Pudong, try **Jinjiang Tours** (161 Changle Lu, Luwan District, tel 6415

1188). Jinjiang's tour costs 250 yuan ($33) and includes lunch. They can also arrange tours by private car for small groups.

Greyline Tours (2 Henshan Lu, Xuhui District, tel 135 1216 9650) offers tours of both the city and outlying areas.

BY BOAT
A great way to momentarily distance yourself from the clamor of Shanghai is to take a boat cruise on the Huang Pu River. This service if offered by **Huangpu River Cruises** (239 Zhongshan Dong Er Lu, tel 6374 4461). The tours depart from The Bund. Both day and nighttime cruises are available and are usually an hour in duration, although longer trips of four hours can take you to the mouth of the Yangtze River. Prices range from 40–100 yuan ($5–13). For a more local experience, join the crowds on the passenger ferry that leaves from the southern end of The Bund and arrives at the southern end of Dongchang Lu in Pudong. This will set you back 1 yuan (about 12 cents).

PRACTICAL ADVICE

BARGAINING

In modern shopping malls and large stores, prices are marked, although you may get a small discount if you ask. Otherwise, serious bargaining is the rule. Hotel shops are the worst place to buy local goods—you'll find similar items at a fraction of the price in local markets. Even here, overcharging foreigners is the rule, so be prepared to bargain.

Expert bargainers use a few tactics worth trying: If you see something you like, ignore it at first, bargain a bit for other items, then "notice" what you really want, and ask about it with disinterest. Rather than immediately make a counteroffer, let the seller continue to reduce his price. Try to negotiate one on one with the seller, without an audience.

Prices are usually shown on a pocket calculator, which is proffered to you to make a counteroffer. Start with 25 percent of the offered price. Be aware that many "antiques" are mass-produced copies, quite nice in their own right but should be priced as the new goods they are. Take your time, keep smiling, and don't let the endeavor be anything other than the fun it should be—you'll find the same item, or maybe something better, in a shop down the street.

COMMUNICATIONS

POST OFFICES
The main post office in Shanghai is located a bit out of the way at 276 Suzhou Beilu. This is where letters addressed to Poste Restante, Shanghai, will be sent. Postal services including Poste Restante are located on the second floor. More convenient are the offices at Shanghai Center, 1376 Nanjing Xilu, and at the Xintiandi shopping arcade. Small packages can be sent from these offices, and packing/wrapping services are available. All of these post offices have separate counters for collectors of Chinese stamps; some of these stamps are quite beautiful.

TELEPHONE
Shanghai's local area code is 021. It can be omitted when making local calls and has not been used througout this guide. The country code for China is 86.

If calling Shanghai from abroad, dial the international access code, then 8621 (omitting the zero), followed by the local number.

If calling from within China, but outside the 021 area code, dial 021 plus the local Shanghai number.

Local directory assistance can be reached at 121. You'll be transferred to an English-speaking operator once they

realize you're a foreigner.

Using the home country direct number, 108, it is possible to be connected with a local operator in your home country, from whom you can place a collect or credit card call. The following numbers are used:

> Australia 108 610
> Canada 108 186
> Hong Kong 108 852
> New Zealand 108 640
> United Kingdom 108 440
> United States 108 11

China Telecom issues Internet Protocol (IP) phone cards that can be used to call abroad at highly attractive rates, especially since the cards are sold at a discount from their face value. There are two types; the cheaper one can only be used from Shanghai, and the other can be used from anywhere in China.

China uses the GSM mobile telephone system common throughout the world except in the U.S., so if you have a GSM phone it's easy to bring it along and buy a local SIM card and a prepaid stored value card. Not only can you be reached immediately from home, you can keep in touch with other members of your traveling group. Basic-model mobile phones are not expensive in China, so those owning the American CDMA mobile phones might find this a good investment—using hotel phones for a couple weeks would exceed the price of a local mobile phone.

INTERNET
China has taken to the Net with a vengeance; despite its efforts, the government has been unable to completely shut this window on the world. Even mainstream news websites such as the BBC are permanently blocked, although savvy locals and expats use the many proxy server websites to circumvent this. E-mail sites, such as Hotmail, will periodically become inaccessible as well.

Internet cafés (*wangba*) are becoming less prevalent in Shanghai as most people in the city now have home computers. Such cafés are mainly the domain of chain-smoking youths playing online games.

The Shanghai Library at 1555 Huaihai Zhonglu in the old French Concession is an exception, with no smoking or drinking allowed. Some local offices of China Telecom also have computer terminals for going online. Hotel business centers offer this service as well, although the hourly rate is inordinately high. If you're staying in a high-end hotel, you'll certainly have broadband access from your room. For those carrying a laptop or handheld computer you'll find many hotel lobbies and chic cafés that are wi-fi hot spots.

CONVERSIONS

Although a traditional measurement system exists, China now follows the metric system.

> 1 kilometer = 0.62 miles
> 1 meter = 1.09 yards
> 1 centimeter = 0.39 inches
> 1 kilogram = 2.2 pounds
> 1 gram = 0.035 ounces
> 1 liter = 0.76 pints
> 0°C = 32°F

ELECTRICITY

China uses a 220-volt electrical system. Although most electrical items intended for overseas travel (such as digital camera and laptop computer battery chargers) are automatically switched between 110 and 220 volts, be sure to check the manual or look for markings on the device itself before plugging it in. Hair dryers and electric shavers intended for use in the U.S. are usually 110 volt only. Transformers are available, but they are either heavy or can overheat and create a fire hazard. A variety of two- and three-pronged, round, flat, and square plugs are used in

China, so bring along a travel conversion plug.

ETIQUETTE & LOCAL CUSTOMS

While the people of Shanghai pride themselves on being the most cosmopolitan of the Chinese, certain cultural traits are worth noting, especially when dealing with people above the age of 40.

Handshakes or slight bows are exchanged as greetings, although the Chinese handshake is soft—powerful handshakes are inappropriate. Chinese surnames precede the given name: thus, Li Dong Feng is Mr., or Madame, Li. Other honorifics are used as well: Doctor, Professor, even Teacher or Engineer Li will be introduced. If you are introduced to a group, you may be applauded. You should applaud in reply.

The concept of saving face is often a stumbling block for foreigners. Although it exists in the West, it is much more important in China. Causing someone to lose face, i.e., making them appear foolish or even wrong about a specific point, is to be avoided. Confrontational behavior will always work against you. Refusals should be indirect: "maybe," "later," "we'll see," and other ambiguities are much better than the definitive "no."

The Chinese are restrained in expressing their feelings. Self-aggrandizing comments and animated hand gestures are much less acceptable in China than in the West.

On the other hand, behavior that would be considered rude in the West is common here, especially in crowded and urban Shanghai. Expect pushing, cutting in lines, people stepping into your path while walking, and the like. Staring is common outside urban Shanghai—don't take it personally. If greeted with a shouted "Hello" from a stranger, just smile or ignore it, since it usually is the extent of the

shouter's English and replying would only produce another "Hello" or gales of laughter.

Spitting, despite the government's numerous campaigns against this disagreeable and infection-spreading practice, is still common.

Avoid discussions that relate to Tibet, Taiwan, or human rights. While the Chinese may disagree with government policies among themselves, no nationality enjoys hearing their country criticized by outsiders.

HOLIDAYS

Official holidays will mean that banks, most companies, and government offices are closed.

New Year's Day—January 1
Chinese New Year, also called Spring Festival, follows the lunar calendar. Upcoming years' dates are as follows:
  February 7, 2008
  January 25, 2009
  February 14, 2010
This date is the beginning of a weeklong period of travel when the Chinese visit their hometowns or just take a trip. Expect transportation and accommodations to be limited.
International Women's Day—March 8
Labor Day—May 1, another weeklong travel binge for millions of Chinese
Youth Day—May 4
Children's Day—June 1
Anniversary of the Founding of the Chinese Communist Party—July 1
Anniversary of the Founding of the People's Liberation Army—August 1
Anniversary of the Founding of the People's Republic of China—October 1. Like Chinese New Year and Labor Day, expect large crowds and travel congestion. These are great fun to watch as long as you have a place to stay and aren't trying to get anywhere. Parades and fireworks can be seen on The Bund.

LIQUOR LAWS

Although the official closing time for bars is 2 a.m., this is Shanghai, and those so inclined can party until dawn. Teenagers are openly served drinks in bars and restaurants. Convenience stores also sell alcoholic beverages 24 hours a day.

MEDIA

The Chinese government keeps a firm grip on both electronic and print media. Books, newspapers, magazines, and websites are regularly censored for information the government feels portrays China in an unflattering light or compromises the morality of the Chinese people.

Government-owned English language publications such as the *China Daily*, while improving, are such obvious propaganda ("grain production soars") that they seem almost counterproductive to the government's intention of portraying the country in a positive light. Privately owned publications, while still subject to government regulation, are much more reliable.

Although it's still best for bibliophiles to bring something along to read, there are some decent bookshops with English language titles in Shanghai (see Shopping, pp. 256).

MAGAZINES

In addition to foreign magazines, which you'll find at hotel shops and bookstores, Shanghai has several good free magazines for visitors and expats that focus on entertainment venues and cultural happenings. These publications also have good feature-length articles covering various aspects of Shanghai's past and present. You'll find them in hotels, restaurants, and bars. Some of the best and their websites:

City Weekend
www.cityweekend.com.cn
That's Shanghai

www.thatssh.com
8 Days
www.8days.sh
Smart Shanghai
www.smartshanghai.com

NEWSPAPERS

In addition to the ubiquitous *International Herald Tribune* and the lifeless *China Daily*, Shanghai offers the government-owned *Shanghai Daily* and the weekly *Shanghai Star*, which often have some informative cultural features. Both have websites:
    Shanghai Daily
    www.shanghaidaily.com
    Shanghai Star
    www.shanghai-star.com.cn

RADIO

Locally, try FM 101.7 for English-language programs. On short-wave, BBC World Service can be found on 17760, 21660, and 9740 kHz, and VOA on 17820 14525, 21840, and 9769 KHz. Both of these services also have radio feeds on their respective websites, which work well when the website has not been blocked by the government.

TELEVISION

Upscale hotels receive BBC, CNN, CNBC, ESPN, and HBO via satellite. One of the channels (CCTV 9) on the government-owned network broadcasts exclusively in English and has some interesting feature programs about Chinese history and culture, albeit with the scent of propaganda.

MONEY MATTERS

The currency of China is the *renminbi* (literally, people's money), abbreviated as RMB, and also called the yuan, or *kuai*. One yuan is divided into 10 *jiao* or *mao*. One jiao is divided into ten *fen*, although this is rarely used.
    Paper bills come in denominations of 100, 50, 20, 10, 5, and 1 yuan. Smaller-size bills are used for 5, 2 and 1 jiao, although these scraps of paper are mercifully being replaced by coins.

The renminbi rate moves only slightly and is usually around eight to one U.S. dollar. Money changers in Hong Kong offer an acceptable exchange rate for renminbi, but elsewhere the currency is either unavailable or sold at unfavorable rates. Be sure to exchange your excess Chinese currency at the airport before leaving. To do this, you will need to present an exchange receipt from a bank proving that you exchanged the Chinese currency from foreign currency.
    There is no black market for Chinese currency—anyone offering you a better rate than what the bank offers is most likely peddling counterfeit notes, which are widespread.

Exchange

Offices of the Bank of China and Hong Kong and Shanghai Banking Corporation (HSBC) exchange renminbi for both major foreign currencies and traveler's checks and can give cash advances for Visa and MasterCard holders, although a commission will be added to the transaction. Hotel cashiers also exchange cash and traveler's checks, although the rate is less favorable than in banks.

CREDIT CARDS

Credit cards are accepted in all big hotels and restaurants, although there is sometimes a service charge of up to 4 percent. If you're settling a large hotel bill, inquire beforehand—it could be well worth your while to walk around the corner and withdraw the needed cash from an ATM. Visa and Master Card are the most widely accepted; American Express and Diners Club are less popular but still accepted in hotels and restaurants that have a foreign clientele.

ATM MACHINES

This is the best way to get Chinese cash in Shanghai. At the ATM machines of both the Bank of China and HSBC, you

can conveniently withdraw Chinese cash at a reasonable rate of exchange. Your card should bear the Cirrus or Maestro logo; debit cards or bank-issued "cash cards" are less likely to function in Chinese ATMs.

OPENING TIMES

Banks, businesses, and government offices are officially open Monday through Friday, 8:30 a.m. to 6 p.m., sometimes with an hour or two lunch break. Temples, museums, zoos, and other tourist sites are generally open daily from 8 or 9 a.m. until 5 p.m. Department stores and privately run boutiques are open until 8 or 9 p.m.

PASSPORTS

You will be asked for your passport when checking into hotels, changing money, and sometimes when buying an airline ticket; otherwise it's best to make a good color photocopy of the page showing your picture, and the one with your Chinese visa, and leave the original in your hotel room safe or the hotel's safe deposit box. Getting a replacement for a lost passport is a time-consuming bureaucratic hassle.

RELIGION

While China is officially atheist, there is now greater religious tolerance, and the Chinese are rediscovering their Buddhist and Taoist faiths. Christianity is also growing in popularity.
    The largest Catholic church in Shanghai is St. Ignatius Cathedral, located at 158 Puxi Lu in Xujiahui District. Mass is held on Sunday at 6 a.m., 7:30 a.m., 10 a.m., and 6 p.m., and at 7 a.m. on weekdays.
    Protestant services are held at the Community Church, located at 53 Hengshan Lu in Xuhui District.
    The Beit Menachem Synagogue, part of the Shanghai Jewish Center, is located at

Shang-Mira Garden, 1720 Hong Qiao Lu in the north-west district of Hongqiao, tel 6278 0225.

Shanghai's largest mosque, Xiao Taoyuan Qingzhensi (Small Peach Garden Mosque), is located at 52 Xiao Taoyan Jie in the Old Town, south of The Bund.

TIME DIFFERENCES

All of China, including Shanghai, marches to Beijing time, which is eight hours ahead of GMT or London time, and 13 hours ahead of New York, 16 hours ahead of Los Angeles, and 2 hours behind Sydney. No daylight savings time is observed.

TIPPING

Although discouraged by the authorities, tipping is one of many foreign customs Shanghai has been quick to adopt. Hotel porters should be tipped 10 yuan per bag; taxi drivers do not expect a tip. In restaurants, give 10 percent, unless a service has been added to the bill.

TOURISM AUTHORITIES

The Tourist Information and Service Centers found throughout Shanghai are more oriented to Chinese visitors than foreigners, thus the level of English spoken varies greatly. They can provide glossy brochures and maps and make hotel bookings. The main office is located at 303 Moling Lu, at the south entrance to the railway station. More central is Century Square office, at 561 Nanjing Donglu. A tourist information hotline can be reached at tel 6252 0000.

TOURIST OFFICES ABROAD

The China National Tourism Office has offices in many countries aboard. The information they provide is useful, including a list of specialized tour operators, but like the government-owned newspapers, the idealized portrait of the country they offer can misinform the traveler. Still, if convenient, the offices are worth a visit for nice brochures and maps.

United States
350 Fifth Ave., Suite 6413
New York, NY 10118
Tel 212/760-8218
www.cnto.org

600 W. Broadway, Suite 320
Glendale, CA 91204
Tel 818/545-7505

Canada
480 University Ave., Suite 806
Toronto, ONT M5G 1V2
Tel 416/599-6636
www.tourismchina-ca.com

United Kingdom
71 Warwick Rd.
London SW5 9HB4
Tel 020/7373-0888
www.cnto.org.uk

Australia
44 Market St., Level 19
Sydney NSW 2000
Tel 02/9299-4057
www.cnto.org.au

TRAFFIC

If you're traveling by taxi, expect near gridlock conditions during morning and evening rush hours. Pedestrians need to be extremely careful in Shanghai. Never expect to be given the right of way, even in a pedestrian crossing with a green light. Be careful of motorcycles and silent electric bicycles that take to the sidewalk. The safest way to navigate the streets is to surround yourself with a crowd of the local pedestrians; they know and follow the unwritten rule of the road, which places pedestrians at the bottom of the food chain.

TRAVELERS WITH DISABILITIES

Shanghai is not easy for the disabled. While the airport, the Metro, and five-star hotels have wheelchair access, the sidewalks are crowded and uneven. Minivan taxis, which can accommodate wheelchairs, are available.

EMERGENCIES

Should you lose your passport, contact your country's consulate in Shanghai, or if there is none, the embassy in Beijing. For this and other emergencies, such as traffic accidents or crime, you should also contact the police, known in China as the Public Security Bureau (PSB). Officiously polite (to foreigners) but glacially bureaucratic, the PSB office (gonganju) in Shanghai is located at 333 Wusong Lu, tel 6357 7925 or 6357 6666.

FOREIGN CONSULATES IN SHANGHAI

Consulates are open only Monday through Friday. It's best to call in advance, since most of them have many Chinese visa applicants and have special times for nationals of the home country to visit and avoid the crowds.

U.S. Consulate General
1038 Nanjing Xilu
Westgate Mall, 8th floor
Metro: Shimen No. 1 Road
Tel 3217 4650
24 hour for emergencies only:
6433 3936
Fax 6217 2071
www.usembassy-china.org.cn/shanghai

Canadian Consulate General
1376 Nanjing Xilu
Shanghai Center
West Tower, Suite 604
Jingan District
Metro: Jingan Temple
Tel 6279 8400
Fax 6279 8401
www.shanghai.gc.ca

British Consulate General
1376 Nanjing Xilu 1376
Shanghai Centre, Suite 301
Jingan District

Metro: Jingan Temple
Tel 6279 7650
Fax 6279 7651
www.uk.cn

Australia Consulate General
1168 Nanjing Xilu
CITIC Square, 22nd Floor
Jingan District
Metro: Jingan Temple
Tel 5292 5500
Fax 5292 5511
www.shanghai.china.embassy
.gov.au

New Zealand Consulate General
989 Changle Lu, The Centre
Room 1605-1607A
Metro: Shanxi Road South
Tel 5407 5858
Fax 5407 5068
www.nzembassy.com

Emergency Phone numbers:
Ambulance: 120
Fire: 119
Police: 110

MEDICAL SERVICES

Given the large expatriate community, it is not surprising that Shanghai has a good reputation for medical services geared to foreigners. Chinese hospitals have special foreigners' wards, and private international clinics are staffed by expat physicians. Some of the best:

Shanghai United Family Hospital
1139 Xian Xialu
Changning District
Tel 5133 1900
24-hour emergency hotline:
5133 1999

Huashan Hospital Foreigners' Clinic
12 Central Wulumuqi Lu
Foreigners Ward on 19th floor
Tel 6248 9999 ext. 1900

For minor ailments, outpatient clinics are more convenient. Try:

World Link Medical Center
Room 203, West Tower
Shanghai Center
(Portman Ritz-Carlton Hotel)
1376 Nanjing Xilu
Jingan District
Tel 6279 7688

Shanghai East International Medical Center
551 Pudong Nanlu
Pudong District
Tel 5879 9999

HEALTH

The most common ailments to afflict travelers in Shanghai are either digestive (diarrhea or stomach cramps) caused by unfamiliar or unclean foods, or respiratory, either from infections such as the common cold or air pollution. Either, while not usually serious, make traveling difficult and are best prevented rather than treated. Drink only bottled water and avoid street food. Don't overexert yourself and be careful of rapid temperature changes. Visit any of the clinics or hospitals mentioned above at the first sign of illness. If you just need an over-the-counter medicine, try the Watson's pharmacies located all over the city, or City Supermarket in Shanghai Center on Nanjing Xilu.

More serious conditions should be guarded against by immunization injections prior to travel. See your doctor three months in advance of your trip, since injections must be given separately. If your trip is limited to Shanghai, the injections required will be less than if you plan to be in rural or subtropical areas.

A good source of current information is your government's travel health website.

United States
www.cdc.gov/travel
Canada
www.hc-sc.gc.ca
United Kingdom
www.dh.gov.uk
Australia
www.smarttraveller.gov.au

New Zealand
www.safetravel.govt.nz

News about avian influenza (bird flu) has frightened many travelers, but the medical evidence shows little cause for alarm. The virus is passed from migratory birds to domestic fowl, such as chickens. Transmission to humans requires close contact with an infected bird. Common sense precautions include avoiding live poultry markets and not eating raw or undercooked chicken or eggs. Wash your hands frequently and see a doctor if you develop a fever.

SAFETY

Violent crime against foreigners is rare, probably due to the consequences for those attempting it. Pickpocketing is a more common problem. Be careful in crowded street markets, on buses, and in the Metro. If you are carrying a handbag, backpack, or waist pack, keep it in front, since razor slicing is a common method used by thieves. The area around the railway station is full of destitute migrants and best avoided. Scam artists ply the tourist areas, so if you are accosted with offers from "art students" wishing to show you their works, or those wishing to practice their English who invite you to have a beer in a nearby café, give a polite but firm refusal. Pickpocket gangs also may use these techniques to distract you. Prostitution flourishes in Shanghai, usually with late night phone calls to your hotel room proposing "massagee." Those foolish enough to accept this invitation can find themselves victims of thugs, sometimes posing as police. Foreign women are seldom the victims of sexual harassment.

FURTHER READING

Shanghai is well represented in 20th-century literature, both in

Chinese and in Western languages. The writers Lu Xun, Mao Dun, and Ba Jin are celebrated in the city's Duolun area, while Western writers, such as Noël Coward (*Private Lives*, 1930), André Malraux (*Man's Fate*, 1934), and J.G. Ballard (*Empire of the Sun*, 1984), wrote in or about the city. Recommended reading includes:

Old Shanghai (pre-1949)

A Short History of Shanghai (1928) by F. Hawks Potts. An intriguing, informed history (reprinted) of the city up to 1928.

Bound Feet and Western Dress (1966) by Pang-Mei Chang. A fascinating biography of the author's aunt, who rejected traditional society to become a banker.

Carl Crow—A Tough Old China Hand (2006) by Paul French. Portrait of the life and times of an American journalist in early 20th-century Shanghai.

The Fall of Shanghai: The Communist Takeover of 1949 (1974) by Noel Barber. A comprehensive account of the events by an informed journalist.

Frenchtown Shanghai (2000) by Tess Johnston and Deke Erh. The best historical and architectural account of the former French Concession.

Old Shanghai: Gangsters in Paradise (1984) by Lynn Pan. An impossible-to-put-down account of Shanghai's underworld in the late 19th and early 20th centuries.

The Rape of Nanking (1997) by Iris Chang. A harrowing account of Japan's worst wartime atrocity in China, an event still denied by Japanese ultranationalists.

Shanghai: Collision Point of Cultures, 1918–1939 (1990) by Harriet Sergeant. A portrait of social life in the 1920s and '30s, from the French Concession through the International Settlement to the Chinese city.

The Soong Dynasty (1985) by Sterling Seagrave. A very readable account of relationships and politics among Shanghai's most influential 20th-century family.

Strange Haven: A Jewish Childhood in Wartime Shanghai (1999) by Sigmund Tobias. Account of a German-Jewish refugee family in wartime Hongkou.

The Shanghai Green Gang: Politics and Organized Crime 1919–1937 (1996) by Brian G. Martin. A compulsive page-turner, well written and documented.

Modern Shanghai (post-1949)

The Bund Shanghai: China Faces West (2007) by Peter Hibbard. A detailed examination of Shanghai's most celebrated thoroughfare then and now.

Daughter of Shanghai (1994) by Tsai Chin. Raised in a liberal, Westernized home, the author left for London in 1949 but here rediscovers her roots.

Life and Death in Shanghai (1995) by Nien Cheng. An insight into conditions during the Cultural Revolution, when the author was accused of espionage and jailed.

New Shanghai: The Rocky Rebirth of China's Legendary City (2001) by Pamela Yatsko. A perceptive analysis by an informed American woman journalist.

Opening Up: Youth, Sex Culture and Market Reform in Shanghai (2002) by James Farrer. Fascinating account of the changing mores of modern Shanghai.

Red Azalea (2006) by Anchee Min. A powerful and well-written account of growing up in Shanghai during the Cultural Revolution.

Shanghai Journal (1969) by Neale Hunter. An eyewitness account of the Cultural Revolution in the powerbase of the Gang of Four.

Fiction

Becoming Madame Mao (2000) by Anchee Min. A surprisingly sympathetic historical novel based on the life of Mao Zedong's fourth wife, Jiang Ching.

Candy (2003) by Mian Mian. A gritty look at drug addiction, prostitution, gambling, and other vice in 1990s Shanghai, written by a former heroin addict.

Empire of the Sun (2005) by J. G. Ballard. Semi-autobiographical tale of the author's childhood internment in a Japanese prison camp in wartime Shanghai.

Man's Fate (1990) by André Malraux. Novel about the White Terror in Shanghai in 1927 when Chiang Kai-shek and the Green Gang attacked the communists.

Midnight (2001) by Mao Dun. A 1933 novel exploring the commercial world of Shanghai from a working class, socialist viewpoint.

The Sing-song Girls of Shanghai (2005) by Han Bangqing. A 1898 novel following the lives of Shanghai courtesans in the late 19th century.

Shanghai Baby (2001) by Zhou Weihui. Praised by some for elegance of language, criticized by others for self-centered lack of substance. A very Shanghainese novel.

When We Were Orphans (2001) by Kazuo Ishiguro. The first part of this celebrated British-Japanese writer's novel is set in Shanghai.

Chinese writers associated with Hongkou & Duolun Lu

A Madman's Diary by Lu Xun. The writer's first work, published in 1918, is a scathing critique of traditional Chinese society.

Dawn Dew Collected at Dusk by Lu Xun. A collection of ironic reminiscences published in 1928, widely considered a masterpiece.

The Goddesses by Guo Moruo. Published in 1921, this is the writer's first anthology of modern Chinese poetry written in the vernacular style.

Mr Pan Weathered the Storm by Ye Shengtao. A collection of short stories published later in the author's life in 1964.

Snowy Morning by Ye Shengtao. An early volume of vernacular Chinese poetry first published in 1922.

The True Story of Ah Q by Lu Xun. An allegorical novel written in the 1920s, this is the author's most celebrated work.

HOTELS & RESTAURANTS

In both sleeping and eating, the choices offered in Shanghai are almost without limit—as long as your budget is equally unlimited. From futuristic to traditional, the accommodation and culinary choices mix the best of East and West. There are exceptions to the high prices in both accommodation and restaurants. A decent meal can be found in the food courts for under $5, and a few budget hostelries can still be found. Still, to enjoy most of what the city has to offer, be prepared to spend more than you would at home. Most visitors leave feeling that, while Shanghai is expensive, considering the experience it offers, it is also a good value.

HOTELS

Shanghai has some of the most spectacular hotels in the world, with prices to match. The target client is the business traveler, and those on an expense account or unlimited budget will find no shortage of excellent accommodation choices. These citadels of opulence are usually found in the business-oriented Pudong area or the central Nanjing Donglu area, and are managed by top international chains. Some companies have expanded their holdings to a second or even third property in Shanghai. Another variety of accommodation is the restored building from the 1930s, which can be equally luxurious, although others are priced within the range of the average traveler. At present, occupancy rates are high, so discounts aren't so common. Rates do fluctuate according to the season, with winter offering relatively lower prices. The rates posted in the hotel's lobby are almost always subject to a discount—ignore this board and ask the price. A hotel building boom is also under way, as Shanghai prepares for the World Expo 2010. This augurs well for a long-term drop in accommodation prices. There are some mid-range modern hotels managed by Chinese companies located throughout the city as well, but they are usually geared to the domestic traveler, so bring along your Chinese phrase book and don't expect impeccable service.

If you are here on business, your choice of hotel should be dictated by where you will be working, which is usually Pudong or Hongqiao, since traffic problems could impede a busy meeting schedule. Those traveling for pleasure would be better served by a hotel either near The Bund or the old French Concession. Given the high occupancy rates, it is a good idea to make advance bookings. Internet bookings can offer good discounts, but try to verify the hotel's description given on the website from other sources.

RESTAURANTS

Shanghai prides itself on being China's capital of the high life, and what better way to express it than in excellent food served in spectacular settings. Both Western and Chinese cuisines are prepared to top standards and served in venues to match. Still, such extravagance is best enjoyed as a special occasion, and there are numerous mid-range restaurants that serve good food in pleasant surroundings—notably the restored villas of the old French Concession. Some of the mid-range restaurants are chains (such as Zen and Shanghai Uncle), but this in no way detracts from their quality.

Likewise, good mid-priced food can be found in the restaurants of the international chain hotels. Street food is becoming hard to find in Shanghai, since the government, with good sense given the city's pollution levels, has limited their locales to suburban areas. The alternative for good cheap eats are the ubiquitous food courts that can be found in every shopping mall or department store, usually in the basement.

WAITAN TO RENMIN GONGYUAN

Given the historical sights on The Bund, great views of the Huangpu River and Pudong, and the proximity of shopping, restaurant, and nightlife venues, this is a good location for visitors to stay. It can, at times feel crowded and noisy.

HOTELS

▥ THE WESTIN BUND
▯ CENTER
$$$$$
(WEISITING DAFANDIAN)
88 HENAN ZHONGLU
TEL 6335 1888
FAX 6335 2888
www.westin.com/shanghai
E-MAIL rsvns-shanghai@westin.com
Three blocks off The Bund, in the 50-story Bund Center, the Westin is a business traveler's favorite, with an atrium lobby, restaurants serving Italian, Thai, Japanese, and even Chinese cuisine. While the luxurious Banyan Tree Spa is located on the premises, those on a tight schedule can book rooms with built-in aerobic exercise machines. Rooms are modern and tastefully decorated, the service ultra efficient.
🛈 580 ▥ East Nanjing Road 🅢 🕭 🔽 🅢 🅢 All major cards

▥ ASTOR HOUSE HOTEL
▯ $$$
(PUJIANG FANDIAN)
15 HUANGPU LU
TEL 6324 6388
FAX 6324 3179
www.pujianghotel.com
E-MAIL sales@pujianghotel.com
This fallen five-star was recently rescued by a renovation. The likes of Charlie Chaplin and Albert Einstein once stayed here, and Shanghai's first electric lightbulbs were installed in 1886. Full of atmosphere, great location on The Bund.
🛈 116 ▥ East Nanjing Road 🅢 🅢 All major cards

HOTELS & RESTAURANTS

HOWARD JOHNSON PLAZA HOTEL
$$$
(GU XIANG DAJIUDIAN)
595 JIUJIANG LU
TEL 3313 4888
FAX 3313 4880
www.hojoshanghai.com
E-MAIL reservations.shanghai
@hojoplaza.com
Like Holiday Inn, this chain's international offerings are decidedly more upscale than in the U.S. This one is located in a 27-story tower just off the Nanjing Donglu pedestrian walkway and within easy walking distance of The Bund.
360 East People's Square or East Nanjing Road   All major cards

RAMADA PLAZA
$$$
(NAN XINYA HUAMEIDA DAJIUDIAN)
700 JIUJIANG LU
HUANGPU DISTRICT
TEL 6350 0000
FAX 6350 6666
www.ramadaplazashanghai.com
E-MAIL marketing@ramadaplaza
shanghai.com
Less opulent and expensive than some of the international chain hotels in Shanghai, the Ramada Plaza, one of four Ramada hotels in Shanghai, is nonetheless quite attractive and represents a good value for the money. The hotel is located in the heart of the Nanjing Lu pedestrian area, has four restaurants, an atrium lobby, and executive floors for business travelers.
333 East Nanjing Road   All major cards

SEAGULL HOTEL
$$$
(HAIOU FANDIAN)
60 HUANGPU LU
TEL 6325 1500
FAX 6324 1263
www.seagull-hotel.com
This comfortable, moderately priced hotel is difficult to miss, especially at night, with its

huge rooftop neon Epson sign perched high above the street. It's certainly worth asking for a riverview room; The Bund, Pudong, Waibaidu Bridge, and the Huangpu River itself are endless sources of entertainment. The Seagull's special business suites are all equipped with their own fax machines, printers, and computers. All rooms contain state-of-the-art plasma televisions.
128 East Nanjing Road   All major cards

CAPTAIN HOSTEL
$$
(CHUANZHANG QINGNIAN JIUDIAN)
37 FUZHOU LU
HUANG PU DISTRICT
TEL 6323 5053
FAX 6321 9331
www.captainhostel.com.cn
E-MAIL captain@captainhostel
com
For those seeking a respite from modern luxury, this favorite of backpackers of all ages is perfect. Located in a 1920's art deco building just off the Bund, the Captain offers not just dorm beds but a selection of nice double rooms with attached bathrooms as well. Only some rooms have a television. The rooftop bar has the same great views of the river as its neighbors at a fraction of the cost. The hostel offers a variety of activities for its guests, such as classes in Chinese cooking and handicraft making. Bicycles are available for rent and there's an internet café in the lobby.
21 East Nanjing Road   All major cards

PACIFIC HOTEL
$$
(JINMNEN DAJIAODIAN)
108 NANJING XILU
HUANGPU DISTRICT
METRO PEOPLE'S SQUARE
TEL 6327 6226

FAX 6372 6374
This building dates from the 1920s and has been well restored and maintained. It's by no means deluxe, although it carries a government mandated three stars, the staff is helpful, and the atmosphere appealing. Try to get a room on one of the upper floors, facing People's Square.
161   All major cards

SHANGHAI MANSIONS
$$
20 SUZHOU BEILU
TEL 6324 6260
FAX 6306 5147
www.broadwaymansions.com
Dating from 1935, this immense 19-story apartment building, once called Broadway Mansions but now Shanghai Mansions Hotel, dominates the north side of Suzhou

Creek. During the 1930s and 40s the upper floors functioned as the Shanghai Foreign Correspondents Club, and today the 18th-floor observation balcony still offers fabulous views south across The Bund and east toward Pudong. Only stay here if you can get a south-facing room—views north across Hongkou offer nothing worth seeing.

🛈 233 🅿 🚇 East Nanjing Road 🔁 🅢 🅐 🅝 🛡 🅢 All major cards

RESTAURANTS

SOMETHING SPECIAL

🍴 JEAN GEORGES

This citadel of haute cuisine was opened by Jean-Georges Vongerichten in 2004 following his successful New York restaurant. French-Asian fusion with a continental flair remains the theme here, both in decor and cuisine. Specialties include fois gras brûlée, sea scallops, kingfish sashimi, and lamb loin with black trumpet mushrooms, all prepared in unique styles. Both set and a la carte menus are presented. Ambience is elegant not splashy, and many consider this Shanghai's best Western restaurant. Prices are high, but proportional to the overall value. Book several days in advance.

$$$$
4TH FLOOR
THREE ON THE BUND
3 ZHONGSHAN DONG YI LU
TEL 6321 7733
🍴 190 🅿 🚇 East Nanjing Road 🔁 🅢 🅐
🅢 All major cards

🍴 M ON THE BUND

$$$$
(MISHI XICANTING)
FIVE ON THE BUND
TEL 6350 9988
www.m-restaurantgroup.com
This is where, in 1999, Shanghai's Western gourmet tradition began. While locals

and expats may have moved on in search of the next big thing, M on the Bund still prepares excellent food in a great setting. It is located on the seventh floor of a Concession-era building (enter from the side at 20 Guangdong Lu) and maintains an elegant art deco atmosphere, coupled with views from the terrace over the river and Huangpu. The menu varies by season, but is concise, and while decidedly continental, has Mediterranean and North African influences. House specialties include leg of lamb and the signature Pavlova dessert. Advance reservations required.

🍴 250 🚇 East Nanjing Road 🅢 🅐 🅢 All major cards

🍴 WHAMPOA CLUB

$$$$
3 ZHONGSHAN DONG YI LU
5TH FLOOR,
THREE ON THE BUND
TEL 6321 3737
One floor above Jean Georges, this restaurant offers spectacular decor and cuisine, but here the Shanghainese cuisine, prepared by renowned chef Jereme Leung, is the draw. The surroundings are plush and warm, with original art works on display. The standard culinary favorites of Shanghai, mainly seafood, are prepared with premium ingredients and surprising but delicious modifications. A signature dish is the yellow braised Australian abalone. Most tables have views on the river. Consistently rated as one of Shanghai's top restaurants. Reservations recommended.

🍴 290 🅿 🚇 East Nanjing Road 🔁 🅢 🅐 🅢 All major cards

🍴 SHANGHAI UNCLE

$$$
(HAISHANG ASHU)
222 YAN'AN DONGLU
BUND CENTER, NEAR HENAN ZHONGLU
TEL 6339 1977

Owned by a Shanghainese-American and son of a New York Times food critic, this restaurant offers Shanghainese food with some interesting twists. In addition to the house specialty of Uncle's crispy pork of flame, try the traditional Shanghai dish of cold smoked fish or Peking pancakes with scallops and XO sauce. The restaurant is located in the basement of The Bund Center, so the only views are of the amusing decor and lively patrons, best seen from booths on the mezzanine. There's a second location on the Pudong side of the river. Reservations recommended.

🍴 500 🚇 East Nanjing Road 🅢 🅢 All major cards

🍴 YUNNAN GOURMET GARDEN

$
(YUNNAN MEISHI YUAN)
268 XIZANG ZHONGLU
RAFFLES CITY B1 19/20
TEL 6340 3076
Located in the basement of the Raffles City shopping mall on The Bund, it's not a garden, or gourmet—just good, basic, inexpensive food from the southeastern Chinese province of Yunnan. The Yunnanese staples include a nourishing chicken steamed with herbs in clay pot (chiguoji), and crossing-the-bridge noodles—various meats, vegetables, and noodles cooked in a piping-hot, oil-layered broth (guoqiao mixian).

🍴 40 🚇 People's Square 🅢 🅢 No credit cards

FUXING TO HUAIHAI

This area feels less frenetic than Nanjing Donglu, with lots of good restaurants, boutiques and galleries, and appealing art deco architecture. Many of the old villas have been converted into attractive boutique hotels.

HOTELS & RESTAURANTS

HOTELS

🏨 88 XINTIANDI
$$$$

380 HUANGPI NANLU
TEL 5383 8833
FAX 5383 8877
www.88xintiandi.com
E-MAIL enquiry@88xintiandi.com
This 53-room boutique hotel in the Xintiandi complex (see pp. 116-117) re-creates the *shikumen*, or stone gate houses, of old Shanghai. The tastefully done rooms are all suites, or at least contain a small kitchenette. Some rooms have lake views, but if your balcony overlooks the shopping area, make sure it's on a high floor, since the activities below can continue quite late.
🛏 53 P 🚇 Huangpi Road South 🛗 🚭 📶 📺 🍽 All major cards

🏨 OKURA GARDEN HOTEL
$$$$

(HUAYUAN FANDIAN)
58 MAOMING NANLU
LUWAN DISTRICT
TEL 6415 1111
FAX 6415 8866
www.gardenhotelshanghai.com
E-MAIL sales@gardenhotelshanghai.com
Situated on the grounds of the former French Sporting Club, the Okura uses the spectacular, old three-story building for its lobby, restaurants, and function rooms. After the French departed, the sweeping staircases, crystal chandeliers, and grand ballroom with a stained-glass dome ceiling appealed to the tastes of Chairman Mao and his top associates, who held regular conferences here. It's now managed by the Japanese Okura group. The guests are mainly Japanese but the staff speaks English as well. Guest rooms are in the less inspiring 33-story annex adjacent to the old building and have a distinct Japanese feeling to them (i.e., tasteful minimalist style), but they're a bit small.

🛏 500 P 🚇 Shanxi Road South 🛗 🚭 📺 🍽 🚇 All major cards

SOMETHING SPECIAL

🏨 HENGSHAN MOLLER VILLA

Once the private residence of a British real estate magnate with a penchant for horseracing. He built this castlelike structure to fulfill the dreams of his youngest daughter. The architecture can only be described as eccentrically pleasing. Steeples and spires, with a leafy garden complete with bronze statuary and meteorites as decor, all somehow fit in with the chandeliers and ornate European-style furniture in the wood-paneled rooms. There are 11 rooms in the original building. The adjacent three-story block is cheaper but not the original.
$$–$$$
(HENGSHAN MALE BIESHU FANDIAN)
30 SHANXI NANLU
JINGAN DISTRICT
TEL 6247 8881
FAX 6289 1020
www.mollervilla.com
E-MAIL sde@mollervilla.com
🛏 40 🚇 Shanxi Road South 🛗 🚭 📺 🍽 🍽 All major cards

🏨 JINJIANG HOTEL
$$–$$$$

(JIN JIANG FANDIAN)
59 MAOMING NANLU
LUWAN DISTRICT
TEL 6258 2582
FAX 6472 5588
www.jinjianghotels.com
E-MAIL marketing@jinjianghotels.com
First opened in the 1920s and called the Cathay Mansions, this complex now comprises the original Cathay, as well as the 1930s Grosvenor House, which has been converted into an all-suite hotel, and the recently renovated South Building. The gardens are magnificent, and the restaurants range from Thai to

Mexican. Classical music concerts are held in the Grand Hall of the former Cathay Mansions. The new Jinjiang Tower is managed as a separate property.
🛏 328 P 🚇 Shanxi Road South 🛗 🚭 📺 🍽 All major cards

🏨 RUIJIN GUESTHOUSE
🍽 **$$$$**

(RUIJIN BINGUAN)
118 RUIJIN ER LU
LUWAN DISTRICT
TEL 6472 5222
FAX 6473 2277
www.shedi.net.cn/outedi/ruijin/
This compound hotel consists of five old villas once belonging to foreign businessmen who lived the high life in 1930s Shanghai. One was an eccentric press baron who raised racing hounds on the premises. All the villas have been well-restored and the 17 acre (7 ha) gardens are also home to the Face Bar, the Lan Na Thai Restaurant and the Hazzara Indian Restaurant.
🛏 62 P 🚇 Shanxi Road South 🚭 🍽 📺

🏨 CITY HOTEL
$$

(CHENGSHI JIUDIAN)
5–7 SOUTH SHANXI NANLU
LUWAN DISTRICT
TEL 6255 1133
FAX 6255 0211
www.cityhotelshanghai.com
E-MAIL reserve@cityhotelshanghai.com
For those wishing to be in the French Concession but wanting the convenience and facilities of a non-boutique hotel, this is a good choice. Although this 30-story building is 20 years old, it has been recently refurbished and boasts good views from the upper floors. The restaurants are forgettable, but you're surrounded by plenty of good restaurants in both the French Concession and Jingan.
🛏 274 P 🚇 Shanxi Road South 🛗 🚭 🍽 🚭 📺 🍽 All major cards

🏨 DONGHU HOTEL
$$

70 DONGHU LU
TEL 6415 8158
FAX 6415 7759
www.donghuhotel.com

Visitors with an interest in old Shanghai should find this converted mansion set in a walled compound with attractive shaded gardens an interesting place to stay. It once belonged to Du Yuesheng, the notorious Green Gang boss and Shanghai mobster. The main four-story building is surrounded by seven smaller villas, which once were home to some of Du's numerous mistresses. Well appointed with all the usual amenities, it's conveniently close to the restaurants of Huaihai Lu.
🛏 310 🅿 🚇 Changshu Road or Shanxi Road South 🚭 🅰 🆑 🏊 🏋 🆂 All major cards

🏨 MASON HOTEL
$$

(MEICHEN DAJIUDIAN)
935 HUAIHAI ZHONGLU
LUWAN DISTRICT
TEL 6466 2020
FAX 6467 1693
www.masonhotel.com

Only four stories tall, the Mason isn't impressive—intimate and functional are more apt descriptions—but the location is great. With broadband Internet service in the rooms, a rooftop beer garden, and a Starbucks branch off the lobby, it attracts a younger clientele who aren't looking for a lot of amenities. All of the rooms on the lower stories are clean, but the ones on the lower floors facing Huaihai Zhonglu are noisy. Try to get one on facing the central courtyard instead.
🛏 120 🚇 Shanxi Road South 🚭 🅰 🆂 All major cards

🏨 OLD HOUSE INN
🍴

Located down a residential alley, this 12-room inn has the feel of the old family home it once was. It is owned and managed by a local architect and has rooms decorated in Chinese style with warm wood paneling. Intimate and charming.
$$
(LAOSHI GUANG LAO SHIGUANG JIUDIAN)
NO. 16
351 LANE HUASHAN LU
TEL 6428 6118
FAX 6429 6869
www.oldhouse.cn
E-MAIL info@oldhouse.cn
🛏 12 🚇 Changshu Road 🅰 🆂 All major cards

🏨 JINGAN HOTEL
$-$$

370 HUASHAN LU
TEL 6248 1888
FAX 6248 2657
www.jinganhotel.net

This old, Spanish-style hotel built in 1934 has seen some changes in its time. After liberation in 1949 the Chinese Communist Party East took control of the building, before passing it on to the Shanghai local Communist Party. It reverted to being a hotel soon after when the party realized that the building was too big for its needs. These days the elegant hotel retains an air of nostalgia with its gracefully pillared ninth-floor restaurant and numerous chandeliers. Rooms are relatively basic but comfortable.
🛏 210 🍴 🅿 🚇 Jingan Temple 🚭 🅰 🆂 All major cards

RESTAURANTS

🍴 T8
$$$-$$$$

HOUSE 8, NORTH BLOCK
XINTIANDI
181 TAICANG LU
TEL 6355 8999

Located in a Xintiandi shikumen that has been decorated with a mixture of traditional and contemporary motifs, the swish T8 caters to a celebrity clientele. The Australian chef's fusion cuisine takes Chinese and Thai flavors and uses them in European-style creations. Everything from the lobster oxtail ravioli starter to the slow-cooked lamb is unique and excellent. The wine list is one of the best in town. Advance reservations suggested for dinner.
🍽 106 🚇 Huangpi Road South 🅰 🆂 All major cards

🍴 HAZARA
$$$

(HAZHALA CANTING)
118 RUIJIN ER LU
BUILDING 4
RUIJIN GUEST HOUSE
LUWAN DISTRICT
TEL 6466 4328

Located within the beautiful grounds of the Ruijin Guesthouse (in fact, downstairs from Lan Na Thai restaurant, below), Hazara presents excellent northern Indian cuisine in a tasteful South Asian atmosphere. The tandoor clay pot oven is put to good use. While aficionados claim the curries lack complexity, the simple *daal* bean soup, cucumber *raita*, samosas, and pulao rice are done perfectly. Reservations required.
🍽 30 🅿 🚇 Shanxi Road South 🅰 🆂 All major cards

🍴 LAN NA THAI
$$$

118 RUIJIN ER LU
BUILDING 4
RUIJIN GUEST HOUSE
LUWAN DISTRICT
TEL 6466 4328

With superb views of the colonial mansion's garden below, the elegant Thai decor of silks and orchids sets the tone for authentic classic Thai cuisine. From the green

---

papaya salad to the green coconut–based chicken curry to the shrimps in basil, everything is piquant but not overly spicy. The chef of course is Thai, and the wait-staff is superbly trained. If you go in the evening, you may want to adjourn to the Face Bar, one of Shanghai's most popular nightspots, which is located below the restaurant. Advance reservations required.

🛏 160 🅿 🚇 Shanxi Road South 🚇 🚫

🍴 YIN
$$$
59 MAOMING NANLU
1ST FLOOR JINJIANG
GOURMET STREET
LUWAN DISTRICT
TEL 5466 5070

Located in the Jinjiang Hotel complex, the decor is old Shanghai, with hardwood floors, carved screens, and qipao-clad waitresses, but contemporary touches of art and lighting have been added. The food centers on local dishes but also covers other Chinese specialties, including Xinjiang-style lamb. A good mixture of style and substance.

🍽 84 🅿 🚇 Shanxi Road South 🚫 🚇 🚫 All major cards

🍴 PAULANER BRAUHAUS
$$$
(BAOLAINA CANTING)
HOUSE 19–20 NORTH BLOCK
181 TAICANG LU
XINTIANDI
LUWAN DISTRICT
TEL 6320 3935

Shanghai's own German microbrewery serves up hearty, even heavy, German food in a raucous beer hall atmosphere spreading over two floors in this Xintiandi shikumen. Choose between the amber-colored bitter called Munich Dark or the sharper wheat beer. Singalongs and good-natured rowdiness add to the atmosphere. If you want a break from delicate sophistication, this is

a good choice. Other branches of the Paulaner Brauhaus are found in Pudong and Xuhui.

🚇 540 🚇 Huangpi Road South 🚫 🚇 🚫 All major cards

🍴 SASHA'S
$$$
11 DONGPING LU
XUHUI DISTRICT
TEL 6474 6628

Although seaped in Chinese history, Sasha's serves Western food. The elegant villa that houses the restaurant was once a home of the Song family and later taken over by Mao's wife, Jiang Qing. Now it's a good place for continental cuisine upstairs or drinks and tapas in the comfortable pub on the ground floor, noted for its vast selection of imported draft beers. When the weather permits, food and drink are served in the garden. Xuhui District is a couple of Metro stops away from the French Concession but has a less touristy feeling to it. Reservations suggested.

🍽 200 🅿 🚇 Hengshan Road 🚫 🚇 🚫 All major cards

🍴 ZEN
$$$
283 HUAIHAI ZHONGLU
3F HONG KONG PLAZA
LUWAN DISTRICT
TEL 6390 6390

Although part of a chain that specializes in Cantonese food, here the emphasis is on taste and good service. Choices include the pomelo salad, crispy roast pork, and steamed crab in rice wine sauce. A choice selection of wines is available.

🍽 320 🚇 Huangpi Road South 🚇 🚫 All major cards

🍴 CRYSTAL JADE RESTAURANT
$$
(FEICUI JIUJIA)
HOUSE 6–7, LANE 123
XINGYE LU
XINTIANDI PLAZA

TEL 6385 8752

If it's made from or wrapped in rice flour, they have it. The open kitchen lets you watch the dough being transformed into noodles, dumplings, and dim sum. The fillings are wide-ranging, from standard pork and chicken to shrimp, crab, and lobster. Heavier fare, such as roast pork and duck, are also served. It's a large restaurant, but partitioned with screens so as not to feel cavernous. This is one of several Shanghai branches of this popular restaurant, and one of the best places to sample the Shanghai favorite dumpling, called *xiao long bao*. Advance reservations recommended.

🍽 200 🚇 Huangpi Road South 🚫 🚇 🚫 All major cards

FONG'S VIETNAMESE
$–$$
2ND FLOOR, LIPPO PLAZA
222 HUAIHAI ZHONGLU
TEL 6387 7228

This is generally believed to be the best Vietnamese restaurant in Shanghai. Fong's attempts to re-create a Southeast Asian atmosphere in an office plaza. The bamboo fixtures and fittings help set the scene, as do the songbirds in cages, but most successful are the local Shanghainese women kitted out in elegant Vietnamese *ao dai* dresses. All the usual Vietnamese specialties, from spring rolls to *pho* noodles and genuine *nuoc mam* sauce are served. Some French dishes are also included on the menu.

🚇 Huangpi Road South 🚭 🏧 All major cards

XINJIANG FENGWEI
$–$$
280 YISHAN LU
TEL 6468 9198

It seems that Shanghai's enduringly popular Uighur restaurants—exotic to local Shanghainese as much as to Westerners—are linked with Uighur dancing and live music as much as delicious Central Asian cuisine. In fact, the far western province has been associated with China proper with twirling dancers and acrobats for well over 1,500 years, and the tradition continues. Singing waiters will take your order and encourage you to join in the dancing. Excellent Uighur food, which is by far the best in Central Asia. English menu. Dinner reservations recommended.

🚇 Yishan Road 🚭 🏧 No credit cards

FRAGRANT CAMPHOR GARDEN
$
(HARN SHEH)
10 HENGSHAN LU
XUHUI DISTRICT
TEL 6433 4385

Although it is called a teahouse, its extensive menu offers both Chinese and Western food ranging from curries to pasta at reasonable prices. A great place to linger over tea or a smoothie and watch the crowds outside on busy Hengshan Lu. A bit far from the French Concession, but a good change in atmosphere.

🚌 300 🚇 Hengshan Road 🚭 🏧 🏧 All major cards

HOT POT KING
$
(LAIFU LOU)
1416 HUAIHAI ZHONGLU
LUWAN DISTRICT
TEL 6474 6380

This is a good place to sample *huo guo*, a Chinese culinary tradition in which a selection of meat, seafood, dumplings, and vegetables are brought to your table uncooked, then simmered in a communal pot of broth. After cooking, you dip them in a selection of sauces. Especially attractive on a cold and rainy Shanghai day. The chain has several branches throughout the city; call for the one nearest you, or if you see the sign, stop in.

🚌 290 🚇 Changshu Road 🚭 🏧 🏧 All major cards

PUDONG

While the area lacks the historical atmosphere of Puxi across the river, it's not far by either Metro or taxi and generally quieter, less polluted, and closer to the international airport. It's where business travelers often stay and is the home to Shanghai's most deluxe accommodations.

HOTELS

SOMETHING SPECIAL

GRAND HYATT
(SHANGHAI JINMAO JINYUEJUNYUE DAJIUDIAN)

Billed as the world's highest hotel—it only starts on the 54th floor of the deceptively 1950s-looking Jinmao Tower—the Grand Hyatt qualifies as a destination in itself. Beginning with the 33-floor atrium lobby, design is key here, with every motif from futuristic to art deco to contemporary Chinese making an appearance somewhere. Surprisingly, it all fits together, and the rooms, with floor-to-ceiling windows, give some incredible views as long as you're not literally in the clouds. Food is superb as well, and the Cloud Nine bar on the 88th floor is fabled in Shanghai.

$$$$$
JINMAO TOWER
(54TH–88TH FLOORS)
88 CENTURY BOULEVARD
PUDONG DISTRICT
TEL 5049 1234
FAX 5049 1111
www.shanghai.hyatt.com
E-MAIL info.ghshanghai@hyatt intl.com

🛏 555 🅿 🚇 Lujiazui
🔄 🚭 🏧 🏊 🏋 🏧 All major cards

PUDONG SHANGRI-LA
$$$$$
(PUDONG XIANGGELILA FANDIAN)
33 FUCHENG LU
PUDONG DISTRICT
TEL 6882 8888
FAX 6882 6688
www.shangri-la.com
E-MAIL slpu@shangri-la.com

The twin 28-story towers offer a less vertiginous but equally luxurious alternative for those wishing to stay in Pudong. Restrained elegance is the theme here, with traditional Chinese design elements and amber wood paneling. The guest rooms are said to be the largest in Shanghai and the CHI day spa is one of the city's best.

🛏 981 🅿 🚇 Lujiazui
🔄 🚭 🏧 🏊 🏋
🏧 All major cards

HOTELS & RESTAURANTS

⌂ ST. REGIS SHANGHAI
$$$$$
(SHANGHAI RUIJI HONGTA
DAJIUDIAN)
889 DONGFANG LU
PUDONG
TEL 5050 4567
FAX 6875 6789
www.stregis.com
This is tasteful luxury at its
finest, including Herman Miller
furniture, Bulgari toiletries,
Bose audio equipment in the
rooms, which are, by the way,
the largest in the city, but
what makes the St. Regis
unique is its Lifestyle Butler
Service. Not limited to
mundane services such as
pressing a shirt or making
dinner reservations, your
butler can also serve as
your personal guide to the
city, showing you the latest
dining and art venues that
only a well-connected local
would know. ⓘ 318 🅿 🚇 Shiji Avenue
🛗 🚫 🚫 🗕
🚫 All major cards

⌂ COURTYARD BY
MARRIOTT
$$$
(SHANGHAI QILU WANYI
DAJIUDIAN)
838 DONGFANG LU
PUDONG DISTRICT
TEL 6886 7886
FAX 6886 7889
www.marriott.com
For the business traveler
looking for convenience and
comfort without the dazzle,
this is a good choice.
ⓘ 318 🅿 🚇 Dongfang
Road 🛗 🚫 🚫 🗕
🚫 All major cards

RESTAURANTS

🍴 FOOK LAM MOON
$$$$
33 FUCHENG LU
2ND FLOOR, PUDONG
SHANGRI-LA HOTEL
PUDONG DISTRICT
TEL 5877 3786
Cantonese cuisine with a local
touch is the speciality. Not

only the chefs but many of
the ingredients as well are
imported from Hong Kong.
Seafood dishes are special
here. Signature dishes are the
hot-and-sour cucumber skins
and braised whole Japanese
dry abalone. Nice views of
The Bund and the Huang Pu
River from a more natural
ground level perspective.
Reservations required.
🍴 160 🅿 🚇 Lujiazui
🛗 🚫 🚫 🗕

🍴 DANIELI'S
$$$
29TH FLOOR, ST. REGIS HOTEL
889 DONGFANG LU
PUDONG DISTRICT
TEL 5050 4567 EXT. 6370
Danieli's is located atop the
Pudong St. Regis Hotel where
the atmosphere is warm and
intimate. The food is classical
Italian, with a good mixture
of pasta, seafood, and meat
courses. Local expats say it's
the best Italian food in the
city. Reserve in advance for
a table by the window.
ⓘ 56 🅿 🚇 Dongfang
Road 🛗 🚫 🚫 🗕 All
major cards

🍴 SOUTH BEAUTY
$$
(QIAO JIANGNAN)
168 LUJIAZUI XILU
10TH FLOOR,
SUPERBRAND MALL
PUDONG DISTRICT
TEL 5047 1917
Serving mainly Sichuanese
food, it also provides a selection of less spicy Chinese
dishes. An elegant but not
overwhelming place with
great views that won't break
the bank.
🍴 800 🚇 Lujiazui 🛗 🚫
🚫 All major cards

🍴 THAI THAI
$
156 LUJIAZUI XILU
5TH FLOOR SUPERBRAND
MALL
PUDONG DISTRICT
TEL 5047 1255
There is a food court in the

basement of this Pudong
shopping mall, but if you'd like
something a bit more relaxing
but still inexpensive, try this.
All the classic Thai favorites,
such as *tom yam kung* (spicy
shrimp soup) and *gang khiaw
wan* (green curry), are
available.
🍴 120 🅿 🚇 Lujiazui 🗕
🚫 🚫 All major cards

The northern part of Shanghai,
which includes the historic
Hongkou district, while distant
from the city center, is undergoing a revival and provides an
interesting hotel and restaurant
alternative to the usual tourist
haunts. The Duolun Road
Cultural Street, a thriving arts
scene gives, this area a less glitzy
atmosphere than better known
parts of Shanghai.

HOTELS

⌂ GRAND MERCURE
BAOLONG HOTEL
$$$
(BAOLONG FANDIAN)
180 YIXIAN LU
TEL 6542 5425
www.accorhotels.com
E-MAIL reservations@baolong
hotel.com
Modern and comfortable, the
Baolong was recently taken
over by this French chain,
bringing it up to international
standards.
ⓘ 400 🅿 🛗 🚫 🚿
🚫 All major cards

⌂ SHANGHAI LUXUN
PARK INN
$
2164 SICHUAN NANLU
TEL 5696 1828
A clean budget hotel located
next to Lu Xun Park.
ⓘ 80 🚫 All major cards

RESTAURANTS

🍴 AFANTI RESTAURANT
$$

(AFANTI SHICHENG)
775 QUYANG LU
TEL 6554 9604
Hearty and authentic Uighur cuisine, the Central Asian fare here is mutton-based, although some vegetable dishes are to be found. Located in the basement of the Tianshan Hotel.
🍴 120 🚫

🍴 OLD FILM CAFÉ
$
123 DUOLUN LU
TEL 5696 4753
Coffee, tea, and light meals served amid a decor of old movies.
🍴 40 🚫 No credit cards

WEST SHANGHAI

West of The Bund and north of the French Concession, Nanjing Xilu and Jingan are quite central and popular with travelers on business or pleasure. Nanjing is a major shopping area, but it's more bustling than atmospheric. Meanwhile, the Hongqiao Development Zone is of interest mainly to business travelers whose work is centered there. It is also near the Hongqiao Airport. The Shanghai Metro doesn't reach Hongqiao, so getting into town requires taking a taxi.

HOTELS

🏨 FOUR SEASONS HOTEL
$$$$$
(SHANGHAI SIJI JIUDIAN)
500 WEIHAI LU
JINGAN DISTRICT
TEL 6256 8888
FAX 6256 5678
www.fourseasons.com
No attempts at futurism here, just classic elegance. A fountain and palm trees in the lobby, offset by marble and rich wood paneling, it's a world away from nearby busy Nanjing Xilu. Staff is welcoming but discreet and the rooms spacious and classic. A jazz club enlivens things on the top floor, and the Cantonese restaurant is one of the best in town.
ℹ️ 439 🅿️ 🚇 Shimen Road No. 1 🔁 🚫 🆒 🏊 🏋️
🚫 All major cards

🏨 PORTMAN RITZ-CARLTON
$$$$$
(SHANGHAI BOTEMAN LIJIA DAJIUDIAN)
1376 NANJING XILU
JINGAN DISTRICT
TEL 6279 8888
FAX 6279 8800
www.ritzcarlton.com
Located in the Shanghai Center and surrounded by excellent restaurants and shopping venues, the Portman Ritz-Carlton is more restrained in its elegance than some of its peers and, mainly because of the service, consistently wins independent hotel survey accolades. The health club includes squash courts, an indoor-outdoor swimming pool, and covers three floors of the 50-story hotel. The restaurants and bars attract both discerning locals and expats.
ℹ️ 564 🅿️ 🚇 Jingan Temple 🔁 🚫 🆒 🏊 🏊 🏋️
🚫 All major cards

🏨 THE REGENT SHANGHAI
$$$$$
(LONGZHIMENG LIJING DAJIUDIAN)
1116 YAN'AN XILU
CHANGNING DISTRICT
TEL 6115 9988
FAX 6115 9977
www.regenthotels.com
Sleek and luxurious with an atrium lobby, the largest indoor pool in Shanghai, a L'Institut de Guerlain spa, large rooms with 42-inch plasma TVs, and sweeping city views, this is an impressive addition to the neighborhood.
ℹ️ 511 🅿️ 🔁 🚫 🆒 🏊
🏋️ 🚫 All major cards

🏨 HILTON HOTEL
$$$$
(JINGAN XIERDUN FANDIAN)
250 HUASHAN LU
JINGAN DISTRICT
TEL 6248 0000
FAX 6248 3848
www.hilton.com
This 43-story hotel was Shanghai's first foreign-owned hotel. It was certainly surpassed in opulence and luxury by later arrivals, but recent renovations have brought it back to its original high standard. The location is excellent, within walking distance of Hengshan Lu and the French Concession. A new health spa and six fine restaurants make it a worthy choice.
ℹ️ 700 🅿️ 🚇 Jingan Temple 🔁 🚫 🆒 🏊 🏋️ 🚫 All major cards

🏨 JW MARRIOTT
🍴 $$$$
TOMORROW SQUARE
399 NANJING XILU
TEL 5359 4969
FAX 6375 5988
www.marriott.com
A recent arrival on the exploding Shanghai luxury accommodation scene, the Marriott opened its doors in 2003. The hotel rises above one of the city's best locations, People's Park, and occupies the top 24 floors of the giant 60-story Tomorrow Square tower. The facilities are staggering and include hydraulic massage showers in the perfectly appointed bathrooms, squash courts, a spa, and a number of excellent restaurants.
ℹ️ 342 🍴 🅿️ 🚇 People's Square 🔁 🚫 🆒 🏊 🏊
🏋️ 🚫 All major cards

🏨 MARRIOTT HOTEL HONGQIAO
$$$$
(SHANGHAI WANHAO HONG QIAO DAJIUDIAN)
2270 HONGQIAO LU
CHANGNING DISTIRCT
TEL 6237 6000

🚫 Non-smoking 🆒 Air-conditioning 🏊 Indoor/🏊 Outdoor swimming pool 🏋️ Health club 🚫 Credit cards

FAX 6237 6222
www.marriott.com
Only eight stories tall, with nice gardens, it's convenient to Hongqiao Airport and the zoo. Primarily a business clientele.
🛏 315 🅿 ⮂ 🚫 📷 🏊
📺 🌐 All major cards

🏨 SHERATON GRAND TAI PING YANG
$$$$
(XI LAI DENG HAO DA TAI PING YANG DA FANDIAN)
5 ZUNYI NANLU
CHANGNING DISTRICT
TEL 6275 8888
FAX 6275 5420
www.sheratongrand-shanghai.com
E-MAIL sheratongrand@un inet.co.ltl
A comfortable oasis for unwinding after a hard day of business meetings. The sports bar momentarily takes you back home, and the deli serves great takeaways for jet lag-induced midnight snackers. Guests with a free day can unwind with a round of golf at the Shanghai International Golf and Country Club.
🛏 496 🅿 ⮂ 🚫 📷 🏊
📺 🌐 All major cards

🏨 CYPRESS HOTEL
$$$
(LONGBAI FANDIAN)
2419 HONGQIAO LU
CHANGNING DISTRICT
TEL 6268 8868
FAX 6268 1878
If you need to be in Hongqiao but want a taste of historic Shanghai, the Cypress is ideal. A modern six-story building on the grounds of what was once a country estate owned by tycoon Victor Sassoon, the 40 acres of gardens and forest are a great escape from modernity. Rooms and service are satisfactory.
🛏 149 🅿 ⮂ 🚫 📷 📺
🌐 All major cards

🏨 GRAND MERCURE HONGQIAO
$$$
369 XIAN XIA

CHANGNING DISTRICT
TEL 5172 7960
FAX 5172 7961
www.grandmercure-asia.com
E-MAIL: reservation@grand mercure-hongqiao-shanghai.com
Just ten minutes from the Hongqiao airport, this twin-towered hotel opened in June 2007 and offers impeccable service.
🛏 496 🅿 ⮂ 🚫 📷 🏊
📺 🌐 All major cards

🏨 PARK HOTEL
$$$
(GUOJI FANDIAN)
170 NANJING XILU
TEL 6327 5225
FAX 6327 6958
www.parkhotel.com.cn
E-MAIL parkhtl@parkhotel.com.cn
An excellently located, historic hotel overlooking People's Square. When it was built in 1934, it was the tallest building in Asia. The Chinese government now recognizes the hotel as an official cultural relic. Art deco architecture sets the tone. The Park is one of the old guard—not the most sophisticated of hotels, but distinguished nonetheless. The building includes Chinese and Western restaurants, a nightclub, and shopping arcade.
🛏 250 🚇 People's Square
⮂ 🚫 📷 🌐 All major cards

RESTAURANTS

🍴 SHINTORI NULL II
$$$$
(XINDULI WUER DIAN)
803 JULU LU
JINGAN DISTRICT
TEL 5404 5252
Some find it incredibly cool, others say it's just plain cold, but no one leaves this postmodern Japanese restaurant without strong impressions. After you pass through the tunnel-like entryway, translucent doors sweep open to admit you. The decor is stark, as in chrome and polished concrete; the main

---

dining area is like a sunken pool; and the presentation includes sashimi on polished stone platters and cold noodles served in bowls of solid ice. The mezzanine tables are more intimate. Opinions vary on the scene, but no one faults the food. Reservations required.
🪑 130 🚇 Changshu Road
🚫 📷 🌐 All major cards

🍴 BARBAROSSA LOUNGE
$$$
231 NANJING XILU
TEL 6318 0220
This North African–themed pleasure dome mixes restaurant, club, and sheesha bar in a three-story, domed-roof venue with an outdoor terrace in once proletarian People's Park. The Middle Eastern cuisine, such as lamb

couscous and Tunisian-style tuna are really quite good, but most diners are here for the arabesque music and the novelty of it all. Quite a scene. Reservations recommended.
🍴 300 🚇 People's Park 🚭 ❄ 🅑 All major cards

🍴 GIOVANNI'S
$$–$$$$
5 ZUNYI NANLU
27TH FLOOR SHERATON
GRAND TAI PING YANG
CHANGNING DISTRICT
TEL 6275 8888
Great views from the top of the Sheraton in Hongqiao, and a good choice of traditional Italian food prepared to top international standards. The menu changes with the season. Not a big place, so reserve in advance.
🍴 40 🅿 🚭 ❄ 🅑 All major cards

🍴 SOPHIA'S TEA RESTAURANT
$$$
480 HUASHAN LU
JINGAN DISTRICT
TEL 6249 9917
In an old house down a small street near the Hilton Hotel, Sophia's is an intimate place for a quiet Chinese meal in pleasant surroundings. Although the emphasis is on Shanghainese food, other regional Chinese cuisines are served here, including Cantonese and northern dishes. Excellent teas are served as drinks, but also incorporated into some of the food, as in the prawns fried in the famous longjin green teas from nearby Hangzhou. Reservations required.
🍴 200 🚇 Jingan Temple 🚭 ❄ 🅑 All major cards

🍴 1221
$$–$$$
(YI ER ER YI)
1221 YAN'AN XILU
CHANGNING DISTRICT
TEL 6213 6585
Quite popular among expats

and visiting businessmen, it's well known for its moderately priced and diverse Chinese cuisine served in a smart atmosphere. Standard favorites include the drunken chicken, Shanghai smoked fish, and spicy Sichuan beef. The tea you see being poured from incongruously long spouts is *babaocha,* (eight treasures tea), which is flavored with dried fruits and nuts. An interesting performance, and it's an excellent digestive after a big meal. Reserve well in advance.
🍴 120 🚭 ❄ 🅑 All major cards

🍴 CHINA MOON
$$–$$$
316–317 CITIC SQUARE
1168 NANJING XILU
JINGAN DISTRICT
JINGAN TEMPLE
TEL 3218 1379
On the third floor of this major shopping and office complex, the China Moon is suitably grand yet subdued and tasteful. Abstract paintings provide the decor, which hints at modern takes on classical Chinese food, mainly Cantonese, Shanghainese, and Sichuan varieties. Some favorite dishes are the crystal abalone, pork in soy sauce, and mandarin fish. Reservations recommended for dinner.
🍴 240 🚇 Changshu Road 🚭 ❄ 🅑 All major cards

🍴 FOLK RESTAURANT
$$–$$$
(XIAN QIANG FANG)
1468 HONGQIAO LU
CHANGNING DISTRICT
TEL 6295 1717
Located on the ground floor of a Tudor-style villa, Folk serves Shanghainese and other regional Chinese cuisines, all with unique interpretations. Antiques enhance the decor. On the third floor of the villa you'll find the Door, which also serves food but is mainly a bar for the super-chic set who find

themselves in Hongqiao with money to burn. It's worth a quick drink for the eclectic music.
🍴 480 🚭 ❄ 🅑 All major cards

SOMETHING SPECIAL

🍴 UIGHUR RESTAURANT
A dependable, clean, and tasty Uighur ashkana serving a variety of Xinjiang delights, including laghman noodles, poluo pilaf rice, manta dumplings filled with mutton and onion, samsa samosas, chushira dumpling soup, delicious nan breads, and a variety of kebabs. The food is, of course, halal, and the atmosphere can only be described as down-to-earth fun, with a Uighur band, dancers in ethnic costume, and distinctively Central Asian Uighur music. English menu. Dinner reservations are required.
$$–$$$
1 SHANXI NANLU
TEL 6255 0843
🚇 Shanxi Nanlu 🚭 ❄ No credit cards

🍴 MALONE'S AMERICAN CAFÉ
$$
(MALONG MEISHI JIULOU)
257 TONGREN LU
JINGAN DISTRICT
TEL 6247 2400
If it's a great burger and draft beer you're craving, this is the place to go. Tex-Mex also finds its way into the menu, as well as steaks, pizza, and even some Chinese dishes. Large-screen TV for sporting events and live music after 10 p.m.
🍴 200 🚇 Jingan Temple ❄ 🅑 All major cards

🍴 BRASIL STEAK HOUSE
$
(BAXI SHAOKAO CANTING)
1649 NANJING XILU
JINGAN DISTRICT
TEL 6255 9898
This features an all-you-can-eat barbeque, known as *churrrascaritas* in the owners'

native Brazil. A semi-buffet is available with roving waiters offering various slices of freshly grilled meats, and a salad bar as well. Nice views into adjacent Jingan Park. The price is right and the restaurant is always busy. A second branch has opened across from the Shanghai Library on Huaihai Zhonglu. No reservations accepted.

🛏 200 🚇 Jingan Temple 🏧 All major cards

🍴 GONGDELIN
$
445 NANJING XILU
HUANGPU DISTRICT
TEL 6327 0218
This vegetarian restaurant is Shanghai's first, having opened in 1922. This is not Western-style vegetarian cuisine; most all the dishes proclaim themselves as meat, but in fact are made from bean curd. The subdued and serene decor are appropriate.

🛏 150 🚇 People's Square 🇸 🇸 🏧 No credit cards

EXCURSIONS SOUTH OF SHANGHAI

The cities to the south of Shanghai provide a base for exploring the Yantze River Delta, from the pilgrimage areas of Putoshan to urban Hangzhou. The accomodations range from simple to a millionaire's country estate.

HANGZHOU

🏨 HYATT REGENCY HANGZHOU
$$$$
(HANGZHOU KAIYUE JIUDIAN)
28 HU BIN LU
TEL 0571 8779 1234
FAX 0571 8779 1818
http://hangzhou.regency.hyatt.com/hyatt/hotels/index.jsp
E-MAIL hangz.reservation@hyattintl.com
Fronting on West Lake, the newer Hyatt Regency is part of an upmarket residential

complex with a shopping mall attached. It's only six stories tall, so it feels part of the environment, but the restaurants are not as diverse as the Shangri-La's.

🛏 390 🅿 🛗 🇸 🇸 🌊 🏧 All major cards

🏨 SHANGRI-LA HOTEL 🍴 HANGZHOU
$$$$
(HANGZHOU XIANGELILA FANDIAN)
78 BEISHAN LU
TEL 0571 8707 7951
FAX 0571 8707 3545
www.shangri-la.com
Located on West Lake's northwest shore in 30 acres (12 ha) of landscaped gardens, the Shangri-La is the most sophisticated port of call in Hangzhou, bursting with fine dining opportunities and an eager-to-please staff. Chinese and Italian restaurants, American bar and café. Snooker/billiards and bike rentals are available.

🛏 387 🅿 🛗 🇸 🌊 🏧 All major cards

🏨 XIHU STATE GUEST HOTEL
$$$
7 XISHAN ROAD, HANGZHOU
TEL 0571 8797 9889
FAX 0571 8797 2348
www.xihusgh.com
E-MAIL sales@xihusgh.com
Located on a 15-acre site on the west side of the West Lake, the guest hotel is composed of eight buildings. Once a local millionaire's country estate, it has a 1.5-mile (2 km) of lake front. It has an outdoor pool and a golf practice range. The property is managed by the local government, so don't expect facilities of an international standard, though the atmosphere compensates.

🛏 180 🅿 🛗 🇸 🌊 🏧
🇸 🏧 All major cards

🍴 LOUWAILOU RESTAURANT
$$

(LOUWAILOU CAIGUAN)
30 GUSHAN LU
TEL 0571 8796 9023
FAX 0571 8799 7264
One of Hangzhou's favorite eateries feeds everyone on immortal local recipes, such as *sudong po* pork and beggar's chicken and offers long views over West Lake. Other specialties: West Lake vinegar fish *(xihu cuyu)* and longjing shrimp *(longjing xiaren)*. English menu.

🛏 1400 🇸 🏧 All major cards

🍴 PEPPINO'S
$$
SHANGRI-LA HOTEL
TEL 0571 8707 7951
An impressive range of Italian flavors finds its way into the pizzas here. English menu.

🛏 140 🏧 🇸 All major cards

MOGANSHAN

SOMETHING SPECIAL

🏨 RADISSON VILLAS

For a taste of history in Moganshan, try this one. Two magnificent villas have been partitioned into rooms and suites. One was the retreat of the notorious Shanghai gangster Du Yue Sheng and the other belonged to a Swedish missionary. Sophisticated, luxurious, expensive.

$$-$$$$
TEL 0572 803 3601
www.radisson.com.cn
E-MAIL hzrph1@mail.hz.zj.cn
🛏 12 🅿 🇸 🏧 All major cards

🏨 BAIYUN HOTEL
$$$
502 MOGANSHAN
TEL 0572 803 3336 or 803 3382
FAX 0572 803 3274
www.mogan-mountain.com
Located at the top of the mountain in Hua Yang Park, this hotel has several buildings, ranging from adequately

comfortable to luxurious.
📞 80 🍽 🚫 All major cards

QINGFENG
SHANZHUANG
$$
240 MOGANSHAN
TEL 0572 803 3275
Moderate accommodation, it
is renowned for excellent
food, which can be enjoyed
on the large terrace.
📞 40 🚫 No credit cards

MOGANSHAN LODGE
$
SONGLIANG SHANZHUANG
343 MOGANSHAN
TEL 0572 803 3011
www.moganshanlodge.com
Located in the Songliang
Shanzhuang Hotel (a nice
place in its own right), the
Moganshan Lodge is managed
by a Chinese lady whose
British husband is the chef.
They provide great Western
breakfasts and lunches, as well
as dinner (reservations
required). A café and bar with
a good choice of wines and
spirits. The English-speaking
source of information for all
things Moganshan.
🚫 No credit cards

PUTUOSHAN

PUTUOSHAN HOTEL
$
93 MEICEN LU
TEL 0580 609 2828
Near Puxi Temple and the
harbor, the hotel is relatively
modern and clean but not of
the highest international
standards.
📞 150 🅿 🍽 🌀 🚫 All
major cards

SANSHENGTANG
HOTEL
$
121 MIAO ZHUANGYAN LU
TEL 0580 609 1277
FAX 0580 609 1140
Once a Buddhist nunnery, the
building has been refurbished
as a hotel but still has a basic
atmosphere in keeping with
the island's sacred character.

Diverse range of rooms, 10-
minute walk from the ferry
terminal, not far from Puzi
Temple. Boat ticketing service.
📞 97 🌀 🚫 No
credit cards

EXCURSIONS WEST
& NORTH OF
SHANGHAI

Electing to stay in one the water
towns provides an opportunity
to enjoy the quiet atmosphere
without the busloads of tourists.
There are a few large and numerous smaller establishments to
choose from.

SUZHOU

SHERATON SUZHOU
HOTEL & TOWER
$$$$
(SUZHOU WUGONG
XILAIDENG DAJIUDIAN)
388 XIN SHI LU
TEL 0512 6510 3388
FAX 0512 6510 0888
www.sheratonintl.com
www.sheraton-suzhou.com
E-MAIL heraton.suzhou@star
woodhotels.com
Located north of the Panmen
scenic area, the Sheraton
Suzhou is the best in town,
deftly embracing the local
architectural vernacular with
its upturned eaves, waterway
bridges, and gorgeous
gardens.
📞 407 🅿 🌀 🌀 🌀 🏊
🍽 🚫 All major cards

MAN PO BOUTIQUE
HOTEL
$$
660 XINHUA LU
TEL 6280 1000
FAX 6280 6606
Well positioned for Shanghai's
Hongqiao Airport, this establishment styles itself a boutique hotel, but it's only by
Shanghai standards. A long
way from the downtown
action (7.5 miles or 10 km
from The Bund), it is nevertheless an excellent option
for late-night arrivals or early
morning airport departures.

The rooms and suites are
comfortable and equipped
with their own cooking
facilities. Two restaurants are
located on site, as well as,
airline ticketing facilities.
📞 76 🅿 🚇 Hongqiao
Road 🌀 🌀 🌀 🚫 All
major cards

BAMBOO GROVE
HOTEL
$$
168 ZHUHUI LU
TEL 0512 6520 5601
FAX 0512 6520 8778
www.bg-hotel.com
E-MAIL bghsz@public1.sz.js.cn
The grounds and restaurant
areas are done in Suzhou
style and surround a rock
pool, which is home to some
amusing ducks. The guest
rooms are in a series of
adjacent modern buildings.
Centrally located. Evening live
music in the foyer bar.
📞 356 🅿 🌀 🌀 🌀 🏊
🍽 🚫 All major cards

SCHOLARS INN
$
(SHUXIANG MENDI
SHANGWU JIUDIAN)
277 JINGDE LUINGDE LU
TEL 0512 6521 7388
FAX 0512 6521 7326
This modern hotel with nods
to Suzhou architectural styles
is centrally located near
Guanqian Lu is a good value.
Chinese food only.
📞 37 🌀 🚫 All major cards

PINE AND CRANE
RESTAURANT
$$
(SONG HE LOU)
141 GUANQIAN JIE
TEL 0512 6727 7006
This local landmark restaurant
has served Suzhou specialties
such as squirrel shaped mandarin fish and gusu marinated
duck for 200 years. English
menu. Priced for tourists.
🍴 220 🌀 🚫 🌀 All
major cards

JIA YOU FANG
Not a restaurant, this is a

street lined with restaurants just north of the Garden of Happiness. Popular with locals (and that's where it counts), there is little to distinguish one eatery from another. Bring your phrase book and be ready to point.

NANJING

SHERATON NANJING KINGSLEY HOTEL & TOWERS
$$$$
169 HANZHONG LU
TEL 025 8666 8888
FAX 025 8666 9999
www.starwoodhotels.com
Spacious rooms, catering largely to business travelers, there's a good fitness center, jogging path, and even an Irish pub.
[i] 350 P ⬍ 🚫 🚭 🏊 🔅 🚭 All major cards

JINGLING HOTEL
$$$
(JINGLING FANDIAN)
2 HANZHONG LU
TEL 025 471 1888
FAX 025 471 1666
www.jinlinghotel.com
This centrally located, first class hotel houses Western and Chinese restaurants, including a revolving one on the 36th floor.
[i] 600 P ⬍ 🚫 🚭 🏊 🔅 🚭 All major cards

NANSHANG HOTEL
$
(NANJING SHIFAN DAXUE NANSHAN JIALOU)
NANJING NORMAL UNIVERSITY
122 NINGHAI LU
TEL 025 371 6440
FAX 025 373 8174
This hotel is centrally located near Xuanwu Lake situated in the quiet heart of Nanjing Normal University, on grounds possessing rare beauty. The rooms are quiet, clean, and quite cheap. Foreign students studying Chinese tend to stay here. It's a great break from the international

tourist circuit.
[i] 200 ⬍ 🚭 🚫 No credit cards

BELLA NAPOLI
$$
(BEILANABOLI YIDALI CANTING)
75 ZHONGSHAN DONGLU
TEL 025 8471 8397
An Italian who has settled in Nanjing offers an extensive menu of his home country's cuisine, from wood-fired pizzas to more substantial fare, including steaks.
🍴 80 🚭 All major cards

GOLDEN HARVEST THAI OPERA CAFE
$–$$
(JINHE TAI CANTING)
HUNAN LU
2 SHIZI QIAO
TEL 025 8324 2525 or 025 8324 1823
For a break from Chinese fare, try the good Thai food here. Tasteful decor and moderate to high prices. It's a favorite of local expats and serves all the spicy curries that make Thailand's cuisine an international favorite. Reservations recommended.
🍴 80 🚭 No credit cards

LAO ZHENG XING
$
CONFUCIUS TEMPLE
Located on the grounds of Nanjing's Confucian Temple, this is a good place to try Nanjing local dishes, such as steamed dumplings. It's a cafeteria, so point and choose ordering is easy. In food court fashion buy tickets and then exchange them for food from each vendor.
🍴 100 🚭 No credit cards

ZHOUZHUANG

ZHOUZHUANG HOTEL
$$
108 QUANFU LU
TEL 0512 5721 6666
Located in the city center, this is a modern hotel, convenient

and clean, but without much else to recommend it.
[i] 108 ⬍ 🚭 🚫 All major cards

TONGLI

ZHENGFU CAOTANG
$
138 MINGQING JIE
TEL 0512 6333 6358 or 0512 6332 0576
www.zfct.net
E-MAIL book@zfct.net
A beautifully restored courtyard home, which truly evokes the atmosphere of old China. The owner plays his *qin* (a traditional Chinese stringed instrument) for guests in the evening. It's a small place, so book in advance.
[i] 12 🚭 🚫 No credit cards

SHANGER RESTAURANT
$$
(XIANGGE JIULOU)
MINGQING JIE
TEL 0512 6333 6988
Although mainly catering to tour groups, it's still good for decent Chinese food and there is an English menu.
🍴 120 🚫 No credit cards

SHANGHAI SHOPPING

The people of Shanghai are known for their sense of style, and what better way to exercise it than through acquiring either the latest trendy goods, or something that expresses your very own sense of taste? Since such bourgeois sentiments were thoroughly disallowed for over 30 years, both Shanghai's shoppers and vendors are back with a vengeance. Your objects of interest will likely differ from those of the locals; Louis Vuitton, Prada, Cartier, and the like—which enthrall the Chinese—are usually more expensive here than in the West due to import duties. In addition to a plethora of local handicrafts based on traditional Chinese motifs, the real jewels of the Shanghai shopping scene are the countless small boutiques offering unique, locally designed goods with modern style and flair. They can range from cute to elegant, without a hint of chinoiserie.

Among local handicrafts, textiles, both silk and woolens (which can be made into beautiful clothing by Shanghai's expert tailors), pearls from Lake Tai, original paintings and calligraphy scrolls, ceramics, reproductions of antique furniture, and even Maoist memorabilia, all compete for your attention.

SHOPPING AREAS

Since the visitor is unlikely to be seeking either imported luxury goods—found in the deluxe emporiums of Nanjing Donglu—or the more everyday domestic items—found at its slightly poorer cousin, Nanjing Xilu—these areas are best seen on sight-seeing not shopping trips. For handicrafts and trendy boutiques, your best choices are either the French Concession or old town, especially around the Yu Garden. Nanshi and upscale Huaihai Lu are best for local handicrafts. Some of the vendors of the closed Xiangyang fakes market—where pirated software and DVDs competed with designer clothing knockoffs—have now reestablished themselves at the Qipu Market in Zhabei District.

MARKETS

Dongtai Road Antiques Market
Off Xizang Lu
Luwan District
Metro: Huangpi Road South
Little you see in the dozens of stalls and small shops here is

truly antique, but many interesting curios such as Mao era memorabilia, recently produced propaganda posters, ceramics, snuff bottles, and other small handicraft items are on offer.

Fuyou Antiques Market
(Fuyou Gongyipin Shichang)
457 Fangbang Zhonglu
Corner of Henan Nanlu
Nanshi Distirct
Metro: Huangpi Road South
Best visited on a weekend morning when sellers come from all over Shanghai and beyond to fill the four-story building. Nonetheless, it's worth a visit any day of the week. Few of the antiques are real, but there are a great selection of porcelains, old coins and prints, and some small-furniture items. Be careful when you are in the vicinity of ceramics—vendors have been known to strategically place items so they can be easily knocked off the shelf and broken, then sold to the unwitting victim at a high price. If you feel you have been a victim of this scam, ask to see the supervisor (jiandi), who knows these stories very well.

Temple Of Town God Market
(Chenghuang Miao Shichang)
265 Fangbang Zhonglu
Nanshi District
Metro: Huangpi Road South
Usually confined to the basement of the Huabao Bulding facing the Yu Garden, on weekends it spills out into the street. A wide range of goods appealing

to visitors is on offer on this section of Fangbang Lu, restored in Qing Dynasty style. Paintings, calligraphy scrolls, and brushes are favorite items. It's also a good place to get a "chop," or stone ink stamp made with your name in Chinese characters.

South Bund Fabric Market
(Nan Waitan Qing Fang Mianliao Shichang)
399 Lujiabang Lu
Dongjiadu District
Metro: Nanpudajiao
Called the Dongjiadu Fabric Market until it was moved indoors and to a new location in 2006, taxi drivers still use the old name, but know the new location, which is in the southeastern section of the old city (Nanshi). Much of the trade is wholesale, so unless you want fabrics by the bolt, the major attractions here are the tailors who work from some of the shops. Bring a favorite item of clothing, chose a fabric from the huge selection available, and return in a week to pick up your new garment. The choice of fabrics is amazing—Chinese and Thai-style silks, cotton, linen, hemp, and woolens.

Qipu Market
(Qipu Fuzhuang Shichang)
Zhabei District
Metro: Baoshan Road
If you want to get away from products directed at foreigners, this is a great place to visit. It's largely clothes and cheap jewelry, and a good place to find the factory overruns and irregulars from the export-oriented garment factories that supply the world. One tip to spot a fake brand name from the real thing—if it reads "Made in USA" on the label, it's a poor-quality fake.

Doulun Road
Near Sichuan Beilu
Hongkou District
Not an open-air market, but a small street with many interesting shops selling antiques, handicrafts, and art. This was the

home of Shanghai's literati in the 1930s, and the buildings have been rebuilt in period style. A more relaxed atmosphere prevails compared to the other shopping areas of Shanghai.

Longhua Temple Market
Longhua Township
Near the Longhua pagoda
Metro: Longcao Road (then a walk)
Located in the southwest outskirts of Shanghai, the Longhua Temple is the site of an interesting annual fair (see Festivals), but a plethora of interesting shops and street stalls along a walking street flourish here all year. The atmosphere is decidedly local and almost rural, but you may find some unique items here. Don't even think about the jade here, however—you will surely be cheated.

BOOKS

Due to government restrictions, there is no book lover's paradise in China, but Shanghai has a few decent selections:

Shanghai City of Books
465 Fuzhou Lu
Huangpu District
Tel 6391 4848

Old China Hand Reading Room
27 Shaoxing Lu
Luwan District
Metro: South Shanxi Road
Tel 6473 2526
Both an attractive café and a bookstore featuring a collection of new and old titles mainly about Shanghai art and architecture.

Shanghai Foreign Language Bookstore
390 Fuzhou Lu
Huangpu District
Metro: Nanjing Road East
Tel 6322 3200
Open 9 a.m.–6 p.m.
A good selection of locally produced books on Chinese art as well as maps and Chinese language learning materials.

ANTIQUES & ARTIFACTS

Henry Antique Warehouse
(Hengli Gudian Jiaju)
3F Building 2, 8 Hongzhong Lu
Changning District
Tel 6401 0831
www.h-antique.com
Although largely dealing in furniture, which has been restored by resident craftsmen, some smaller items are available. Traditional Chinese, art deco, and even modern creations are on view. Affiliated with nearby Tongji University, student craftsmen are trained in both restoration and creation of classical and modern Chinese furniture.

Shanghai Antique and Curio Store
(Shanghai Wenwu Shangdian)
200–242 Guangdong Lu
Huangpu District
Metro: Henan Middle Road
Tel 6321 5868
If you're not the bargaining type, this is the best place for you. It is owned by the government, and all prices are fixed, with official certificates for pre-1949 items. Hand-painted fans, old jades, ceramics, sculpture, tapestries, and cloisonné-inset screens are among the most attractive items.

Chine Antiques
1660 Hongqiao Lu
Hongqiao District
Metro: Hongqiao Road
Tel 6270 1023
Like many of Shanghai's best antique warehouses, this is located a bit far from the city's center, in the western district of Hongqiao. The emphasis is on furniture, with some beautiful true antiques carrying certificates of authenticity. Not for the bargain-hunter.

Hu & Hu Antiques
1685 Wu Zhonglu
Hongkou District
Metro: Zhong Shan Road
Tel 6405 1212
Open 9 a.m.–6 p.m.
Large selection of furniture and

smaller pieces in the showroom and warehouse. Fixed prices.

Zhongzhong Jiayuan Gongsi
3050 Hechuan Lu
Tel 6406 4066
Probably the largest collection of antique furniture in Shanghai, including an immense warehouse of items awaiting restoration. Like many of Shanghai's best antique warehouses, it is located a bit far from the center, in the western district of Hongqiao. The emphasis is on furniture, with some beautiful true antiques carrying certificates of authenticity. Not for the bargain-hunter.

ARCADES & MALLS

Raffles City
286 Xizang Zhonglu
Huangpu District
Metro: People's Square
Part of a Singaporean chain, you'll find all sorts of Western clothing, electronics, and home furnishings here, as well as a food court, a gym, and a Watson's pharmacy.

Citec Square
1168 Nanjing Xilu
Huangpu District
Metro: Shimen No. 1
Another view of the West for the Chinese masses. Upmarket imported goods, as well as a McDonald's.

Plaza 66
1266 Nanjing Xilu
Huangpu District
Metro: Shimen No. 1
The most upmarket of Nanjing Lu's shopping malls. Tasteful displays, not crowded, and some excellent restaurants.

Westgate Mall
1038 Nanjing Xilu
Huangpu District
Metro: Shimen No. 1
An attractive atrium-type building with slightly less exclusive brands than Plaza 66, but still featuring high-quality Western imports. There is a good food court in the basement.

ART & DESIGN GALLERIES

Eddy Tam's Gallery
20 Maoming Nanlu
Metro: Shanxi Road South
Tel 6253 6715
This street is full of galleries showing contemporary art and design. Eddy's is one of the best.

Shanghai Arts & Crafts Museum
(Shanghai Gongyi Meishuguan)
79 Fenyang Lu
Xujiahui District
Metro: Changshu Road
Tel 6437 0509
It is called a museum, but the true attraction of this French Concession area mansion is the fine crafts made and sold here. Ceramics, hand-painted snuff bottles, calligraphy, and painted kites are all great gift items.

Chinese Ink Painting Shop
(Moxiiang Gongyipin Shanghang)
134 Nanchang Lu
Tel 5386 3997
Metro: Shanxi Road South
Original scroll paintings by the resident artist. Bird, flower, and calligraphic motifs. Reasonably priced, but still negotiable.

Shanghai Museum Art Store
201 Renmin Dadao
Metro: People's Square
Part of the Shanghai Museum, the shop sells art books, cards, and prints too elegant to be called souvenirs. Also available are high-quality (and expensive) reproductions of the ceramic pieces found in the museum.

Art Scene
8 Lane 37 Fuxing Xilu
Xuhui District
Metro: Changshu Road
Tel 6437 0631
Housed in a restored French villa, Art Scene specializes in contemporary Chinese art and represents well-known and up-and-coming artists.

ShanghART Gallery
50 Moganshan Lu
Buildings 16 & 18
Tel 6359 3923
Fax 6359 4570
www.shanghartgallery.com
Open 10 a.m.–7 p.m.
Located in the gallery district of Moganshan Lu, this contemporary art gallery opened in 1995. In the two gallery spaces, there are a variety of exhibitions covering painting, sculpture, film, video, and performance art.

BizArt
50 Moganshan Lu
Building 7, 4th floor
Tel 6377 5358
www.biz-art.com
Don't be misled by the name—it comes from both "bizarre" and "business," as the website explains. In fact it's a non-profit center that supports young artists via exhibitions, seminars, and residency programs.

Jingdezhen Porcelain Artware
(Jingdezhen Yishu Taoqi)
1175 Nanjing Xilu
Jingan District
Metro: Shimen No. 1 Road
Tel 6253 8865
A good place for high-quality traditional porcelain, in both the classic blue and white and more subdued celadon styles. Shipping can be arranged.

Bokhara Carpets
679 Xianxia Lu
Changning District
Tel 6290 1745
Open 10 a.m.–6:30 p.m.
Carpets from Iran, Afghanistan, and Central Asia.

DEPARTMENT STORES

Shanghai No. 1 Department Store
800 Nanjing Xilu
Huangpu District
Metro: People's Square
This 11-story government-owned emporium is the antithesis of the upscale malls. The locals shop here for just about everything under the sun.

Next Age
501 Zhangyang Lu
Pudong
Metro: Dongchang Road
Tel 5830 1111
Another government-owned department store, this 10-story building has it all, and the prices are fixed.

CLOTHING

Silk King
(Zhensi Da Wang)
590 Huaihai Zhonglu
Metro: Huangpi Road South
Tel 6372 0561
An excellent selection of quality silks and woolens. Resident tailors can cut the fabrics to measure either as the traditional Chinese high-collared qipao dress or Western-style clothing for both women and men, but allow a week for the job to be completed. Yardage and ready-to-wear garments also available.

Shanghai Tang
Promenade Shop E
59 Maoming Nanlu
Luwan District
Metro: Shanxi Road South
Tel 5466 3006
Originally from Hong Kong, this citadel of chic is famous for its modern interpretations of the Chinese classics, qipaos for the ladies and jackets for men, with a good selection of accessories and home furnishings as well. Pricey.

Jooi Design
No. 21 Lane 210
Taikang Lu
Luwan District
Metro: Shanxi Road South
Tel 6473 6193
A Danish designer interprets Chinese traditional designs. Strong on accessories such as silk handbags and scarves.

La Vie
No. 7 Lane 210
Taikang Lu
Luwan District
Metro: Shanxi Road South
Tel 6445 3585
Some element of Chinese style

is visible but avant-garde is the word here.

Yi Hui
No. 15 210 Taikang Lu
Luwan District
Metro: Shanxi Road South
Tel 6466 5429
Traditional but carries modern interpretations of Chinese designs. Specializes in evening wear.

Insh
No. 3 Lane 210 Taikang Lu
Luwan District
Metro: Shanxi Road South
Tel 6473 1921
Insh is short for "in Shanghai," characterizing the informality of their designs, often with a humorous take on Shanghai and the fashion world's pretensions. From T-shirts to jackets, it's all whimsical and amusing.

Hanyi
217 Changle Lu
Luwan District
Metro: Shanxi Road South
Tel 5404 4727
Tradition reigns here—it's the best place for ladies to be fitted for a high-quality silk *qipao*. If you choose a highly embroidered design, be prepared for a month long wait while the garment is created. Simpler designs can be picked up in a few days.

Chinese Printed Blue Nankeen Exhibition Hall
(Zhongguo Lanyinhua Bu Guan)
House 24, 637 Changle Lu
Xuhui District
Metro: Changshu Road
Tel 5403 7947
If you would like traditional Chinese fabric, but not silk, the indigo-dyed batiks (*nankeen*) provide a subdued alternative. This folk art tradition has been revived by the shop's owner, a Japanese artist who has run the enterprise for more than 20 years. The fabric is sold by the meter, or as shirts, tablecloths, and other household accessories.

FOOD & DRINK

City Supermarket
Shanghai Center
1376 Nanjing Xilu
Jingan District
Tel 6279 8018
Shanghai's most extensive collection of imported food and household items. If you're homesick for some special product, you'll most likely find it here, although not at the price you're used to. A good selection of wines, books, and magazines as well.

Shanghai Huanshang Tea Company
853 Huaihai Lu
Huangpu District
Tel 6711 4919
In addition to a good selection of teas sold by weight, a selection of teapots and paraphernalia, with pots in both porcelain and the unglazed Yixing ceramics favored by connoisseurs. Tasting is free. The method of preparation, while not as ritualized as the Japanese tea ceremony, is well worth observing.

JEWELRY

Amy Lin's Pearls and Jewelry
580 Nanjing Xilu, 3rd floor
Jingan District
Metro: Shimen No. 1 Road
Tel 5228 2372
Shanghai's best place for both freshwater pearls from Lake Tai and saltwater pearls from the South Pacific. More expensive than small shops, but the quality is better.

Pearl Village
(Zhenzhu Cun)
288 Fuyou Lu
Nanshi District
Metro: Henan Middle Road
Tel 6355 3418
A collection of pearl shops located in the larger First Asia Jewelry Plaza across the street from the Yu Garden, carrying both local freshwater and saltwater cultured pearls. Price follows the quality.

Lao Feng Xiang Jewelers
(Lao Feng Xiang Yinlou)
432 Nanjing Donglu
Huangpu District
Metro: Henan Middle Road
Tel 6322 0033
This establishment has been in business since the Qing Dynasty, albeit with ups and downs according to the political winds. They continue to purvey top quality jade, pearls, and precious metal jewelry.

SPECIALIZED SHOPPING

COMPUTERS AND ELECTRONICS
Cybermart
282 Huaihai Zhonglu
Luwan District
Metro: Huangpi Road South
From laptop computers to MP3 players they have it all, as well as accessories and repairs. No cheaper than in the West, though, unless you opt for a local brand.

TOYS
Tots
77 Ruijin Lu
Metro: South Shanxi Road
A good selection of amusing and educational ways to keep the young ones occupied. There is also a branch in Raffles City on Nanjing Donglu.

Bao Da Xiang
685 Nanjing Donglu
Metro: East Nanjing Road
Tel 6322 5122
Five full floors with toys for kids of all ages.

OUTDOOR GEAR
Ye Huo Huwai Yongpin Dian
296 Changle Lu
Metro: South Shanxi Road
Tel 5386 0591
Excellent selection of backpacks, tents, hiking shoes, and other outdoor gear, all export quality but not inexpensive.

ENTERTAINMENT

Shanghai's entertainment scene is at once the most sophisticated, varied, and vibrant in China. After 30 years of repression, the people of Shanghai are keen both to reestablish their position at the cutting edge of the nation's cultural scene and to have a good time. There are plenty of expatriates to help them do so, and with their numbers their influence on the clubbing, music, and bar scene grows. The city has its fair share of theaters, opera houses, and cinemas, as well as dance halls, clubs, and a very lively bar scene, notably around Xintiandi and Maoming Roads. Several monthly listings magazines are published in English, including *That's Shanghai* and *SH Magazine*—look for them in bars, restaurants and at hotel reception desks.

ENTERTAINMENT CENTERS

THEATER

With several impressive venues, Shanghai's performing arts scene is truly of an international standard. Tickets are available in advance from the venue's box office, or through your hotel concierge. Avoid dealing with scalpers outside the venue; you're likely to be cheated.

Shanghai Grand Theatre

300 Renmin Dadao
Metro: People's Square
Tel 6386 8686
This is Shanghai's premier venue for Western opera, ballet, and Broadway musicals. In addition to visiting classical orchestras it is the home of the Shanghai Philharmonic. Chinese opera performances round out the bill.

Shanghai Concert Hall

523 Yan'an Donglu
Metro: People's Square
Tel 6386 2836
This impressive Art Deco building from the 1930s hosts classical performances, both local and from abroad.

Shanghai Oriental Art Centre

(Shanghai Dongfang Yishu Zhongxin)
425 Dingxiang Lu
Metro: Science and Technology Museum
Tel 6854 7757
Located in Pudong, this architecturally spectacular hall, with a steel-and-glass exterior mellowed by wooden interiors with

superb acoustics in all its three halls hosts major foreign troupes.

OPERA HOUSES

Yifu Theatre/Beijing Opera

701 Fuzhou Lu
People's Square
Metro: People's Square
Tel 6351 4668
Chinese Opera is definitely an acquired taste. Needless to say, the plot will escape those not fluent in archaic Chinese, and the music, using stringed instruments and gongs, can seem cacophonous. Still the costumes are beautiful and the acrobatic element needs no translation. The Yifu Theatre is Shanghai's top venue for the local version, *kunhu* that is easier on the ear since it uses woodwind instruments.

Shanghai Centre Theatre

Shanghai Centre
1376 Nanjing Xilu
Metro: Jingan Temple
Tel 6279 8948
A good alternative to Chinese opera is an acrobatic performance, and the Shanghai troupes are the best in China. Nightly performances feature tightrope walking, plate balancing, human pyramids, and magicians.

CINEMA

Since the government not only censors foreign and domestic films, but also limits the number of foreign films to less than 50 per year, China is not a good place to visit the cinema. The Shanghai International Film Festival, which takes place in June, is interesting for the art film aficionado. If you're determined

to visit a Chinese cinema, try the Peace Cinema on The Bund, which has an IMAX theater.

MUSEUMS

Shanghai Museum

201 Renmin Dadao
People's Square
Huangpu District
Metro: People's Square
Tel 6372 3500
www.shanghaimuseum.com
Open Sun.–Fri. 9 a.m.–5 p.m.,
Sat. 9 a.m.–8 p.m.
$$ Adult; $ Student
Excellent display of Chinese art over 50 centuries. Many consider this the best museum in China.

Shanghai Art Museum

325 Nanjing Xilu
People's Square
Huangpu District
Metro: People's Square
Tel 6327 4030
www.sh-artmuseum.org.cn
Open 9 a.m.–5 p.m.
$
Regularly changing exhibitions featuring Chinese and international artists, both in contemporary and classical styles.

Bund Museum

1 Zhongshan Dong Er Lu
Huangpu District
Metro: Nanjing Road East
Tel 6321 6542
Open 9 a.m.–12:30 p.m.
$
Mainly period photographs, but a nice shop and observation deck.

Duolun Museum of Modern Art

27 Duolun Lu
Hongkou District
Metro: East Baoxing Road
Tel 6587 2530
www.duolunart.com
Open Tue.–Sun. 10 a.m.–6 p.m., closed Monday
$
Publicly funded, noncommercial, offering by far the best public display of modern Chinese art in the world.

Lu Xun Museum

2288 Sichuan Beilu
Hongkou Park

Hongkou District
Metro: East Baoxing Road
Tel 6540 4378
Open 9 a.m.–4 p.m.
$
Commemorates the leading figure of Chinese modern literature. Letters, photographs, and period furniture.

Museum of Sex Culture
479 Nanjing Donglu
Huangpu District
Metro: Nanjing Road East
Open 10 a.m.–9 p.m.
$
Taking a historical perspective, it is risqué yet informative. Under 18 not admitted.

Zendai Museum of Modern Art
Building 28, 199 Fang Dian Lu
Pudong District
Tel 5033 9801
www.zendaiart.com
Open Tues.–Sun. 10 a.m.–9 p.m.
$ (free on Sun.)
A good display of modern art in Pudong.

First Communist Party Congress Museum
78 Xingye Lu
Luwan District
Metro: Huangpi Road South
Tel 6328 5266
Open 9 a.m.–5 p.m.
$
Located in a French villa where the future leaders of China first met.

Ohel Moshe Synagogue Museum
62 Changyang Lu
Hongkou District
Metro: East Baoxing Road
Tel 6327 9900
Open Mon.–Fri. 9–11:30 a.m. & 1–4 p.m.
No longer used for prayer, this synagogue chronicles Jewish history in Shanghai.

Museum of Contemporary Art/MOCA
231 Nanjing Xilu
People's Park
Huangpu District

Metro: People's Square
Tel 6327 9900
www.mocashanghai.org
Open 10 a.m.–6 p.m. (until 10 p.m. Wed.)
$
Beautiful building, eclectic art works.

Museum of Folk Art
1551 Zhongshan Nan Yi Lu
Nanshi District (Old Town)
Tel 6313 5582
Open 9 a.m.–4 p.m.
$
Housed in a former merchants' guild hall of great architectural merit, the museum showcases folk art from all over China.

Propaganda Poster Art Center
868 Huashan Lu
Basement Level, Building B
Changning District
Tel 6211 1845
Open 10 a.m.–3 p.m.
$
Posters from the Mao era. Both an exhibition and art gallery; select pieces are for sale.

Shanghai Science and Technology Museum
(Shanghai Keji Guan)
2000 Shiji Dadao
Pudong District
Metro: Science & Technology Museum
Tel 6862 2000
Open Tues.–Sun. 9 a.m.–5 p.m.
$$ Adults; $ children under 12
With interactive robotics, a simulated rain forest, and an iWerks theater, this museum brings science to life for the young. World class, it is crowded on weekends, and school excursions on weekday mornings.

Shanghai Discovery Children's Museum
330 Yangqu Lu
Zhabei District
Metro: Shanghai Tiyuguan
Tel 5688 0844
www.shanghaidiscovery.org
Open Tues.–Sun. 9 a.m.–5 p.m.
$
Interactive exhibits for kids up to 12, teaches science and the arts.

MUSEUMS OUTSIDE SHANGHAI
Museum of Ancient Chinese Sex Culture
Tuisi Garden
Tongli
Tel 0512 6332 2972
Open 8 a.m.–5 p.m.
$
This is the original sex museum from Shanghai, now relocated with its extensive collection.

China Silk Museum
Yuhuang Shan
Hangzhou
Tel 0571 8703 2060
www.chinasilkmuseum.com
Open 7:30 a.m.–5:00 p.m.
$
All aspects of the cultivation and manufacture of silk are covered.

Zhejiang Provincial Museum
25 Gushan Lu
Hangzhou
Tel 0571 8797 1177
www.zhejiangmuseum.com
Open Mon. noon–4 p.m. & Tues.–Sun. 9 a.m.–4 p.m.
$

Kunqu Opera Museum
Maanshan Donglu
Tinglin Park
Suzhou
Open 8 a.m.–5 p.m.
$
Exhibits include masks, costumes, manuscripts, and ancient instruments.

Suzhou Silk Museum
661 Renmin Lu
Suzhou
Tel 0512 6753 6538
Open 9 a.m.–5 p.m.
$

NIGHTLIFE

Shanghai's bar scene has something for everyone. From big band jazz to trance clubs, with a good middle ground of tasteful and comfortable venues catering to expats. Bars are supposed to close at 2 a.m., but the wilder carry on until dawn. Male travelers should be aware that some of the ladies they meet on the town could be practicing the world's oldest profession.

FOR JAZZ
CJW
1st floor, 2 Lane 123
Xingye Lu
Metro: Huangpi Road South
Tel 6385 6677
CJW stands for cigars, jazz and wine. Modern jazz played by excellent local and foreign musicians. Upscale ambiance and prices. Another branch on the 50th floor of The Bund Center is more of a restaurant, and has stunning views as well.

Cotton Club
8 Fuxing Lu
Xuhui District
Metro: Changshu Road
Tel 6437 7110
A Shanghai institution, this is more relaxed than deluxe and has a good combination of jazz and blues, usually performed by the house musicians. Busy on weekends, with a mixed crowd of foreigners and Chinese.

House of Blues and Jazz
158 Maoming Nanlu
Metro: Shanxi Road South
Tel 6347 5280
Maoming Lu, in the French Concession, has calmed down a bit, but this old-time favorite still keeps the beat. It's got an art deco atmosphere and a mixture of jazz fusion and blues bands.

DANCE CLUBS
Attica
15 Zhongshan Donglu,
11th floor
Huangpu District
Metro: East Nanjing Road
Tel 6373 3588
Located on top floor of an older building on The Bund, it has great views of the river and Pudong skyline from the outdoor terraces. Inside there are two separate dancing venues, techno and hip-hop. Expensive.

Guandii
2 Gaolan Lu
Fuxing Park

Luwan District
Metro: Shanxi Road South
Tel 3308 0726
This is the epicenter of hip-hop and house music. Popular with younger Taiwanese and visitors from Hong Kong. If white kids can rap, why not Chinese? Open until 4 a.m. on weekends.

Mint
333 Tongren Lu
2nd floor
Jingan District
Metro: Jingan Temple
Tel 6247 9666
Constructed in a converted greenhouse, Mint is a smallish club that specializes in house music. Nice outdoor terrace.

Monsoon Lounge
Pier One, 82 Yichang Lu
Tel 5155 8318
Located in the Pier One complex in a renovated Art Deco brewery overlooking Suzhou Creek, this is a classy rooftop venue that plays an eclectic mixture of dance tunes and even has a 10-person hot tub.

Rojam
(Long Shu)
4th floor, Hong Kong Plaza
283 Huaihai Zhonglu
Luwan District
Metro: Huangpi Road South
Tel 6390 7181 or 6390 7161
Two floors of dancing, the upper one being relatively more laid-back, but expect strobe lights and a big beat mixture of trance and techno music.

BARS & PUBS

Cloud 9 and Sky Lounge
Jin Mao Tower
88 Century Avenue, Pudong
Metro: Lujiazui
Tel 5049 1234
On the 87th floor of the Grand Hyatt, currently claiming the title of the world's highest bar. It takes three elevators to get here, but the views are worth it. The upstairs Sky Lounge is the more intimate of the two bars.

Cotton's
132 Anting Lu
Xuhui District
Metro: Hengshan Road
Tel 6433 7995
Located in a restored villa in the French Concession, it's a cozy place with fireplaces and comfortable couches, and a beautiful garden bar when the weather permits.

DR Bar
15 North Block
Xintiandi District
Metro: Huangpi Road South
Tel 6311 0358
A sleek and elegant martini bar in trendy Xintiandi. Champagne is also a favorite of the chic clientele. The marble walls, black furniture, and silver bar create a sense of calm, enhanced by the elegantly-clad staff.

Face Bar
Ruijin Guesthouse
118 Ruijin Lu
Luwan District
Metro: Shanxi Road South
Tel 6466 4328
Located on the grounds of the Ruijin Guesthouse in the French Concession, Face's candlelit garden and stylish bar provide relaxation and people-watching. Two excellent restaurants are located in the same villa.

Bar Rouge
18 Zhongshan Dong Yi Lu
7th Floor, 18 On The Bund
Huangpu District
Metro: Henan Central Road
Tel 6339 1199
A glamorous place for Shanghai's super chic to see and be seen. Great views, a cool terrace, inspired cocktail menu, and after 10 p.m., dancing.

O'Malley's
42 Taojiang Lu
Metro: Changshu Road
Tel 6474 4533
A Shanghai expat institution, with smooth leather booths and memorabilia on the wall, and of course the obligatory draught Guinness stout. Evenings feature Irish music and major sporting

events on large screen. In summer, enjoy a beer on terrace.

FESTIVALS

In addition to the three major holidays of Chinese New Year (usually February), Labor Day (May 1), and National Day (Oct. 1)—essentially week long vacations for Chinese workers—some festivals are worth noting, since they often have a deep cultural significance for the locals.

Anting Kite Festival
Located in the once village, now suburb of Shanghai, this festival is great for kids. In addition to flying and design competitions, there are exhibitions showing kites of the past and the chance to build your own high flier. Held annually on April 4–5.

Birthday of the Sakyamuni Buddha
More a ceremony than a festival, monks chant in the temples and ritually cleanse the Buddha images. The Jingan Temple on Nanjing Lu welcomes foreign visitors (dress appropriately). Lunar-based, usually occurs in May.

Dragon Boat Festival
This festival celebrates the memory of Qu Yuan, a poet of the 3rd century B.C., who drowned himself to protest the corruption of the emperor. Legend states that the saddened citizens attempted to keep the fish from feeding on his body by throwing rice dumplings wrapped in bamboo leaves into the sea, and beating the waters with staves. The tradition lives on with the casting of bamboo wrapped rice dumplings and traditionally constructed boats rowed with long oars. Races are held in May on both the Huangpu River and Suzhou Creek.

International Tea Culture Festival
Held at the Shanghai Railway station from mid- to late April,

there are tea exhibits, tastings, and tours of the tea gardens outside Shanghai. This is a serious event for the committed tea aficionado.

Lantern Festival
Based on a Taoist tradition that dictated hanging a red lantern outside one's house to call in the blessings of the Lord of Happiness, this is now celebrated mostly at the Yu Garden in the Old City. Beautifully cut paper lanterns and traditional sweets are on sale. The date is lunar but falls 15 days after Chinese New Year.

Longhua Temple Fair
Next to Longhua Park in Xuhui District, this temple celebrates the future arrival of Maitreya, also called the Laughing Buddha. In addition to the religious rites, a lively (and crowded) fair flourishes in and around the temple, with jugglers, stilt walkers, and a panoply of traditional crafts. A lunar festival, this usually occurs in April.

Mid-Autumn Festival
Called the Moon Festival by the Chinese, this festival celebrates the abundance of the recently gathered harvest. Moon-shaped pastries are exchanged and families gather to admire the full harvest moon.

Qingming
This is the time when Chinese pay respects to their ancestors. In addition to sweeping the tombs in rural areas, you'll notice packets of false bank notes and other goods being burned in the streets, destined for those in the other worlds. Usually falls in March.

SPORTS & ACTIVITIES

Many hotels have state-of-the-art fitness centers, and if that sounds too strenuous, what's better than a relaxing massage? If you have a passion for other sports—from basketball to soc-

cer, check the local entertainment magazines. You are bound to find a group of like-minded folks who organize games on weekends.

GYMS AND FITNESS CENTERS

Clark Hatch Fitness Center
Radisson Plaza Hotel
78 Xingguo Lu
Changning District
Tel 6212 9998
With machines, a pool, squash courts, tai chi, yoga classes, and massage services.

Kerry Center
1515 Nanjing Xilu
Jingan District
Metro: Jingan Temple
Tel 6279 4625
Weight training, aerobics classes, tennis courts, and even a rock-climbing wall.

Total Fitness Club
6F Zhong Chuang Building
819 Nanjing Xilu
Huangpu District
Metro: Nanjing Road
Tel 6255 3535
Massage and spas available.

Banyan Tree
Westin Hotel 3rd floor
88 Henan Zhonglu
Metro: East Nanjing Road
Tel 6335 1888
Shanghai's most luxurious spa. In addition to massage, they offer facials and body scrubs in an atmosphere of ancient Asian opulence. Prices? Don't ask.

CHI, The Spa
Pudong Shangri-La Hotel
6th Floor Tower 2
33 Fucheng Lu
Pudong District
Metro: Lujiazui
Tel 6882 8888, ext. 460
A Tibetan motif that carries into the therapies themselves, including a scrub with tsampa, the Tibetan staple made from roasted barley. Facials, body wraps, and healing hot stone massages in an atmosphere of serenity.

Dragonfly
206 Xinle Lu
Luwan District
Metro: Shanxi Road South
Tel 5403 9982
This is the main location, although there are now 11 branches in Shanghai. A relaxing Zen atmosphere, a simple but comprehensive treatment menu.

Funing Feining Blind Massage Center
597 Fuxing Zhonglu
Luwan District
Metro: Shanxi Road South
Tel 6347 8378
Massage therapy is an occupation historically undertaken by the blind in China. These establishments don't try for attractive ambiance, but the massage is good and the price is right.

Ming
298 Wulumuqi Nanlu
Dapuqiao District
Metro: Hengshan Road
Tel 5465 2501
Japanese-style decor and great treatments in a classy ambiance.

GOLF
There are more than 20 golf courses in the greater Shanghai area. Largely a sport of the well-off, so usually expensive, and some courses require membership. Expect green fees of up to 800 yuan ($104) on weekdays and twice that on weekends, when reservations are a must. Check with your local country club to find if any courses here offer reciprocal privileges.

Binhai Golf Club
Binhai Resort
Baiyulan Dadao
Nanhui
Pudong
Tel 5805 8888
Open to non-members. Scottish style—hard, fast fairways and greens, and numerous traps.

Shanghai East Asia Golf Club
135 Jianguo Xilu
Tel 6433 1198

Not a course, since it is located downtown, but a good place to hit a few buckets of balls on the two-level driving range.

Shanghai International Golf and Country Club
Xinyang Village
Zhujiajiao
Qingpu County
Tel 5972 8111
Robert Trent Jones, Jr. designed course and includes a water hazard on most holes. Considered the city's best course, but must be introduced to a member, or be a guest at the Sheraton Grand Tai Ping Hotel.

Shanghai Riviera Golf Resort
277 Yangzi Lu
Nanxiang Town
Tel 5912 6888
At least an hour's drive from Shanghai, but the course is lighted for night play.

Tianma Country Club
Zhaokun Lu
Tianma Town
Songjiang District
Tel 5766 1666
Open to non-members and has nice views of the nearby Sheshan Mountain.

CYCLING
As opposed to becoming another fish in the sea of urban bicycle commuters, it is possible to enjoy real mountain biking in the countryside toward Hangzhou and Suzhou.

Cycle China
1/F No. 25, Lane 1984
Nanjing Xilu
Tel 139 1707 1775
www.cyclechina.com
Organizes trips in and around Shanghai as well as elsewhere in China. Provides bikes and English-speaking guides.

Shanghai Bike Club
Suite 2308, Building 2
2918 North Zhong Shan Lu
Tel 5266 9013
As an adjunct to selling mountain bikes as Bohdi Bikes, they

rent good-quality machines and arrange day tours for all levels of cycling abilities.

BOWLING
Orden Bowling Center
10 Hengshan Lu
Xiujiahui District
Metro: Xiujiahui
Tel 6474 6666
Open 24 hours

TENNIS
Many hotels have courts, but here you can meet local and expat tennis enthusiasts.

Changning Tennis Club
Lane 1038, Caojiayan Lu
Changning District
Metro: Jiangsu Road
Tel 6252 4436

Luwan Tennis Center
128 Zhaojiabang Lu
Metro: Shanxi Road South
Tel 6467 5245

Pudong Tennis Center
Yuansheng Stadium
9 Yushan Lu
Tel 5821 5850

Shanghai Jiabao Tennis Club
118 Xincheng Lu
Jiading Sports Center
Tel 5999 7151

Shanghai Racquet Club
Lane 555, Jinfeng Lu
Hua Cao Town
Minhang District
Tel 2201 0100

TAI CHI, WU SHU, AND QI GONG
Take a morning walk anywhere in China, and you will see groups and individuals engaged in this ancient practice, which looks like slow motion shadow boxing. Qi gong mainly involves stationery positions, tai chi moves slowly, and wu shu is the most active branch.

Long Wu International Kung Fu Centre
1 Maoming Nanlu
Luwan District
Tel 6287 1258

ENTERTAINMENT

Metro: Shanxi Road South
The emphasis is on martial arts
here, but they also offer courses
in the softer tai chi.

Mingwu International
Kungfu Club
3/F 359 Hongzhong Lu
Changning
Tel 6465 9806
Martial arts, tai chi, yoga, and
tae kwon do for different age
groups. Classes taught bilingually.

Tai Chi and Pushing Hands
2/F Jingwu Building
157 Dongbaoxing Lu
Hongkou District
Tel 130 2012 4902
Soft form of this ancient practice.

Karma Yoga Center
3–4/F, 172 Pucheng Lu
Pudong District
Tel 3887 0669
www.karmayoga.com
This center offers a wide range
of classes, for experts to begin-
ners. Also has a spa and café.

Shanghai Wushu Center
595 Nanjing Xilu
Huangpu District
Metro: Nanjing Road West
Tel 6215 3599

THEME PARKS
Aquaria 21
Gate 4, Changfeng Park
451 Daduhe Lu
Tel 6223 5280
www.oceanworld.com.cn
$$
This South American–themed
park has penguins and sharks, as
well as a mammal show. Basic
diving instruction with PADI-
certified teachers.

Dino Water Park
78 Xinzhen Lu, near Gudai Lu
Qibao Town
Tel 6478 3333
www.ty04.com
$$
With Asia's biggest wave pool
and the biggest man-made beach
in Shanghai, it's a great family-
oriented place.

PUBLIC PARKS
Century Park
1001 Jinxiu Lu
Pudong District
Metro: Century Park
Spacious and airy, good for pic-
nics and kite flying, with a children's area and climbing walls.

Shanghai Binjiang Forest
Park
3 Lingqiao Lu
Gaoshatan
Gaoqiao Town
Tel 5864 8426
Located in northern Pudong on
the Huangpu, it's an escape from
urban life. Offers bicycles for
rent, pedal boats, and an aviary.

Shanghai Botanical Gardens
1111 Longwu Lu
Xuhui District
Tel 5436 3369
Open 7 a.m.–5:30 p.m.
$
More than 200 acres of botani-
cal specimens, organized my
type, including medicinal plants,
orchids, and bonsai.

Taipingqiao Lake & Gardens
Madang Lu
Luwan District
Metro: Huangpi Road South
Small, but centrally located next
to the Xintiandi area, an oasis of
relative quiet.

Fuxing Park
2 Gaolan Lu
Luwan District
Metro: Huangpi Road South
Tel 6372 6083
Open 6 a.m.–6 p.m.
Once only open to French resi-
dents, it has trees, fountains and
flower beds, children's play-
ground, and cafés and clubs.

SPECTATOR SPORTS
Foreign soccer teams often visit
and frequent other team athletic
events occur. Check the local
magazines for happenings. Most
big events take place at the
Shanghai Stadium. The Shanghai
Open Tennis Tournament takes
place in September. The Shanghai Sharks basketball team, the
original team of Yao Ming, play

at Luwan Stadium from
November to April.

Shanghai International
Circuit
2000 Yining Lu
Jiading District
Tel 6956 9999
www.icsh.sh.cn
In addition to the Formula One
and Moto GP, the track hosts a
variety of motor sports competitions throughout the year.

Luwan Stadium
135 Jianguo Xilu
Metro: Shanxi Road South
Tel 6467 4239
An indoor venue hosting both
sporting and musical events.

Hongkou Stadium
444 Dongjiangwan Lu
Metro: Hongkou Stadium
Tel 6540 0009
Outdoor football stadium, home
to the local Shanghai Shenhua
team. Also hosts international
soccer competitions.

Shanghai Sports Palace
444 Dongjiangwan Lu
Putuo District
Tel 6265 3338
Shanghai's local baseball team,
the Golden Eagles, play here.

Shanghai Stadium
666 Tianyaoqiao Lu
Xujiahui District
Metro: Shanghai Stadium
Tel 6426 6666, ext. 2567
Seats 80,000, hosting major
sports and musical events.

Shanghai Circus World
2266 Gonghe Xin Lu
Zhabei District
Metro: Shanghai Circus World
Tel 5665 6622, ext. 202
A 1,600-seat amphitheater with
revolving stage hosts both circus
and acrobatic performances.

LANGUAGE GUIDE

USEFUL WORDS AND PHRASES
Hello *ni hao*
Goodbye *zaijian*
Thank you *xiexie*
Pardon me *dui bu qi*
I *wo*
We, us *women*
You (sing.) *ni*
You (plur.) *nimen*
He, she *ta*
Them, they *tamen*
My name is... *wo jiao...*
What is your name? *ni gui xing?*
I want... *wo yao...*
Do you have...? *ni you mei you...?*
I do not have... *wo mei you...*
I understand *wo mingbai*
I don't understand *wo bu mingbai*
No problem *mei wenti*
I am American *wo shi meiguoren*
I am English *wo shi yingguoren*
I am Australian *wo shi aodaliyaren*
America *meiguo*
England *yingguo*
Australia *aodaliya*
Canada *jianada*
New Zealand *xinxilan*
China *zhongguo*
France *faguo*
Germany *deguo*
Toilet *cesuo*
Where is...? *zai nar...?*
Where is the toilet? *cesuo zai nar?*
How much is...? *duoshao qian...?*
Beer *pijiu*
Water *shui*
How much is the beer? *pijiu duoshao qian?*
Too expensive *tai gui le*
Vegetables *cai*
Fruit *shuiguo*
Money *qian*
I don't like... *wo bu xihuan...*

NUMBERS
one *yi*
two *er*
two (when followed by a noun) *liang*
three *san*
four *si*
five *wu*
six *liu*
seven *qi*
eight *ba*
nine *jiu*
ten *shi*
11 *shiyi*
20 *ershi*
21 *ershiyi*
30 *sanshi*
100 *yi bai*
200 *liang bai*
1,000 *yi qian*
10,000 *yi wan*
1,000,000 *yi bai wan*
0 *ling*

RESTAURANT
Chopsticks *kuaizi*
Coffee *kafei*
Coke *kele*
Fork *chazi*
Knife *daozi*
Menu *caipu/caidan*
Plate *panzi*
Tea *cha*
Waitress *xiaojie!*
Water *shui*
Wine *putaojiu*
I am vegetarian *wo chisu*
Warm/hot *re*
Cold *leng*
The bill, please *qing jiezhang*

HOTEL
Do you have any rooms? *you mei you kong fangjian?*
Bed *chuangwei*
Check out *tuifang*
Deluxe room *haohuafang*
Double room *shuangrenfang*
Passport *huzhao*
Reception *zongfuwutai*
Standard room *biaozhunfang*
Suite *taofang*
Toilet paper *weishengzhi*

TIME
Today *jintian*
Tomorrow *mingtian*
Yesterday *zuotian*
What time is it? *ji dian zhong?* \

GETTING AROUND
Airplane *feiji*
Airplane ticket *jipiao*
Airport *jichang*
Bicycle *zixingche*
Boarding card *dengjika*
Bus *gonggong qiche/bashi*
Car *qiche*
Map *ditu*
Medium-size bus *zhongba*
Seat *zuowei*

Small bus *xiaoba*
Subway *ditie*
Taxi *chuzu qiche*
Ticket *piao*
Train *huoche*
I want to go to... *wo xiang qu...*
How far is it? *duo yuan?*
Give me a receipt, OK? *gei wo yi ge shoutiao, hao bu hao?*

EMERGENCY
Ambulance *jiuhuche*
Antibiotics *kangjunsu*
Doctor *yisheng*
Fire! *zhao huo le!*
Help! *jiuming a!*
Hospital *yiyuan*
Police *jingcha*
Public Security Bureau (PSB) *gonganju*
I feel ill *wo bu shufu*

DIRECTIONS
North *bei*
South *nan*
East *dong*
West *xi*
Left *zuo*
Right *you*
Inside *limian*
Outside *waimian*

POST OFFICE
Envelope *xinfeng*
Letter *xin*
Post office *youju*
Telephone *dianhua*

SIGHTSEEING
Avenue *dadao*
Lake *hu*
Main street *dajie*
Mountain *shan*
River *he, jiang*
Road *lu*
Street *jie*
Temple *simiao/si/guan*

MENU READER

The following are recommended dishes found throughout Shanghai at regional restaurants or in some of the larger establishments.

SHANGHAI/EASTERN CHINESE DISHES

Beggar's chicken *jiaohua ji*
Brine duck *yanshui ya*
Cold spiced beef *xuxiang niurou*
Crab with ginger and scallions *jiang cong chaoxie*
Drunken chicken *zuiji*
Drunken pigeon with wine sauce *zuixiang ruge*
Drunken shrimps *zuixia*
Fermented tofu *chou doufu*
Fish in tomato sauce *qiezhi yukuai*
Fish with corn and pine nuts *songren yumi*
Fried crab with salty egg *xiandan chaxie*
Fried shrimp *youbao xiaren*
Green peppers in sweet chili sauce *hupi jianjiao*
Hairy crab *dazhaxie*
Hot and sour squid *suanla youyu*
Longjing shrimp *longjing xiaren*
Quick-fried freshwater shrimp *qingchao xiaren*
Red-cooked pork *hong shao zhu rou*
Shanghai crab in wine *zuixie*
Shanghai dumplings *xiaolongbao*
Smoked fresh yellow fish *xun xinxian huangyu*
Steamed Mandarin fish *tangcu guiyu*
Sweet and sour pork spare ribs *tangcu xiaopai*
West Lake soup *xihu chuncai tang*

BEIJING (PEKING), NORTH & NORTH-EASTERN DISHES

Beijing Duck *Beijing kaoya*
Braised fish in soy sauce *hongshao yu*
Braised spare ribs in soy sauce *hongshai paigu*
Chicken in lotus leaf *qing xiang shao ji*
Deep-fried mutton *jiao zha yangrou*
Drunken crab *zuixie*
Dumplings *shuijiao*
Egg and tomato soup *xihongshi jidan tang*
Fish with ham and vegetables *huotui sucai yupian*

Hotpot *huoguo*
Mongolian barbecue *menggu kaorou*
Pork tenderloin with coriander *yuan bao li ji*
Red-cooked lamb *hong shao yangrou*
Sliced bean curd with Chinese cabbage *san mei doufu*
Steamed crab *qingzheng pangxie*
Stewed pork with rice noodles *zhurou dun fentiao*
Stewed ribs with potatoes *paigu dun tudou*

CANTONESE/ CHAOZHOU & SOUTHERN CHINESE DISHES

Dim Sum:
Barbecued pork buns *cha shao bao*
Crispy suckling pig *kao ruzhu*
Deep-fried shrimps in bread crumbs *suzha fengwei xia*
Fried dumplings *guo tie*
Pork and shrimp dumplings *shao mai*
Rice-flour rolls with shrimp or pork *chang fen*
Shrimp dumplings *xia jiao*
Spare ribs *paigu*
Spring rolls *chun juan*

Other dishes:
Barbecued pork *chashao*
Beef with oyster sauce *haoyou niurou*
Curried chicken *gali ji*
Deep-fried stuffed chicken wings *cuipi niang jiyi*
Five flower pork *wuhuarou*
Roast crispy pigeon with soya sauce *shengchou huang cuipi ruge*
Salt-baked chicken *dongjiang yanju ji*
Shark's fin soup *dayuchi tang*
Steamed crab *zhengxie*
Sweet and sour pork *gulao rou*

SICHUAN & WESTERN DISHES

Chicken with chili *lazi jiding*
Crispy dried yogurt *rubing*
Eggplant in hot fish sauce *yuxiang qiezi*

Fish and cabbage in spicy sauce *suancai yu*
Hot-and-sour soup *suanla tang*
Tofu with pork in spicy sauce *mapo doufu*
Meat strips in hot fish sauce *yuxiang rousi*
Pork slices in chili *shuizhu roupian*
Shredded chicken in hot pepper sauce *bangbang ji*
Spicy beef slices *shuizhu niurou*
Spicy chicken with peanuts *gongbao jiding*
Spicy noodles *dandan mian*
Twice cooked pork *huiguo rou*
Wind-cured ham *huotui*

UIGHUR DISHES

Bread with garlic or sesame topping *nan*
Dumpling soup with spicy peppers *chushira*
Dumplings filled with mutton and onion *manta*
Rice pilaf *poluo*
Samosa *samsa*
Stir-fried noodles with mutton *laghman*

EVERYDAY DISHES ACROSS CHINA

Noodle soup *tangmian*
Chicken and cashew nuts *yaoguo jiding*
Crispy aromatic duck *xiangsuya*
Eel with black beans *douche zhengshan*
Egg fried with tomatoes *fanqie chaodan*
Lemon chicken *ningmeng ji*
Pork and mustard greens *jiemo roupian*
Pork and water chestnut *mati zhurou*
Pork chop with rice *paigu fan*
Roast duck *kaoya*
Shredded pork with garlic and chili *dasuan lajiao chaoroupian*
Spicy eggplant *xiangqiezitiao*
Wonton soup *huntun tang*

FRUIT

Apple *pingguo*
Banana *xiangjiao*
Grape *putao*
Mango *mangguo*
Orange *chengzi*
Peach *taozi*
Pear *li*
Plum *lizi*

ILLUSTRATIONS CREDITS

Cover and all interior photographs by David Butow, unless otherwise noted: 26-27, The Mary Evans Picture Library/The Image Works; 28, NGS Archives; 30, Bettmann/ CORBIS; 32-33, Alinari Archive/The Image Works; 34, AFP/Getty Images; 36-37, Bettmann/CORBIS; 38, Hulton-Deutsch Collection/CORBIS; 39, Topical Press Agency/Getty Images; 41, Henri Cartier-Bresson/Magnum Photos; 42, Bettmann/ CORBIS; 48, The Picture Desk; 49 (UP), Bettmann/CORBIS; 49 (LO), Time Life Pictures/Pictures Inc./Time Life Pictures/Getty Images; 57, Aly Song/Reuters/Corbis; 58-59, Aly Song/Reuters/Corbis; 60, Aly Song/Reuters/Corbis; 79, The Shanghai Museum; 103, AFP/Getty Images; 123, LANCASHIRE/Sipa; 161, Library of Congress; 225, The Granger Collection, NY.